M
Spanish

phrasebooks
and
Rafael & Cecilia Carmona

Mexican Spanish phrasebook
1st edition – October 2003

Published by
Lonely Planet Publications Pty Ltd ABN 36 005 607 983
90 Maribyrnong St, Footscray, Victoria 3011, Australia

Lonely Planet Offices
Australia Locked Bag 1, Footscray, Victoria 3011
USA 150 Linden St, Oakland CA 94607
UK 72-82 Rosebery Ave, London, EC1R 4RW

Cover illustration
¡Viva la vida de la bebida! by Patrick Marris

ISBN 1 74059 495 9

text © Lonely Planet Publications Pty Ltd 2003
cover illustration © Lonely Planet Publications Pty Ltd 2003

10 9 8   6 5 4 3 2 1

Printed through Colorcraft Ltd, Hong Kong
Printed in China

acknowledgments

This phrasebook is the product of a close collaboration between editors, translators, designers and publishing staff of all stripes. Editor Piers Kelly would like to thank everyone involved in bringing it into existence.

Special thanks to the terrific translators Rafael and Cecilia Carmona who remained involved right through to the final stages. These prodigies would never have been spotted without the intuition of two talented talent scouts: commissioning editors Karina Coates and Karin Vidstrup Monk.

Their labour would not have borne fruit without the ongoing assistance of the *three amigos* – managing editor Annelies Mertens who kept it running, and fellow editors Francesca Coles and Ben Handicott who kept it real.

Layout designer Patrick Marris transformed his miraculous visions into the front cover and inside illustrations, and pieced everything together with help from layout designer Sally Darmody. Series designer Yukiyoshi Kamimura was responsible for the book design and layout checks together with layout manager Adriana Mammarella.

Thanks also to JenniKate Estavillo and Isa Haviland for offering additional linguistic intelligence and cultural insights, Gerilyn Attebery for patiently explaining the peculiarities of *gringo* English, and David Burnett and Nick Stebbing for technical assistance.

We'd be lost without the marvellous map produced by cartographer Valentina Kremenchutskaya, cartographic designer Wayne Murphy and managing cartographer Paul Piaia. And where would we be without the guidance of project manager Fabrice Rocher and his *bandido* in crime, Charles Rawlings-Way?

Finally, nobody would have known why we were doing it in the first place without the masterminding of publishing manager Jim Jenkin and his successor Peter D'Onghia .

acknowledgments

make the most of this phrasebook ...

Anyone can speak another language! It's all about confidence. Don't worry if you can't remember your school language lessons or if you've never learnt a language before. Even if you learn the very basics (on the inside covers of this book), your travel experience will be the better for it. You have nothing to lose and everything to gain when the locals hear you making an effort.

finding things in this book

For easy navigation, this book is in sections. The Tools chapters are the ones you'll thumb through time and again. The Practical section covers basic travel situations like catching transport and finding a bed. The Social section gives you conversational phrases, pick-up lines, the ability to express opinions – so you can get to know people. Food has a section all of its own: gourmets and vegetarians are covered and local dishes feature. Safe Travel equips you with health and police phrases, just in case. Remember the colours of each section and you'll find everything easily; or use the comprehensive Index. Otherwise, check the two-way traveller's Dictionary for the word you need.

being understood

Throughout this book you'll see coloured phrases on the right-hand side of each page. They're phonetic guides to help you pronounce the language. You don't even need to look at the language itself, but you'll get used to the way we've represented particular sounds. The pronunciation chapter in Tools will explain more, but you can feel confident that if you read the coloured phrase slowly, you'll be understood.

communication tips

Body language, ways of doing things, sense of humour – all have a role to play in every culture. 'Local talk' boxes show you common ways of saying things, or everyday language to drop into conversation. 'Listen for ...' boxes supply the phrases you may hear. They start with the phonetic guide (because you'll hear it before you know what's being said) and then lead in to the language and the English translation.

contents

5

mexican spanish

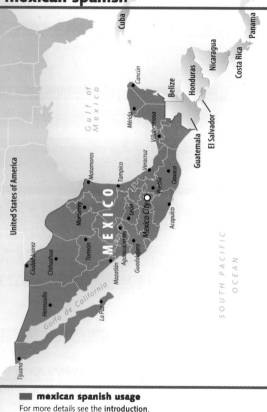

mexican spanish usage

For more details see the **introduction**.

INTRODUCTION
introducción

When the Spanish conquistador Hernándo Cortés landed in Mexico he was confronted by a vast and complex Aztec civilisation in which Nahuatl and Mayan languages predominated. It's difficult to imagine how Cortés, with his relatively small band of followers, managed to overthrow one of the most powerful empires of its time.

The key to the conquest of Mexico was not brute force but language. As every Mexican knows, it was the indigenous mistress of Cortés – a Mayan girl known as La Malinche – who facilitated the Spanish conquest by acting as an interpreter between the warring parties. Though reviled by many as a traitor, in recent years she has been reinvented as a symbol of Mexico's unique hybrid culture.

In many ways, the multilingual La Malinche is also the mother of Mexican Spanish, a language that still bears the birthmark of the early interaction between Mexico and Europe.

at a glance ...

language name:
Mexican Spanish

names in language:
español, castellano,
español mexicano

language family: Romance

**approximate number of
speakers:** 98 million

close relatives: Castilian
Spanish, Latin American
Spanish, Italian, French,
Portuguese

donations to English:
tomato, chocolate,
avocado, coyote

Today Mexican Spanish has evolved from that first significant encounter. Variations in grammar and pronunciation distinguish Mexican Spanish from the Castilian Spanish spoken in Spain. Mexicans do not 'lisp' the letters *c* and *z*, as the Spanish do, and the use of the Spanish form *vosotros* ('you' plural) is limited to remote areas of the southern state of Chiapas. Perhaps the most obvious distinguishing feature of Mexican Spanish is its colloquial vocabulary that sets it apart from Castilian Spanish, as well as the forms of Spanish spoken in neighbouring Latin American countries (see Lonely Planet's Spanish Phrasebook, Costa Rica Spanish Phrasebook and Latin American Spanish Phrasebook).

The indigenous languages that first baffled Cortés have had a considerable impact on Mexican Spanish, especially in words to do with food, flora, fauna and place names (including the word *México* itself). Nahuatl words, such as *avocado* and *tomato*, have even made it into the English language. These days US English is possibly the strongest influence on Mexican Spanish, particularly in the northern border areas where Mexicans are known to accommodate some English words in everyday conversation.

Getting acquainted with Mexican Spanish is easy. In many ways, the pronunciation is similar to English, and visitors soon fall for the beauty of the Mexican accent with its cantering rhythm and plaintive rising and falling. If you're already familiar with the Spanish spoken in Spain or elsewhere in Latin America you'll have no problem learning the basic differences, and locals will warm to your efforts to use the appropriate Mexican words and expressions.

This book gives you all the practical vocabulary and phrases you need to get by as well as all the fun, spontaneous phrases that lead to a better understanding of Mexico and its people. Need more encouragement? Remember, the contact you make using Mexican Spanish will make your travels unique. Local knowledge, new relationships and a sense of satisfaction are on the tip of your tongue, so don't just stand there, say something!

abbreviations used in this book

m	masculine	**sg**	singular	**pol**	polite
f	feminine	**pl**	plural	**inf**	informal

TOOLS > pronunciation
herramientas de pronunciación

Mexican Spanish pronunciation isn't hard, as many sounds are similar to sounds used in English. The best way to learn the correct pronunciation is to listen carefully to people around you.

Mexican Spanish pronunciation differs from the Castilian Spanish spoken in Spain. The most obvious difference is the lack of the lisping 'th' sound which is found in Castilian Spanish. With a bit of practice you'll soon get the basics and even if you can't roll your r's like Speedy González, you'll still be understood.

vowel sounds

vocales

symbol	english equivalent	spanish example
a	run	*agua*
e	red	*número*
ee	bee	*día*
o	dog	*ojo*
oo	book	*gusto*

Vowels in Mexican Spanish are quite short and fairly closed. Unlike some English vowels, the sound remains level, and each vowel is pronounced as an individual unit. There are, however, a number of cases where two vowel sounds become very closely combined (so-called 'diphthongs'):

symbol	english equivalent	spanish example
ai	a**i**sle	*bailar*
ay	s**ay**	*seis*
ow	h**ou**se	*autobús*
oy	b**oy**	*hoy*

consonant sounds

symbol	english equivalent	spanish example
b	**b**ig	**b**arco
ch	**ch**ili	**ch**ica
d	**d**in	**d**inero
f	**f**un	**f**iesta
g	**g**o	**g**ato
k	**k**ick	**c**abeza/**qu**eso
kh	as in the Scottish lo**ch**	**g**ente/**j**ardín/Mé**x**ico
l	**l**oud	**l**ago
m	**m**an	**m**añana
n	**n**o	**n**uevo
ny	ca**ny**on	se**ñ**ora
p	**p**ig	**p**adre
r	**r**un, but strongly 'rolled', especially in words with 'rr'	**r**itmo/ma**r**iposa/bu**rr**o
s	**s**o	**s**emana/**X**ochimilco
t	**t**in	**t**ienda
v	a soft 'b', halfway between 'v' and 'b'	**v**einte
w	**w**in	g**u**ardia/O**a**xaca
y	**y**es	**ll**ave/**vi**aje

word stress

Words in Spanish have stress, which means you emphasise one syllable over another. Rule of thumb: when a written word ends in *n*, *s* or a vowel, the stress falls on the second-last syllable. Otherwise, the final syllable is stressed. If you see an accent mark over a syllable, it cancels out these rules and you just stress that syllable instead. Don't worry if you can't remember this rule – our coloured phonetic guides give you the stressed syllable in *italics*.

plunge in!

¡anímate!

Don't worry too much about pronunciation. Speaking another language is a little like acting, so if you can talk the talk like Benicio del Toro you're halfway there. The coloured phonetic guides we've provided for every phrase give you all the correct sounds and the stressed syllables.

mexican spanish alphabet					
a	a	*j*	*kho*·ta	*r*	er
b	be *lar*·ga	*k*	ka	*rr*	*e*·re
c	se	*l*	e·le	*s*	*e*·se
ch	che	*ll*	*do*·ble *e*·le	*t*	te
d	de	*m*	e·me	*u*	oo
e	e	*n*	e·ne	*v*	be *kor*·ta
f	*e*·fe	*ñ*	e·nye	*w*	*do*·ble be
g	khe	*o*	o	*x*	e·kees
h	*a*·che	*p*	pe	*y*	ee·*grye*·ga
i	ee	*q*	koo	*z*	*se*·ta

pronunciation

11

spellbound

The relationship between Mexican Spanish sounds and their spelling is quite straightforward and consistent. The following rules will help you read any written Mexican Spanish you may come across:

c	before *e* or *i* pronounced as the 's' in 'so'	**c**erveza, **c**inco
	before *a*, *o* and *u* pronounced as the 'k' in 'kick'	**c**arro, **c**orto, **c**ubo
g	before *e* or *i* pronounced as the 'ch' in 'loch' – a harsh, breathy sound	**g**igante
gue, gui	pronounced as the 'g' in 'go' (the *u* is not pronounced in these combinations unless there are two dots over the *u*)	**g**uerra, **G**uillermo, **g**üiski
h	never pronounced (silent)	**h**aber
j	harsh and breathy as the 'ch' in 'loch'	**j**ardín
ll	pronounced as the 'y' in 'yes'	**ll**ave
ñ	pronounced as the 'ny' in 'canyon'	ni**ñ**o
qu	pronounced as the 'k' in 'kick' (*u* is not pronounced)	**qu**ince
x	usually pronounced as the 'ch' in 'loch'	Mé**x**ico
	as an 's' in some indigenous place names	**X**ochimilco
	as a 'ks' in other words (See also the box on page 84)	pró**x**imo
z	pronounced as the 's' in 'soup'	**z**orro

TOOLS

12

a–z phrasebuilder
construyendo frases

Differences in vocabulary and pronunciation distinguish Mexican Spanish from the Spanish spoken in Spain. But Mexicans will also structure their sentences slightly differently. If you're already familiar with some Spanish, take note of how Mexicans use **diminutives** (page 17) and the plural form of **you** (page 26).

This chapter is designed to help you build your own sentences. It's arranged alphabetically for ease of navigation. If you can't find the exact phrase you need in this book, remember that with just a little grammar, a few gestures and a couple of well-chosen words, you'll generally get the message across.

a/an & some

I'd like a ticket and a postcard.

Quisiera un boleto   kee·*sye*·ra oon bo·*le*·to
y una postal.   ee *oo*·na pos·*tal*
(lit: I-would-like a ticket
   and a postcard)

Spanish has two words for 'a/an': *un* and *una*. The gender of the noun determines which one you use. *Un* and *una* have plural forms, *unos* and *unas*, meaning 'some'.

masculine	*un* sg	*un taco* oon *ta*·ko	**a taco**
	unos pl	*unos tacos* oo·nos *ta*·kos	**some tacos**
feminine	*una* sg	*una casa* oo·na *ka*·sa	**a house**
	unas pl	*unas casas* oo·nas *ka*·sas	**some houses**

adjectives see describing things

articles see a/an & some and the

be

Spanish has two words for the English verb 'be': *ser* and *estar*.

use *SER* to express	examples	
permanent characteristics of persons/things	*Cecilia es muy amable.* se·*see*·lya es mooy a·*ma*·ble	Cecilia is very nice.
occupations or nationality	*Marcos es de México.* *mar*·kos es de me·*khee*·ko	Marcos is from Mexico.
the time & location of events	*Son las tres.* son las tres	It's 3 o'clock.
possession	*¿De quién es esta mochila?* de kyen es es·ta mo·*chee*·la	Whose backpack is this?

use *ESTAR* to express	examples	
temporary characteristics of persons/things	*La comida está fría.* la ko·*mee*·da es·ta *free*·a	The meal is cold.
the time & location of persons/things	*Estamos en Coyoacán.* es·*ta*·mos en ko·yo·a·kan	We are in Coyoacán.
the mood of a person	*Estoy contento/a.* m/f es·*toy* kon·*ten*·to/a	I'm happy.

I	am	a journalist	yo	soy	reportera
you sg inf	are	from Chihuahua	tú	eres	de Chihuahua
you sg pol	are	an artist	usted	es	artista
he/she	is	an artist	él/ella m/f	es	artista
we	are	single	nosotros/as m/f	somos	solteros/as m/f
you pl pol&inf	are	students	ustedes m&f	son	estudiantes
they	are	students	ellos/as m/f	son	estudiantes

I	am	well	yo	estoy	bien
you sg inf	are	angry	tú	estás	enojado/a m/f
you sg pol	are	drunk	usted	está	borracho/a m/f
he/she	is	drunk	él/ella	está	borracho/a m/f
we	are	happy	nosotros/as m/f	estamos	contentos/as m/f
you pl pol&inf	are	reading	ustedes	están	leyendo
they	are	reading	ellos/as m/f	están	leyendo

describing things

I'm looking for a comfortable hotel.

> *Estoy buscando un hotel* es·toy boos·*kan*·do oon o·*tel*
> *cómodo.* *ko*·mo·do
> (lit: I-am looking-for a hotel
>   comfortable)

When using an adjective to describe a noun, you need to use a different ending depending on whether the noun is masculine or feminine, and singular or plural. Most adjectives have four forms which are easy to remember:

	singular	**plural**
masculine	*fantástico*	*fantásticos*
feminine	*fantástica*	*fantásticas*

un hotel fantástico	oon o·*tel* fan·*tas*·tee·ko	a fantastic hotel
una hamaca fantástica	*oo*·na a·*ma*·ka fan·*tas*·tee·ka	a fantastic hammock
unos libros fantásticos	*oo*·nos *lee*·bros fan·*tas*·tee·kos	some fantastic books
unas tortillas fantásticas	*oo*·nas tor·*tee*·yas fan·*tas*·tee·kas	some fantastic tortillas

Adjectives generally come after the noun in Spanish. However, adjectives of quantity (such as 'much', 'a lot', 'little/few', 'too much') and adjectives expressing possession (eg, 'my' and 'your') always precede the noun.

muchos turistas	*moo*·chos too·*rees*·tas	many tourists
primera clase	pree·*me*·ra *kla*·se	first class
mi sombrero	mee som·*bre*·ro	my hat

diminutives

Mexicans frequently use diminutives which are nouns whose endings have been altered in order to soften their intensity, emphasise smallness, express endearment or even show politeness. A person's name can be made diminutive as a way of expressing affection, especially towards a child or younger sibling.

Diminutives are created by changing the ending of the noun to *-ito* for a masculine noun, or *-ita* for a feminine noun. Less commonly, diminutives may be formed with *-illo* and *-illa* endings.

noun	diminutive noun	used to express
un momento **one moment**	*un momentito* **just a moment** (lit: a moment-little)	show politeness
dos semanas **two weeks**	*dos semanitas* **just two weeks** (lit: two weeks-little)	soften intensity
gato **cat**	*gatito* **kitten** (lit: cat-little)	emphasize smallness
Pablo **Paul**	*Pablito* **(dear) Paul** (lit: Paul-little)	endearment/ affection

gender

In Mexican Spanish, all nouns – words which denote a thing, person or concept – are either masculine or feminine.

The dictionary will tell you what gender a noun is, but here are some handy tips to help you determine gender:

- gender is masculine when talking about a man and feminine when talking about a woman
- words ending in *-o* are often masculine
- words ending in *-a* are often feminine
- words ending in *-d*, *-z* or *-ión* are usually feminine

In this book, masculine forms appear before the feminine forms. If you see a word ending in -o/a, it means the masculine form ends in -o, and the feminine form ends in -a (that is, you replace the -o ending with the -a ending to make it feminine). The same goes for the plural endings -os/as. If you seen an (a) between brackets on the end of a word, eg, *escritor(a)*, it means you have to add that in order to make that word feminine. In other cases we spell out the whole word.

See also **a/an & some**, **describing things**, **possession** and **the**.

have

I have two brothers.
> *Tengo dos hermanos.*   *ten·go dos er·ma·nos*
> (lit: I-have two brothers)

Possession can be indicated in various ways in Mexican Spanish. The easiest way is by using the verb *tener*, 'have'.

I	have	a ticket	yo	tengo	un boleto
you sg inf	have	the key	tú	tienes	la llave
you sg pol	have	the key	usted	tiene	la llave
he/she	has	aspirin	él/ella	tiene	aspirinas
we	have	matches	nosotros/as m/f	tenemos	cerillos
you pl pol&inf	have	tequila	ustedes	tienen	tequila
they	have	problems	ellos/as m/f	tienen	problemas

See also **my & your** and **somebody's**.

is & are see be

more than one

I would like two tickets.
> *Quisiera dos boletos.*   kee·*sye*·ra dos bo·*le*·tos
> (lit: I-would-like two tickets)

In general, if the word ends in a vowel, you add -s for a plural. If the nouns ends in a consonant (or *y*), you add -*es*:

| bed | *cama* | *ka*·ma | beds | *camas* | *ka*·mas |
| woman | *mujer* | moo·*kher* | women | *mujeres* | moo·*khe*·res |

my & your

This is my daughter.
> *Ésta es mi hija.*   *es*·ta es mee *ee*·kha
> (lit: this is my daughter)

A common way of indicating possession is by using possessive adjectives before the noun they describe. As with any other adjective, they always agree with the noun in number (singular or plural) and gender (masculine or feminine).

	singular		plural	
	masculine	**feminine**	**masculine**	**feminine**
	gift	room	friends	sisters
my	*mi regalo*	*mi habitación*	*mis amigos*	*mis hermanas*
your sg inf	*tu regalo*	*tu habitación*	*tus amigos*	*tus hermanas*
your sg pol	*su regalo*	*su habitación*	*sus amigos*	*sus hermanas*
his/her/its	*su regalo*	*su habitación*	*sus amigos*	*sus hermanas*
our	*nuestro regalo*	*nuestra habitación*	*nuestros amigos*	*nuestras hermanas*
your pl pol&inf	*su regalo*	*su habitación*	*sus amigos*	*sus hermanas*
their	*su regalo*	*su habitación*	*sus amigos*	*sus hermanas*

See also **have** & **somebody's**.

negative

Just add the word *no* before the main verb of the sentence:

I don't like bullfights.
No me gustan las corridas de toros.
(lit: not me they-please the bullfights)

no me *goo*·stan las ko·*ree*·das de *to*·ros

planning ahead

As in English, you can talk about your plans or future events by using the verb *ir* (go) followed by the word *a* (to) and the infinitive of another verb, for example:

Tomorrow, I'm going to travel to Real de Catorce.

Mañana, yo voy a viajar   ma·*nya*·na yo voy a vya·*khar*
a Real de Catorce.   a re·*al* de ka·*tor*·se
(lit: tomorrow I go-I to travel
   to Real de Catorce)

I	am going	to call	yo	voy	a llamar
you sg inf	are going	to sleep	tú	vas	a dormir
you sg pol	are going	to dance	usted	va	a bailar
he/she	is going	to drink	él/ella	va	a beber
we	are going	to sing	nosotros/as m/f	vamos	a cantar
you pl pol&inf	are going	to eat	ustedes	van	a comer
they	are going	to write	ellos/as m/f	van	a escribir

plural see more than one

pointing something out

To point something out the easiest phrases to use are *es* (it is), or *eso es* (that is). To say 'this is' use *este es* if it's a masculine object and *esta es* if it's a feminine.

Es una guía de Mérida.	es *oo*·na *gee*·a de me·*ree*·da	It's a guide to Mérida.
Eso es mezcal.	e·so es mes·*kal*	That is mezcal.
Este es mi pasaporte.	es·to es mee pa·sa·*por*·te	This is my passport.
Esta es mi licencia.	es·ta es mee lee·*sen*·sya	This is my drivers license.

See also **this & that**.

possession see **have, my & your** and **somebody's**

pronouns

Subject pronouns corresponding to 'I', 'you', 'he', 'she', 'it', 'we' and 'they' are often omitted, as verb endings make it clear who the subject is. Use them if you want to emphasise the subject.

singular		plural	
I	*yo*	**we**	*nosotros/as* m/f
you inf	*tú*	**you** pl inf	*ustedes*
you pol	*usted*	**you** pl pol	*ustedes*
he/she/it	*él/ella*	**they**	*ellos/as* m/f

See also **be, have** and **you**.

questions

Is that the main square?
   ¿Eso es el zócalo?   e·so es el *so*·ka·lo
   (lit: that is the main-square)

When asking a question, simply make a statement, but raise your intonation towards the end of the sentence, as you can do in English. The inverted question mark in written Spanish prompts you to do this.

question words

Who?	*¿Quién?* sg *¿Quiénes?* pl	kyen *kye*·nes
Who is it?	*¿Quién es?*	kyen es
Who are those men?	*¿Quiénes son estos hombres?*	*kye*·nes son es·tos om·bres
What?	*¿Qué?*	ke
What are you saying?	*¿Qué está usted diciendo?*	ke es·*ta* oo·*sted* dee·*syen*·do
Which?	*¿Cuál?* sg *¿Cuáles?* pl	kwal *kwa*·les
Which restaurant is the cheapest?	*¿Cuál es el restaurante más barato?*	kwal es el res·tow·*ran*·te mas ba·*ra*·to
Which local dishes do you recommend?	*¿Cuáles platos típicos puedes recomendar?*	*kwa*·les *pla*·tos *tee*·pee·kos *pwe*·des re·ko·men·*dar*
When?	*¿Cuándo?*	*kwan*·do
When does the next bus arrive?	*¿Cuándo llega el próximo pesero?*	*kwan*·do *ye*·ga el *prok*·see·mo pe·*se*·ro
Where?	*¿Dónde?*	*don*·de
Where can I buy tickets?	*¿Dónde puedo comprar boletos?*	*don*·de *pwe*·do kom·*prar* bo·*le*·tos
How?	*¿Cómo?*	*ko*·mo
How do you say that in Spanish?	*¿Cómo se dice eso en español?*	*ko*·mo se *dee*·se es·o en es·pa·*nyol*
How much is it?	*¿Cuánto cuesta?*	*kwan*·to *kwe*·sta
How many?	*¿Cuántos/as?* m/f pl	*kwan*·tos/*kwan*·tas
For how many nights?	*¿Por cuántas noches?*	por *kwan*·tas *no*·ches
Why?	*¿Por qué?*	por ke
Why is the museum closed?	*¿Por qué está cerrado el museo?*	por ke es·*ta* se·*ra*·do el moo·*se*·o

some see a/an & some

somebody's

In Spanish, ownership is expressed through the word *de* (of).

That's my friend's backpack.
Esa es la mochila   *e·*sa es la mo·*chee·*la
de mi amigo.   de mee a·*mee·*go
(lit: that is the backpack
  of my friend)

See also **have** and **my & your**.

the

The articles *el* and *la* both mean 'the'. Whether you use *el* or *la* depends on the gender of the thing, person or idea talked about, which in Spanish will always be either masculine or feminine. The gender is not really concerned with the sex of something, for example a toucan is a masculine noun, even if it's female! There's no rule as to why, say, the sea (*el mar*) is masculine but the beach (*la playa*) is feminine.

When talking about plural things, people or ideas, you use *los* in stead of *el* and *las* instead of *la*.

	singular	plural
masculine	*el*	*los*
feminine	*la*	*las*

el burro	el *boo·*ro	the donkey
la tienda	la *tyen·*da	the shop
los burros	los *boo·*ros	the donkeys
las tiendas	las *tyen·*das	the shops

See also **gender** and **a/an** & **some**.

this & that

There are three 'distance words' in Spanish, depending on whether something or someone is close (this), away from you (that) or even further away in time or distance (that over there).

masculine	singular	plural
close	*éste* (this)	*éstos* (these)
away	*ése* (that)	*ésos* (those)
further away	*aquél* (that over there)	*aquéllos* (those over there)
feminine		
close	*ésta* (this)	*éstas* (these)
away	*ésa* (that)	*ésas* (those)
further away	*aquélla* (that over there)	*aquéllas* (those over there)

See also **pointing something out**.

word order

Sentences in Mexican Spanish have a basic word order of subject-verb-object, just as English does.

I study business.

Yo estudio comercio.   yo es·*too*·dyo ko·*mer*·syo
(lit: I study-I business)

However, the subject pronoun is generally omitted: '*Estudio comercio*' is enough.

yes/no questions

It's not impolite to answer questions with a simple *sí* (yes) or *no* (no) in Mexico. There's no way to say 'Yes it is/does', or 'No, it isn't/doesn't', as in English.

See also **questions**.

you

Mexicans use two different words for 'you'. When talking to someone familiar to you or younger than you, it's usual to use the informal form *tú*, too, rather than the polite form *usted*, oos·*ted*. The polite form should be used when you're meeting someone for the first time, talking to someone much older than you or when you're in a formal situation (eg, when talking to the police, customs officers etc).

In this phrasebook we have often chosen the appropriate form for the situation, so you don't have to think twice about whether you are being polite enough. If both forms could be handy we give you the polite option first, followed by the informal option. For example:

Did you like it?
   ¿Le/Te gustó? pol/inf   le/te goos·to

Note that in Mexcio you use the word *ustedes* when you mean 'you' plural – whether or not it's a formal situation. This is different to the Spanish spoken in Spain where you would distinguish between formal speech (*ustedes*) and informal speech (*vosotros/as* m/f).

language difficulties
dificultades con el idioma

Do you speak (English)?
¿Habla/Hablas (inglés)? pol/inf   a·bla/a·blas (een·gles)

Does anyone speak (English)?
¿Hay alguien que   ai al·gyen ke
hable (inglés)?   a·ble (een·gles)

Do you understand?
¿Me entiende/entiendes? pol/inf   me en·tyen·de/en·tyen·des

I understand.
Entiendo.   en·tyen·do

I don't understand.
No entiendo.   no en·tyen·do

I speak (Spanish).
Hablo (español).   a·blo (es·pa·nyol)

I don't speak (Spanish).
No hablo (español).   no a·blo (es·pa·nyol)

I speak a little (Spanish).
Hablo un poquito   a·blo oon po·kee·to
(de español).   (de es·pa·nyol)

I speak (English).
Hablo (inglés).   a·blo (een·gles)

How do you pronounce this?
¿Cómo se pronuncia ésto?   ko·mo se pro·noon·sya es·to

How do you write 'ciudad'?
¿Cómo se escribe   ko·mo se se es·kree·be
'ciudad'?   syoo·dad

What does 'güey' mean?
¿Qué significa 'güey'?   ke seeg·nee·fee·ka gway

Could you please …?	¿Puede …, por favor?	pwe·de … por fa·vor
repeat that	repertirlo	re·pe·teer·lo
speak more slowly	hablar más despacio	a·blar mas des·pa·syo
write it down	escribirlo	es·kree·beer·lo

false friends

Beware of false friends – words which look, and sound, like English words but have a different meaning altogether. Using them in the wrong context could confuse, or even amuse locals.

injuria   een·khoo·ree·a   insult
     not 'injury' which is *herida*, e·ree·da

parientes   pa·ryen·tes   relatives
     not 'parents' which is *padres*, pa·dres

éxito   ek·see·to   success
     not 'exit' which is *salida*, sa·lee·da

embarazada   em·ba·ra·sa·da   pregnant.
     not 'embarrassed' which is *avergonzado/a* m/f
     a·ver·gon·sa·do/a

Spanish visitors to Mexico frequently embarrass themselves by using the verb *coger* which in Spain means 'to take' or 'to catch' but in Mexico means 'to fuck'.

numbers & amounts
los números & las cantidades

cardinal numbers

los números cardinales

0	*cero*	*se*·ro
1	*uno*	*oo*·no
2	*dos*	dos
3	*tres*	tres
4	*cuatro*	*kwa*·tro
5	*cinco*	*seen*·ko
6	*seis*	says
7	*siete*	*sye*·te
8	*ocho*	*o*·cho
9	*nueve*	*nwe*·ve
10	*diez*	dyes
11	*once*	*on*·se
12	*doce*	*do*·se
13	*trece*	*tre*·se
14	*catorce*	ka·*tor*·se
15	*quince*	*keen*·se
16	*dieciséis*	dye·see·*says*
17	*diecisiete*	dye·see·*sye*·te
18	*dieciocho*	dye·see·*o*·cho
19	*diecinueve*	dye·see·*nwe*·ve
20	*veinte*	*vayn*·te
21	*veintiuno*	vayn·tee·*oo*·no
22	*veintidós*	vayn·tee·*dos*
30	*treinta*	*trayn*·ta
40	*cuarenta*	kwa·*ren*·ta
50	*cincuenta*	seen·*kwen*·ta
60	*sesenta*	se·*sen*·ta
70	*setenta*	se·*ten*·ta
80	*ochenta*	o·*chen*·ta
90	*noventa*	no·*ven*·ta
100	*cien*	syen
200	*doscientos*	do·*syen*·tos
1,000	*mil*	meel
2,000	*dos mil*	dos meel
1,000,000	*un millon*	oon mee·*yon*

ordinal numbers

1st	*primero/a* m/f	pree·*me*·ro/a
2nd	*segundo/a* m/f	se·*goon*·do/a
3rd	*tercero/a* m/f	ter·*se*·ro/a
4th	*cuarto/a* m/f	*kwar*·to/a
5th	*quinto/a* m/f	*keen*·to/a

fractions

las fracciones

a quarter	*un cuarto*	oon *kwar*·to
a third	*un tercio*	oon *ter*·syo
a half	*un medio*	oon *me*·dyo/a
three-quarters	*tres cuartos*	tres *kwar*·tos
all (of it)	*todo/a* m/f sg	*to*·do/*to*·da
all (of them)	*todos/as* m/f pl	*to*·dos/*to*·das
none	*nada*	*na*·da

useful amounts

cantidades útiles

How much?	*¿Cuánto/a?* m/f	*kwan*·to/*kwan*·ta
How many?	*¿Cuántos/as?* m/f pl	*kwan*·tos/*kwan*·tas
Please give me ...	*Por favor, deme ...*	por fa·*vor de*·me ...
(just) a little	*(sólo) un poco*	*(so*·lo) oon *po*·ko
some	*algunos/as* m/f pl	al·*goo*·nos/as
much	*mucho/a* m/f	*moo*·cho/a
many	*muchos/as* m/f pl	*moo*·chos/as
less	*menos*	*me*·nos
more	*más*	mas

telling the time

When telling the time in Mexico 'It is …' is expressed by *Son las …* followed by a number. The exceptions are *Es la una* (It's one o'clock), *Es mediodía* (It's midday) and *Es medianoche* (It's midnight).

What time is it?	*¿Qué hora es?*	ke *o*·ra es
It's one o'clock.	*Es la una.*	es la *oo*·na
It's (ten) o'clock.	*Son las (diez).*	son las (dyes)
Quarter past one.	*Es la una y cuarto.*	es la *oo*·na ee *kwar*·to
Twenty past one.	*Es la una y veinte .*	es la *oo*·na ee *vayn*·te
Half past (eight).	*Son las (ocho) y media.*	son las (*o*·cho) ee *me*·dya
Twenty to (eight).	*Son veinte para las (ocho).*	son *vayn*·te pa·ra las (*o*·cho)
Quarter to (eight).	*Son cuarto para las (ocho).*	son *kwar*·to pa·ra las (*o*·cho)
in the morning/am	*de la mañana*	de la ma·*nya*·na
in the afternoon/pm	*de la tarde*	de la *tar*·de
in the evening/pm	*de la noche*	de la *no*·che
at night/pm	*de la noche*	de la *no*·che
At what time …?	*¿A qué hora …?*	a ke *o*·ra …
At one.	*A la una.*	a la *oo*·na
At (eight).	*A las (ocho).*	a las (*o*·cho)
At (4.40 pm).	*A las (cuatro y cuarenta de la tarde).*	a las (*kwa*·tro ee kwa·*ren*·ta de la *tar*·de)

days of the week

Monday	*lunes*	*loo·*nes
Tuesday	*martes*	*mar·*tes
Wednesday	*miércoles*	*myer·*ko·les
Thursday	*jueves*	*khwe·*ves
Friday	*viernes*	*vyer·*nes
Saturday	*sábado*	*sa·*ba·do
Sunday	*domingo*	do·*meen·*go

the calendar

el calendario

months

January	*enero*	e·*ne·*ro
February	*febrero*	fe·*bre·*ro
March	*marzo*	*mar·*so
April	*abril*	a·*breel*
May	*mayo*	*ma·*yo
June	*junio*	*khoo·*nyo
July	*julio*	*khoo·*lyo
August	*agosto*	a·*gos·*to
September	*septiembre*	sep·*tyem·*bre
October	*octubre*	ok·*too·*bre
November	*noviembre*	no·*vyem·*bre
December	*diciembre*	dee·*syem·*bre

dates

What date?	*¿Qué día?*	ke *dee·*a
What' today's date?	*¿Qué día es hoy?*	ke *dee·*a es oy
It's (17 November).	*Es (el diecisiete de noviembre).*	es (el *dye·see·sye·*te de no·*vyem·*bre)

TOOLS

seasons

summer	*verano*	ve·*ra*·no
autumn	*otoño*	o·*to*·nyo
winter	*invierno*	een·*vyer*·no
spring	*primavera*	pree·ma·*ve*·ra

present

now	*ahora*	a·*o*·ra
right now	*ahorita*	a·o·*ree*·ta
this ...		
afternoon	*esta tarde*	*es*·ta *tar*·de
morning	*esta mañana*	*es*·ta ma·*nya*·na
month	*este mes*	*es*·te mes
week	*esta semana*	*es*·ta se·*ma*·na
year	*este año*	*es*·te *a*·nyo
today	*hoy*	oy
tonight	*esta noche*	*es*·ta *no*·che

past

(three days) ago	*hace (tres días)*	*a*·se (tres *dee*·as)
day before yesterday	*antier*	an·*tyer*
last ...		
month	*el mes pasado*	el mes pa·*sa*·do
night	*anoche*	a·*no*·che
week	*la semana pasada*	la se·*ma*·na pa·*sa*·da
year	*el año pasado*	el *a*·nyo pa·*sa*·do
since (May)	*desde (mayo)*	*des*·de (*ma*·yo)
yesterday	*ayer*	a·*yer*
yesterday ...	*ayer ...*	a·*yer ...*
afternoon	*en la tarde*	en la *tar*·de
evening	*en la noche*	en la *no*·che
morning	*en la mañana*	en la ma·*nya*·na

time & dates

33

future

day after tomorrow	*pasado mañana*	pa·*sa*·do ma·*nya*·na
in (six) days	*en (seis) días*	en (says) *dee*·as
next ...		
month	*el mes que viene*	el mes ke *vye*·ne
week	*la próxima*	la *prok*·see·ma
	semana	se·*ma*·na
year	*el año que viene*	el *a*·nyo ke *vye*·ne
tomorrow	*mañana*	ma·*nya*·na
tomorrow ...	*mañana en la ...*	ma·*nya*·na en la ...
afternoon	*tarde*	*tar*·de
evening	*noche*	*no*·che
morning	*mañana*	ma·*nya*·na
until (June)	*hasta (junio)*	*as*·ta (*khoo*·nyo)

mañana, mañana ...

It's worth remembering that the word *mañana* means 'tomorrow', but *la mañana* means 'morning'. More rarely, *mañana* can mean 'later on' (especially in bureaucratic situations). Also, *madrugada* can mean 'daybreak' or 'the small hours of the morning', depending on the context.

during the day

afternoon	*tarde* f	*tar*·de
dawn	*madrugada* f	ma·droo·*ga*·da
day	*día* m	*dee*·a
evening	*noche* f	*no*·che
morning	*mañana* f	ma·*nya*·na
night	*noche* f	*no*·che
sunrise	*amanecer* m	a·ma·ne·*ser*
sunset	*puesta* f *del sol*	*pwes*·ta del sol

money
dinero

How much is it?
¿Cuánto cuesta? — kwan·to kwes·ta

How much is this?
¿Cuánto cuesta ésto? — kwan·to kwes·ta es·to

It's free.
Es gratis. — es gra·tees

It's (10) pesos.
Cuesta (diez) pesos. — kwes·ta (dyes) pe·sos

Can you write down the price?
¿Puede escribir el precio? — pwe·de es·kree·beer el pre·syo

Do you change money here?
¿Se cambia dinero aquí? — se kam·bya dee·ne·ro a·kee

Do you accept …?	*¿Aceptan …?*	a·sep·tan …
credit cards	*tarjetas de crédito*	tar·khe·tas de kre·dee·to
debit cards	*tarjetas de débito*	tar·khe·tas de de·bee·to
travellers cheques	*cheques de viajero*	che·kes de vya·khe·ro

I'd like to …	*Me gustaría …*	me goos·ta·ree·a …
cash a cheque	*cobrar un cheque*	ko·brar oon che·ke
change money	*cambiar dinero*	kam·byar dee·ne·ro
change a travellers cheque	*cambiar un cheque de viajero*	kam·byar oon che·ke de vya·khe·ro
withdraw money	*sacar dinero*	sa·kar dee·ne·ro

What's the …?	*¿Cuál es …?*	kwal es …
commission	*la comisión*	la ko·mee·syon
exchange rate	*el tipo de cambio*	el tee·po de kam·byo

What's the charge for that?

¿Cuánto hay que pagar por eso?	kwan·to ai ke pa·gar por e·so

Do I need to pay upfront?

¿Necesito pagar por adelantado?	ne·se·see·to pa·gar por a·de·lan·ta·do

I'd like …, please.

Quisiera …, por favor.	kee·sye·ra … por fa·vor
a receipt *un recibo*	oon re·see·bo
my change *mi cambio*	mee kam·byo
my money back *que me devuelva el dinero*	ke me de·vwel·va el dee·ne·ro

I have already paid for this.

Ya pagué ésto.	ya pa·ge es·to

There's a mistake in the bill.

Hay un error en la cuenta.	ai oon e·ror en la kwen·ta

I don't want to pay the full price.

No quiero pagar el precio total.	no kye·ro pa·gar el pre·syo to·tal

Where's the nearest automatic teller machine?

¿Dónde está el cajero automático más cercano?	don·de es·ta el ka·khe·ro ow·to·ma·tee·ko mas ser·ka·no

---

pieces of eight

During the colonial era, the imperial currency circulated in Mexico was a silver coin known as the *Ocho Reales* (lit: eight royals) although in common usage it was referred to by its present name, the *peso* (lit: weight). Since the end of the 15th century, Mexico began to lead the world in the production of silver, and the *Ocho Reales* was traded all over the globe. In English-speaking countries it earned the name 'pieces of eight', in Holland the *Real van Achten*, and in Italy, the *colonnato* (lit: with-columns) alluding to the pillars of Hercules stamped on the coin. The Egyptians mistook these pillars for cannons and gave it the name *abu madfa*, meaning 'two cannons'.

getting around

desplazándose

What time does the ... leave?	¿A qué hora sale el ...?	a ke o·ra sa·le el ...
boat	barco	bar·ko
bus (city)	camión	ka·myon
bus (intercity)	autobús	ow·to·boos
metro	metro	me·tro
minibus	pesero	pe·se·ro
plane	avión	a·vyon
train	tren	tren
trolleybus	trolebús	tro·le·boos

What time's the ... bus?	¿A qué hora sale el ... autobús?	a ke o·ra sa·le el ... ow·to·boos
first	primer	pree·mer
last	último	ool·tee·mo
next	próximo	prok·see·mo

Can I have a lift in your ...?	¿Me puede dar un aventón en su ...?	me pwe·de dar oon a·ven·ton en soo ...
trailer	trailer	tray·ler
truck	camión	ka·myon
ute/pick-up	pickup	pee·kop
van	camioneta	ka·myo·ne·ta

bussing it

Originally, a small bus was simply called a *colectivo* but in the '70s, small public transport vehicles (including cars and vans) came to be classified as *peseros* – so called because the trip cost one peso. During the '80s, the goverment began introducing new minibuses known as *microbuses* or just *micros*. While all these terms are still widely used, the general word is *pesero*, though today a lift will cost you a lot more than one peso!

How long will it be delayed?
¿Cuánto tiempo habrá
de retraso?
*kwan·to tyem·po a·bra
de re·tra·so*

When's the next flight to (Mexico City)?
¿Cuándo sale el próximo
vuelo para (México)?
*kwan·do sa·le el prok·see·mo
vwe·lo pa·ra (me·khee·ko)*

Can you tell me when we get to (Puerto Vallarta)?
¿Me puede avisar cuándo
lleguemos a (Puerto Vallarta)?
*me pwe·de a·vee·sar kwan·do
ye·ge·mos a (pwer·to va·yar·ta)*

I want to get off here.
¡Aquí me bajo!
a·kee me ba·kho

Is this seat free?
¿Está libre este asiento?
es·ta lee·bre es·te a·syen·to

That's my seat.
Ése es mi asiento.
e·se es mee a·syen·to

buying tickets

comprando boletos

Where can I buy a ticket?
¿Dónde puedo comprar
un boleto?
*don·de pwe·do kom·prar
oon bo·le·to*

Do I need to book?
¿Tengo que reservar?
ten·go ke re·ser·var

Can I get a stand-by ticket?
¿Puede ponerme en la
lista de espera?
*pwe·de po·ner·me en la
lees·ta de es·pe·ra*

**I'd like to ... my
ticket, please.**
  cancel
  change
  confirm

*Me gustaría ... mi
boleto, por favor.*
  cancelar
  cambiar
  confirmar

*me goos·ta·ree·a ... mee
bo·le·to por fa·vor*
  kan·se·lar
  kam·byar
  kon·feer·mar

PRACTICAL

A ... ticket (to Oaxaca), please.	Un boleto ... (a Oaxaca), por favor.	oon bo·le·to ... (a wa·kha·ka) por fa·vor
1st-class	de primera clase	de pree·me·ra kla·se
2nd-class	de segunda clase	de se·goon·da kla·se
child's	infantil	een·fan·teel
one-way	viaje sencillo	vya·khe sen·see·yo
return	redondo	re·don·do
student's	de estudiante	de es·too·dyan·te

I'd like a/an ... seat.	Quisiera un asiento ...	kee·sye·ra oon a·syen·to ...
aisle	de pasillo	de pa·see·yo
(non-)smoking	en la sección de (no) fumar	en la sek·syon de (no) foo·mar
window	junto a la ventana	khoon·to a la ven·ta·na

Is there (a) ...?	¿Hay ...?	ai ...
air- conditioning	aire acondicionado	ai·re a·kon·dee·syo·na·do
blanket	una cobija	oo·na ko·bee·kha
toilet	sanitarios	sa·nee·ta·ryos
video	video	vee·de·o

How much is it?
¿Cuánto cuesta?   kwan·to kwes·ta

How long does the trip take?
¿Cuánto dura el viaje?   kwan·to doo·ra el vya·khe

Is it a direct route?
¿Es un viaje directo?   es oon vya·khe dee·rek·to

What time do I have to check in?
¿A qué hora tengo que documentar?   a ke o·ra ten·go ke do·koo·men·tar

For phrases about entering and leaving countries, see **border crossing**, page 47.

luggage

My luggage hasn't arrived.
Mis maletas no han llegado.
mees ma·*le*·tas no an ye·*ga*·do

My luggage has been …	*Se … mis maletas.*	se … mees ma·*le*·tas
damaged	*dañaron*	da·*nya*·ron
lost	*perdieron*	per·*dye*·ron
stolen	*robaron*	ro·*ba*·ron

I'd like …	*Quisiera …*	kee·*sye*·ra …
a luggage locker	*un casillero*	oon ka·see·*ye*·ro
some coins	*unas monedas*	oo·nas mo·*ne*·das
some tokens	*unas fichas*	oo·nas *fee*·chas

bus, trolleybus & metro

Which city/intercity bus goes to …?
¿Qué camión/ autobús va a …?
ke ka·*myon*/ ow·to·*boos* va a …

This/That one.
Éste/Ése.
es·te/*e*·se

Bus/Trolleybus number (11).
El camión/trolebús número (once).
el ka·*myon*/tro·le·*boos* *noo*·me·ro (*on*·se)

How many stops (to the market)?
¿Cuántas paradas son (al mercado)?
kwan·tas pa·ra·das son (al mer·*ka*·do)

train

What station is this?
¿Cuál es esta estación? kwal es *es*·ta es·ta·*syon*

What's the next station?
¿Cuál es la próxima estación? kwal es la *prok*·see·ma es·ta·*syon*

Does this train stop at (Chihuahua)?
¿Para el tren a (Chihuahua)? *pa*·ra el tren a (chee·*wa*·wa)

Do I need to change trains?
¿Tengo que cambiar de tren? *ten*·go ke kam·*byar* de tren

Which is the dining car?
¿Cuál es el vagón comedor? kwal es el va·*gon* ko·me·*dor*

Which carriage is …?	*¿Cuál es el tren …?*	kwal es el tren …
1st class	*de primera clase*	de pree·*me*·ra *kla*·se
for (Querétaro)	*para (Querétaro)*	*pa*·ra (ke·*re*·ta·ro)

boat

el barco

Are there life jackets?
¿Hay chalecos salvavidas? ai cha·*le*·kos sal·va·*vee*·das

What's the sea like today?
¿Cómo está el mar hoy? *ko*·mo es·*ta* el mar oy

I feel seasick.
Estoy mareado/a. m/f es·*toy* ma·*re*·a·do/a

taxi

el taxi

I'd like a taxi …	*Quisiera un taxi …*	kee·*sye*·ra oon *tak*·see …
at (9am)	*a las (nueve de la mañana)*	a las (*nwe*·ve de la ma·*nya*·na)
now	*ahora*	a·o·ra
tomorrow	*mañana*	ma·*nya*·na

Is this taxi free?
¿Está libre este taxi? es·ta lee·bre es·te tak·see

How much is it to …?
¿Cuánto cuesta ir a …? kwan·to kwes·ta eer a …

Please put the meter on.
Por favor, ponga el taxímetro. por fa·vor pon·ga el tak·see·me·tro

Please take me to (this address).
Por favor, lléveme a (esta dirección). por fa·vor ye·ve·me a (es·ta dee·rek·syon)

Please …	*Por favor …*	por fa·vor …
slow down	*vaya más despacio*	va·ya mas des·pa·syo
wait here	*espere aquí*	es·pe·re a·kee

Stop …	*Pare …*	pa·re …
at the corner	*en la esquina*	en la es·kee·na
here	*aquí*	a·kee

car & motorbike

car & motorbike hire

I'd like to hire a/an ...	Quisiera rentar ...	kee·sye·ra ren·tar ...
4WD	un cuatro por cuatro	oon kwa·tro por kwa·tro
automatic (car)	un (coche) automático	oon (ko·che) ow·to·ma·tee·ko
car	un coche	oon ko·che
manual (car)	un (coche) manual	oon (ko·che) ma·nwal
motorbike	una moto	oo·na mo·to

with/without ...	con/sin ...	kon/seen ...
air-conditioning	aire acondicionado	ai·re a·kon·dee·syo·na·do
a driver	chofer	cho·fer

How much for ... hire?	¿Cuánto cuesta la renta ...?	kwan·to kwes·ta la ren·ta ...
daily	diaria	dya·rya
hourly	por hora	por o·ra
weekly	semanal	se·ma·nal

on the road

What's the speed limit ...?	¿Cuál es el límite de velocidad ...?	kwal es el lee·mee·te de ve·lo·see·dad ...
in town	en las calles	en las ka·yes
on the highway	en las carreteras	en las ka·re·te·ras

Is this the road to (Palenque)?
¿Por aquí se va a (Palenque)?   por a·kee se va a (pa·len·ke)

Where's a petrol station?
¿Dónde hay una gasolinera?   don·de ai oo·na ga·so·lee·ne·ra

Please fill it up.
Lleno, por favor.   ye·no por fa·vor

I'd like (30) pesos worth.
Quiero (treinta) pesos.   kye·ro (trayn·ta) pe·sos

diesel	diesel	dee·sel
petrol	gasolina	ga·so·lee·na
unleaded petrol	gasolina sin plomo	ga·so·lee·na seen plo·mo
regular unleaded	Magna	mag·na
premium unleaded	Premium	pre·mee·oom

Please check the ...	*Por favor, revise ...*	por fa·vor re·vee·se ...
oil	el nivel del aceite	el nee·vel del a·say·te
tyre pressure	la presión de las llantas	la pre·syon de las yan·tas
water	el nivel del agua	el nee·vel del a·gwa

petrol
gasolina f
ga·so·lee·na

windscreen
parabrisas m
pa·ra·bree·sas

battery
batería f
ba·te·ree·a

engine
motor m
mo·tor

headlight
faro m
fa·ro

tyre
llanta f
yan·ta

(How long) Can I park here?
¿(Por cuánto tiempo)   (por *kwan*·to *tyem*·po)
Puedo estacionarme aquí?   pwe·do es·ta·syo·*nar*·me a·*kee*

Where do I pay?
¿Dónde se paga?   *don*·de se *pa*·ga

road signs

Alto	*al*·to	Stop
Ceda el Paso	*se*·da el *pa*·so	Give Way
Cuota	*kwo*·ta	Toll
Entrada	en·*tra*·da	Entrance
Estacionamiento	es·ta·syo·na·*myen*·to	Parking
Peligro	pe·*lee*·gro	Danger
Prohibido el Paso	pro·ee·*bee*·do el *pa*·so	No Entry
Prohibido	pro·ee·*bee*·do	No Parking
Estacionar	es·ta·syo·*nar*	
Salida	sa·*lee*·da	Exit
Un Sólo Sentido	oon *so*·lo sen·*tee*·do	One Way

problems

I need a mechanic.
Necesito un mecánico.   ne·se·*see*·to oon me·*ka*·nee·ko

The car has broken down (at the intersection).
El coche se descompuso   el *ko*·che se des·kom·*poo*·so
(en la intersección).   (en la een·ter·sek·*syon*)

I had an accident.
Tuve un accidente.   *too*·ve oon ak·see·*den*·te

The motorbike won't start.
La moto no arranca.   la *mo*·to no a·*ran*·ka

I have a flat tyre.
Tengo una llanta ponchada.   *ten*·go *oo*·na *yan*·ta pon·*cha*·da

I've lost my car keys.
Perdí las llaves de   per·*dee* las *ya*·ves de
mi coche.   mee *ko*·che

I've locked the keys inside.
Dejé las llaves dentro   de·*khe* las *ya*·ves *den*·tro
del coche.   del *ko*·che

I've run out of petrol.
Me quedé sin gasolina.   me ke·*de* seen ga·so·*lee*·na

Can you fix it (today)?
¿Puede arreglarlo (hoy)?   *pwe*·de a·re·*glar*·lo (oy)

How long will it take?
¿Cuánto tardará?   *kwan*·to tar·da·*ra*

listen for ...

ke *mar*·ka/mo·*de*·lo es
   ¿Qué marca/modelo es?   **What make/model is it?**

ten·go ke pe·*deer* e·sa re·fak·*syon*
   Tengo que pedir esa   **I have to order that part.**
   refacción.

bicycle

la bicicleta

Where can I ...?	*¿Dónde puedo ...?*	*don*·de *pwe*·do ...
buy a second-	*comprar una*	kom·*prar* oo·na
hand bike	*bicicleta*	bee·see·*kle*·ta
	usada	oo·*sa*·da
hire a bicycle	*rentar una*	ren·*tar* oo·na
	bicicleta	bee·see·*kle*·ta
How much is it	*¿Cuánto cuesta*	*kwan*·to *kwes*·ta
per ...?	*por ...?*	por ...
afternoon	*una tarde*	oo·na *tar*·de
day	*un día*	oon *dee*·a
hour	*hora*	*o*·ra
morning	*una mañana*	oo·na ma·*nya*·na

I have a puncture.
Se me ponchó una llanta.   se me pon·*cho* oo·na *yan*·ta

I'm here …
in transit
on business
on holiday
to visit relatives

Estoy aquí …
en tránsito
de negocios
de vacaciones
visitando a
mis parientes

es·*toy* a·*kee* …
en tran·see·to
de ne·*go*·syos
de va·ka·*syo*·nes
vee·see·*tan*·do a
mees pa·*ryen*·tes

I'm here for …
(10) days
(two) months
(three) weeks

Voy a estar …
(diez) días
(dos) meses
(tres) semanas

voy a es·*tar* …
(dyes) *dee*·as
(dos) *me*·ses
(tres) se·*ma*·nas

listen for …

soo … por fa·*vor*
pa·sa·*por*·te
tar·*khe*·ta de
too·*rees*·ta
vee·sa

Su …, por favor.
pasaporte
tarjeta de
turista
visa

Your …, please.
passport
tourist card

visa

es·*ta*
vya·*khan*·do …
en *groo*·po
kon soo fa·*mee*·lya

so·lo/a

¿Está
viajando …?
en grupo
con su familia

solo/a m/f

Are you
travelling …?
in a group
with your
family
on your own

For phrases about payment and receipts, see **money**, page 35.

I have nothing to declare.
No tengo nada
que declarar.

no *ten*·go *na*·da
ke de·kla·*rar*

I have something to declare.
Quisiera declarar algo.

kee·*sye*·ra de·kla·*rar* al·go

I didn't know I had to declare it.
No sabía que tenía que
declararlo.

no sa·*bee*·a ke te·*nee*·a ke
de·kla·*rar*·lo

Do you have this form in English?
¿Tiene esta forma
en inglés?

tye·ne *es*·ta *for*·ma
en een·*gles*

signs

Aduana	a·*dwa*·na	Customs
Artículos Libres	ar·*tee*·koo·los *lee*·bres	Duty-free
de Impuestos	de eem·*pwes*·tos	Goods
Control de	kon·*trol* de	Passport
Pasaportes	pa·sa·*por*·tes	Control
Inmigración	een·mee·gra·*syon*	Immigration

Where's (the bank)?
   ¿Dónde queda (el banco)?   don·de ke·da (el ban·ko)

I'm looking for (the cathedral).
   Busco (la catedral).   boos·ko (la ka·te·dral)

Which way's (the main square)?
   ¿Cómo se llega (al zócalo)?   ko·mo se ye·ga (al so·ka·lo)

How do I get to …?
   ¿Cómo llego a …?   ko·mo ye·go a …

How far is it?
   ¿A qué distancia está?   a ke dees·tan·sya es·ta

Can you show me (on the map)?
   ¿Me lo puede señalar   me lo pwe·de se·nya·lar
   (en el mapa)?   (en el ma·pa)

It's …	Está …	es·ta …
behind …	detrás de …	de·tras de …
(three) blocks from here	a (tres) cuadras	a (tres) kwa·dras
far away	lejos	le·khos
here	aquí	a·kee
in front of …	en frente de …	en fren·te de …
left	a la izquierda	a la ees·kyer·da
near	cerca	ser·ka
next to …	al lado de …	al la·do de …
on the corner	en la esquina	en la es·kee·na
one block from here	a una cuadra	a oo·na kwa·dra
opposite …	frente a …	fren·te a …
right	a la derecha	a la de·re·cha
straight ahead	todo derecho	to·do de·re·cho
there	ahí	a·ee

Turn ...	De vuelta a la ...	de vwel·ta a la ...
left/right	izquierda/	ees·kyer·da/
	derecha	de·re·cha
at the corner	en la esquina	en la es·kee·na
at the	en el semáforo	en el se·ma·fo·ro
traffic lights		

It's ...	Está a ...	es·ta a ...
(100) metres	(cien) metros	(syen) me·tros
(two) kilometres	(dos) kilómetros	(dos) kee·lo·me·tros
(30) minutes	(treinta)	(trayn·ta)
	minutos	mee·noo·tos

by bus (city)	en camión	en ka·myon
by car	en coche	en ko·che
by metro	en metro	en me·tro
by minibus	en pesero	en pe·se·ro
by taxi	en taxi	en tak·see
by train	en tren	en tren
on foot	a pie	a pye

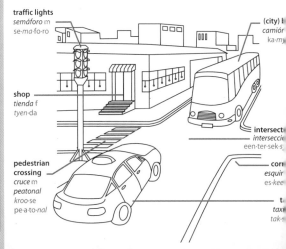

traffic lights
semáforo m
se·*ma*·fo·ro

shop
tienda f
tyen·da

pedestrian
crossing
cruce m
kroo·se
peatonal
pe·a·to·*nal*

(city) b
camión
ka·my

intersecti
intersecció
een·ter·sek·s

corr
esquir
es·*kee*

t
taxi
tak·s

PRACTICAL

accommodation

alojamiento

finding accommodation

buscando alojamiento

Where's a …?	*¿Dónde hay …?*	don·de ai …
camping ground	*un área para*	oon *a·re·a pa*·ra
	acampar	a·kam·*par*
guesthouse	*una pensión*	*oo*·na pen·*syon*
hotel	*un hotel*	oon o·*tel*
room	*una habitación*	*oo*·na a·bee·ta·*syon*
youth hostel	*un albergue*	oon al·*ber*·ge
	juvenil	khoo·ve·*neel*
Can you	*¿Puede*	*pwe*·de
recommend	*recomendarme*	re·ko·men·*dar*·me
somewhere …?	*alojamiento …?*	a·lo·kha·*myen*·to …
cheap	*barato*	ba·*ra*·to
good	*bueno*	*bwe*·no
luxurious	*lujoso*	loo·*kho*·so
nearby	*cercano*	ser·*ka*·no
romantic	*romántico*	ro·*man*·tee·ko

CHILES

a room with a view

In Mexico you'll find lodging to suit all budgets and lifestyles. Look out for some of the following popular accommodation options:

cabaña f	ka·*ba*·nya	cabin
casa f *de*	*ka*·sa de	lodging house
huespedes	*wes*·pe·des	
departamento m	de·par·ta·*men*·to	apartment
posada f	po·*sa*·da	inn

accommodation

What's the address?
¿Cuál es la dirección?   kwal es la dee·rek·*syon*

What's the telephone number?
¿Cuál es el teléfono?   kwal es el te·*le*·fo·no

<table>
<tr><td colspan="3">local talk</td></tr>
<tr><td>dive</td><td>lugar m de
mala muerte</td><td>loo·gar de
ma·la mwer·te</td></tr>
<tr><td>rat-infested</td><td>plagado/a m/f
de ratas</td><td>pla·ga·do/a
de ra·tas</td></tr>
<tr><td>top spot</td><td>lugar m
de moda</td><td>loo·gar
de mo·da</td></tr>
</table>

booking ahead & checking in

reservando & registrándose

Do you have	¿Tiene una	*tye*·ne *oo*·na
a ... room?	habitación ...?	a·bee·ta·*syon* ...
double	*doble*	*do*·ble
single	*sencilla*	sen·*see*·ya
triple	*triple*	*tree*·ple
twin	*con camas*	kon *ka*·mas
	individuales	een·dee·vee·*dwa*·les
with/without (a) ...	*con/sin ...*	kon/seen ...
air-conditioning	*aire*	*ai*·re
	acondicionado	a·kon·dee·syo·*na*·do
bathroom	*baño*	*ba*·nyo
fan	*ventilador*	ven·tee·la·*dor*
sea view	*vista al mar*	*vees*·ta al mar
street view	*vista a la calle*	*vees*·ta a la *ka*·ye
TV	*televisión*	te·le·vee·*syon*
How much is	¿Cuánto cuesta	*kwan*·to *kwes*·ta
it per ...?	por ...?	por ...
night	*noche*	*no*·che
person	*persona*	per·*so*·na
week	*semana*	se·*ma*·na

I'd like to book a room, please.
*Quisiera reservar una
habitación.*

kee·sye·ra re·ser·var oo·na
a·bee·ta·syon

I have a reservation.
Tengo una reservación.

ten·go oo·na re·ser·va·syon

My name's …
Me llamo …

me ya·mo …

For (three) nights/weeks.
Por (tres) noches/semanas.

por (tres) no·ches/se·ma·nas

From (30 July) to (4 August).
*Del (treinta de julio)
al (cuatro de agosto).*

del (trayn·ta de khoo·lyo)
al (kwa·tro de a·gos·to)

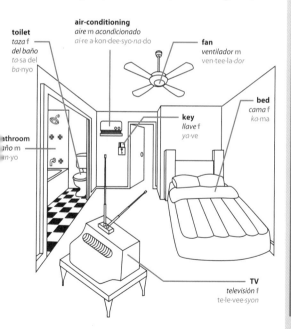

toilet
taza f
del baño
ta·sa del
ba·nyo

air-conditioning
aire m *acondicionado*
ai·re a·kon·dee·syo·na·do

fan
ventilador m
ven·tee·la·dor

bed
cama f
ka·ma

key
llave f
ya·ve

bathroom
baño m
ba·nyo

TV
televisión f
te·le·vee·syon

Can I see it?
¿Puedo verla?   pwe·do ver·la

It's fine. I'll take it.
Está bien, la tomo.   es·ta byen la to·mo

Do I need to pay upfront?
¿Necesito pagar por   ne·se·see·to pa·gar por
adelantado?   a·de·lan·ta·do

Can I pay ...?	*¿Puedo pagar ...?*	pwe·do pa·gar ...
by credit card	*con tarjeta*	kon tar·khe·ta
	de crédito	de kre·dee·to
by travellers	*con cheques*	kon che·kes
cheque	*de viajero*	de vya·khe·ro
with cash	*con efectivo*	kon e·fek·tee·vo

For more on payment, see **money**, page 35.

listen for ...

kon·soo·myo al·go del mee·nee·bar
¿Consumió algo del   **Did you use the**
minibar?   **mini-bar?**

la ya·ve es·ta en la re·sep·syon
La llave está en la   **The key is at**
recepción.   **reception.**

lo syen·to no ai va·kan·tes
Lo siento, no hay vacantes.   **I'm sorry, we're full.**

por kwan·tas no·ches
¿Por cuántas noches?   **For how many nights?**

soo pa·sa·por·te por fa·vor
Su pasaporte, por favor.   **Your passport, please.**

requests & queries

When/Where's breakfast served?
¿Cuándo/Dónde se sirve
el desayuno?
kwan·do/don·de se seer·ve
el de·sa·yoo·no

Do you have room service?
¿Tiene servicio al cuarto?
tye·ne ser·vee·syo al kwar·to

Please wake me at (seven).
Por favor, despiérteme a
las (siete).
por fa·vor des·pyer·te·me a
las (sye·te)

Can I get (another towel)?
¿Puede darme (otra toalla)?
pwe·de dar·me (o·tra to·a·ya)

Can I use the …?	*¿Puedo usar …?*	pwe·do oo·sar …
kitchen	*la cocina*	la ko·see·na
laundry	*la lavandería*	la la·van·de·ree·a
telephone	*el teléfono*	el te·le·fo·no

Do you have a/an …?	*¿Hay …?*	ai …
dry-cleaning service	*servicio de tintorería*	ser·vee·syo de teen·to·re·ree·a
elevator	*elevador*	e·le·va·dor
gym	*gimnasio*	kheem·na·syo
laundry service	*servicio de lavandería*	ser·vee·syo de la·van·de·ree·a
message board	*pizarrón de anuncios*	pee·sa·ron de a·noon·syos
safe	*caja fuerte*	ka·kha fwer·te
swimming pool	*alberca*	al·ber·ka

Do you … here?	*¿Aquí …?*	a·kee …
arrange tours	*organizan tours*	or·ga·nee·san toors
change money	*cambian dinero*	kam·byan dee·ne·ro

Can I leave a message for someone?
¿Puedo dejar un   *pwe·*do de·*khar* oon
mensaje para alguien?   men·*sa·*khe *pa·*ra *al·*gyen

Is there a message for me?
¿Hay algún mensaje   ai al·*goon* men·*sa·*khe
para mí?   *pa·*ra *mee*

I'm locked out of my room.
Dejé la llave dentro   de·*khe* la *ya·*ve *den·*tro
del cuarto.   del *kwar·*to

The (bathroom) door is locked.
La puerta (del baño) está   la *pwer·*ta (del *ba·*nyo) es·*ta*
cerrada con llave.   se·*ra·*da kon *ya·*ve

complaints

quejas

The room is	*La habitación*	la a·bee·ta·*syon*
too ...	*es muy ...*	es mooy ...
cold	*fría*	*free·*a
dark	*oscura*	os·*koo·*ra
expensive	*cara*	*ka·*ra
light/bright	*iluminada*	ee·loo·mee·*na·*da
noisy	*ruidosa*	rwee·*do·*sa
small	*pequeña*	pe·*ke·*nya

The (air-conditioning) doesn't work.
No funciona (el aire   no foon·*syo·*na (el *ai·*re
acondicionado).   a·kon·dee·syo·*na·*do)

This (blanket) isn't clean.
Esta (cobija) no está   es·ta (ko·*bee·*kha) no es·*ta*
limpia.   *leem·*pya

For more things you might want in your room, see the **dictionary**.

Who is it?	¿Quién es?	*kyen* es
Just a moment.	Un momentito.	oon mo·men·*tee*·to
Come in.	Pase.	*pa*·se
Come back later, please.	¿Puede volver más tarde, por favor?	*pwe*·de vol·*ver* mas *tar*·de por fa·*vor*

checking out

pagando la cuenta

What time is checkout?
¿A qué hora hay que dejar la habitación?
a ke *o*·ra ai ke de·*khar* la a·bee·ta·*syon*

Can I have a late checkout?
¿Puedo dejar la habitación más tarde?
pwe·do de·*khar* la a·bee·ta·*syon* mas *tar*·de

How much extra to stay until (6 o'clock)?
¿Cuánto cuesta quedarse hasta (las seis)?
kwan·to *kwes*·ta ke·*dar*·se *as*·ta (las says)

Can I leave my luggage here?
¿Puedo dejar mis maletas aquí?
pwe·do de·*khar* mees ma·*le*·tas a·*kee*

Can you call a taxi for me (for 11 o'clock)?
¿Me puede pedir un taxi (para las once)?
me *pwe*·de pe·*deer* oon *tak*·see (*pa*·ra las *on*·se)

There's a mistake in the bill.
Hay un error en la cuenta.
ai oon e·*ror* en la *kwen*·ta

I'm leaving now.
Me voy ahora.
me voy a·*o*·ra

Could I have my ..., please?	¿Me puede dar ..., por favor?	me *pwe*·de dar ... por fa·*vor*
deposit	mi depósito	mee de·*po*·see·to
passport	mi pasaporte	mee pa·sa·*por*·te
valuables	mis objetos de valor	mees ob·*khe*·tos de va·*lor*

accommodation

57

I'll be back ...	*Volveré ...*	vol·ve·*re* ...
in (three) days	*en (tres) días*	en (tres) *dee*·as
on (Tuesday)	*el (martes)*	el (*mar*·tes)

I had a great stay, thank you.
Tuve una estancia muy   *too*·ve *oo*·na es·*tan*·sya mooy
agradable, gracias.   a·gra·*da*·ble *gra*·syas

You've been terrific.
Han sido estupendos. pl   an *see*·do es·too·*pen*·dos

I'll recommend it to my friends.
Se lo recomendaré a mis   se lo re·ko·men·da·*re* a mees
amigos.   a·*mee*·gos

camping

acampando

Where's the	*¿Dónde está ...*	*don*·de es·*ta* ...
nearest ...?	*más cercana?*	mas ser·*ka*·na
campsite	*el área para*	el *a*·re·a *pa*·ra
	acampar	a·kam·*par*
shop	*la tienda*	la *tyen*·da
Do you have ...?	*¿Tiene ...?*	*tye*·ne ...
electricity	*electricidad*	e·lek·tree·see·*dad*
a site	*un lugar de*	oon loo·*gar* de
	acampado	a·kam·*pa*·do
shower facilities	*regaderas*	re·ga·*de*·ras
tents for hire	*tiendas de*	*tyen*·das de
	campaña en	kam·*pa*·nya en
	renta	*ren*·ta
How much is it	*¿Cuánto es*	*kwan*·to es
per ...?	*por ...?*	por ...
person	*persona*	per·*so*·na
tent	*tienda*	*tyen*·da
vehicle	*vehículo*	ve·*ee*·koo·lo

Can I …?	¿Se puede …?	se *pwe*·de …
camp here	*acampar aquí*	a·kam·*par* a·*kee*
park next to	*estacionar al lado*	es·ta·syo·*nar* al *la*·do
my tent	*de la tienda*	de la *tyen*·da

Who do I ask to stay here?
¿Con quién tengo que hablar   kon kyen *ten*·go ke a·*blar*
para quedarme aquí?   pa·ra ke·*dar*·me a·*kee*

Could I borrow (a mallet)?
¿Me puede prestar   me *pwe*·de pres·*tar*
(un martillo)?   (oon mar·*tee*·yo)

Where's the toilet block?
¿Dónde están los   *don*·de es·*tan* los
sanitarios?   sa·nee·*ta*·ryos

Is it coin-operated?
¿Funciona con monedas?   foon·*syo*·na kon mo·*ne*·das

Is the water drinkable?
¿El agua es potable?   el *a*·gwa es po·*ta*·ble

For more words related to camping, see the **dictionary**.

renting

renting

I'm here about the … for rent.
Vengo por el/la … en renta. m/f   *ven*·go por el/la … en *ren*·ta

Do you have	¿Tiene …	*tye*·ne …
a/an … for rent?	*en renta?*	en *ren*·ta
apartment	*un departamento*	oon de·par·ta·*men*·to
cabin	*una cabaña*	*oo*·na ka·*ba*·nya
house	*una casa*	*oo*·na *ka*·sa
room	*una recámara*	*oo*·na re·*ka*·ma·ra
villa	*una villa*	*oo*·na *vee*·ya

(partly) furnished	*(parcialmente)*	(par·syal·*men*·te)
	amueblado/a m/f	a·mwe·*bla*·do/a
unfurnished	*sin amueblar*	seen a·mwe·*blar*

How much is it for ...?	¿Cuánto cuesta por ...	kwan·to kwes·ta por ...
(one) week	(una) semana	(oo·na) se·ma·na
(two) months	(dos) meses	(dos) me·ses

Are bills extra?
¿Los servicios se pagan aparte?   los ser·vee·syos se pa·gan a·par·te

staying with locals

Can I stay at your place?
¿Me puedo quedar en su/tu casa? pol/inf   me pwe·do ke·dar en soo/too ka·sa

Is there anything I can do to help?
¿Puedo ayudar en algo?   pwe·do a·yoo·dar en al·go

I have my own ...	Tengo mi propio/a ... m/f	ten·go mee pro·pyo/a ...
hammock	hamaca f	a·ma·ka
mattress	colchón m	kol·chon
sleeping bag	bolsa f de dormir	bol·sa de dor·meer

Can I ...?	¿Puedo ...?	pwe·do ...
bring anything for the meal	traer algo para la comida	tra·er al·go pa·ra la ko·mee·da
do the dishes	lavar los platos	la·var los pla·tos
set/clear the table	poner/quitar la mesa	po·ner/kee·tar la me·sa
take out the rubbish	sacar la basura	sa·kar la ba·soo·ra

Thanks for your hospitality.
Gracias por su/tu hospitalidad. pol/inf   gra·syas por soo/too os·pee·ta·lee·dad

If you're dining with your hosts, see **eating out**, page 139, for additional phrases.

looking for ...

Where's (a supermarket)?
¿Dónde hay (un   *don·*de ai (oon
supermercado)?   soo·per·mer·*ka*·do)

Where can I buy (bread)?
¿Dónde puedo comprar (pan)? *don*·de *pwe*·do kom·*prar* (pan)

For more items and shopping locations, see the **dictionary**.
Want to know how to get there? See **directions**, page 49.

making a purchase

I'd like to buy ...
Quisiera comprar ...   kee·*sye*·ra kom·*prar* ...

I'm just looking.
Sólo estoy mirando.   *so*·lo es·*toy* mee·*ran*·do

How much is this?
¿Cuánto cuesta ésto?   *kwan*·to *kwes*·ta es·to

Can you write down the price?
¿Puede escribir el precio?   *pwe*·de es·kree·*beer* el *pre*·syo

Do you have any others?
¿Tiene otros?   *tye*·ne *o*·tros

Can I look at it?
¿Puedo verlo?   *pwe*·do *ver*·lo

I don't like it.
No me gusta. — no me *goos*·ta

Does it have a guarantee?
¿Tiene garantía? — *tye*·ne ga·ran·*tee*·a

Could I have it wrapped?
¿Me lo podría envolver? — me lo po·*dree*·a en·vol·*ver*

Can I have it sent overseas/abroad?
¿Pueden enviarlo a otro país? — *pwe*·den en·*vyar*·lo a o·tro pa·*ees*

Can you order it for me?
¿Me lo puede pedir? — me lo *pwe*·de pe·*deer*

When can I pick it up?
¿Cuándo lo puedo recoger? — *kwan*·do lo *pwe*·do re·ko·*kher*

Can I pick it up later?
¿Puedo recogerlo más tarde? — *pwe*·do re·ko·*kher*·lo mas *tar*·de

It's faulty/broken.
Está defectuoso/roto. — es·*ta* de·fek·*two*·so/*ro*·to

Do you accept ...?	*¿Aceptan ...?*	a·*sep*·tan ...
cash	*efectivo*	e·fek·*tee*·vo
credit cards	*tarjetas de crédito*	tar·*khe*·tas de *kre*·dee·to
debit cards	*tarjetas de débito*	tar·*khe*·tas de *de*·bee·to
travellers cheques	*cheques de viajero*	*che*·kes de vya·*khe*·ro

Could I have a ..., please?	*¿Podría darme ..., por favor?*	po·*dree*·a *dar*·me ... por fa·*vor*
bag	*una bolsa*	*oo*·na *bol*·sa
box	*una caja*	*oo*·na *ka*·kha
receipt	*un recibo*	oon re·*see*·bo

I'd like ..., please.	*Quisiera ..., por favor.*	kee·*sye*·ra ... por fa·*vor*
my change	*mi cambio*	mee *kam*·byo
my money back	*que me devuelva el dinero*	ke me de·*vwel*·va el dee·*ne*·ro
to return this	*devolver ésto*	de·vol·*ver* es·to

bargaining

That's too expensive.
Es demasiado caro/a. m/f   es de·ma·*sya*·do *ka*·ro/a

The price is very high.
El precio es muy alto.   el *pre*·syo es mooy *al*·to

Can you lower the price?
¿Podría bajar un poco   po·*dree*·a ba·*khar* oon *po*·ko
el precio?   el *pre*·syo

Do you have something cheaper?
¿Tiene algo más barato?   *tye*·ne *al*·go mas ba·*ra*·to

I'll give you …
Le doy …   le doy …

What's your final price?
¿Cuál es su precio final?   kwal es soo *pre*·syo fee·*nal*

local talk

bargain	*ganga* f	*gan*·ga
bargain hunter	*cazador/*	ka·sa·*dor*/
	cazadora m/f	ka·sa·*do*·ra
	de ofertas	de o·*fer*·tas
rip-off	*estafa* f	es·*ta*·fa
specials	*rebajas* f pl	re·*ba*·khas
sale	*venta* f	*ven*·ta

clothes

Can I try it on?
¿Me lo puedo probar?   me lo *pwe*·do pro·bar

It doesn't fit.
No me queda bien.   no me *ke*·da byen

It's too (big).
Está demasiado (grande).   es·*ta* de·ma·*sya*·do (*gran*·de)

My size is ...	Soy talla ...	soy *ta*·ya ...
small	chica	*chee*·ka
medium	mediana	me·*dya*·na
large	grande	*gran*·de
(40)	(cuarenta)	(kwa·*ren*·ta)

For different types of clothes, see the **dictionary**.

repairs

reparaciones

Can I have my ...	¿Puede reparar	*pwe*·de re·pa·*rar*
repaired here?	mi ... aquí?	mee ... a·*kee*
backpack	mochila	mo·*chee*·la
camera	cámara	*ka*·ma·ra

When will my	¿Cuándo estarán	*kwan*·do es·ta·*ran*
... be ready?	listos mis ...?	*lees*·tos mees ...
shoes	zapatos	sa·*pa*·tos
(sun)glasses	lentes (de sol)	*len*·tes (de sol)

hairdressing

en la estética

I'd like (a) ...	Quisiera ...	kee·*sye*·ra ...
blow wave	un secado a mano	oon se·*ka*·do a *ma*·no
colour	un tinte	oon *teen*·te
haircut	un corte de pelo	oon *kor*·te de *pe*·lo
highlights	unos reflejos	*oo*·nos re·*fle*·khos
my beard	que me recorte	ke me re·*kor*·te
trimmed	la barba	la *bar*·ba
shave	que me afeite	ke me a·*fay*·te
trim	que me despunte	ke me des·*poon*·te
	el pelo	el *pe*·lo

Do you do …?	*¿Aquí …?*	a·kee …
facials	*hacen*	a·sen
	tratamientos	tra·ta·*myen*·tos
	faciales	fa·*sya*·les
manicure	*hacen manicure*	a·*sen* ma·nee·*kyoor*
massage	*dan masajes*	dan ma·*sa*·khes
waxing	*depilan*	de·*pee*·lan

Don't cut it too short.
No me lo corte   no me lo *kor*·te
demasiado corto.   de·ma·*sya*·do *kor*·to

Shave it all off!
¡Rápeme!   *ra*·pe·me

Please use a new blade.
Por favor, use una   por fa·*vor* oo·*se* oo·na
navaja nueva.   na·*va*·kha *nwe*·va

I should never have let you near me!
¡No debería haberme   no de·be·*ree*·a a·*ber*·me
cortado con usted!   kor·*ta*·do kon oos·*ted*

For colours, see the **dictionary**.

---

his & hers

A *salón de belleza* is a hairdressing salon specifically for women, while a *peluquería* is for men. If you need a neutral word for 'hairdresser' use *estética*.

---

books & reading

libros & lectura

Is there a/an (English-language) …?	*¿Hay alguna … (con material en inglés)?*	ai al·*goo*·na … (kon ma·te·*ryal* en een·*gles*)
bookshop	*librería*	lee·bre·*ree*·a
section	*sección*	sek·*syon*

Do you have a book by (Rosario Castellanos)?
¿Hay algún libro de   ai al·*goon* lee·bro de
(Rosario Castellanos)?   (ro·*sa*·ree·o kas·te·*ya*·nos)

Can you recommend a book for me?
¿Me puede recomendar   me *pwe*·de re·ko·men·*dar*
algún libro?   al·*goon* lee·bro

Do you have Lonely Planet guidebooks?
¿Tiene libros de   *tye*·ne *lee*·bros de
Lonely Planet?   *lon*·lee *pla*·net

I'd like a ...	Quisiera ...	kee·*sye*·ra ...
dictionary	un diccionario	oon deek·syo·*na*·ryo
guidebook	una guía	oo·na *gee*·a
	turística	too·*rees*·tee·ka
magazine	una revista	oo·na re·*vees*·ta
map	un mapa	oon *ma*·pa
newspaper	un periódico	oon pe·*ryo*·dee·ko
(in English)	(en inglés)	(en een·*gles*)

listen for ...

no no te·*ne*·mos
   No, no tenemos.   **No, we don't have any.**

see te·*ne*·mos al·*goo*·nas *gee*·as
   Sí, tenemos algunas guías. **Yes, we have some**
                             guidebooks.

music

música

I'd like ...	Quisiera ...	kee·*sye*·ra ...
a blank tape	un cassette	oon ka·*set*
	vírgen	*veer*·khen
a CD	un cómpact	oon *kom*·pakt
headphones	unos audífonos	oo·nos ow·*dee*·fo·nos

I heard a band called (Maná).
Escuché a un grupo que se   es·koo·*che* a oon *groo*·po ke se
llama (Maná).   *ya*·ma (ma·*na*)

I heard a singer called ...
Escuché a un cantante   es·koo·*che* a oon kan·*tan*·te
que se llama (Luis Miguel)   ke se *ya*·ma (*loo*·ees mee·*gel*)

What's his/her best recording?
¿Cuál es su mejor disco?   kwal es soo me·*khor dees*·ko

Can I listen to this?
¿Puedo escucharlo?   *pwe*·do es·koo·*char*·lo

photography

I need ... film for this camera.	*Necesito un rollo ... para esta cámara.*	ne·se·*see*·to oon *ro*·yo ... *pa*·ra *es*·ta *ka*·ma·ra
APS	*Advantix*	ad·*van*·teeks
B&W	*blanco y negro*	*blan*·ko y *ne*·gro
colour	*de color*	de ko·*lor*
slide	*de transparencias*	de trans·pa·*ren*·syas
(400) speed	*ASA (cuatrocientos)*	*a*·sa (*kwa*·tro·*syen*·tos)
a 35 mm	*de treinta y cinco milímetros*	de *trayn*·ta ee *seen*·ko mee·*lee*·me·tros
Can you ...?	*¿Puede ...?*	*pwe*·de ...
develop this film	*revelar este rollo*	re·ve·*lar es*·te *ro*·yo
load my film	*cargar la cámara*	kar·*gar* la *ka*·ma·ra
I'd like ...	*Quisiera ...*	kee·*sye*·ra ...
borders	*marcos*	*mar*·kos
double copies	*dos copias*	dos *ko*·pyas
glossy	*en papel brillante*	en pa·*pel* bree·*yan*·te
matte	*en papel mate*	en pa·*pel ma*·te
panoramic	*panorámica*	pa·no·*ra*·mee·ka

How much is it to develop this film?

¿Cuánto cuesta revelar   *kwan·*to *kwes·*ta re·ve·*lar*
este rollo?   *es·*te *ro·*yo

When will it be ready?

¿Cuándo estará listo?   *kwan·*do es·ta·*ra lees·*to

I need passport photos taken.

Necesito fotos tamaño   ne·se·*see·*to *fo·*tos ta·*ma·*nyo
pasaporte.   pa·sa·*por·*te

I'm (not) happy with these photos.

(No) Estoy satisfecho/a con   (no) es·*toy* sa·tee·*fe·*cho/a kon
estas fotos. m/f   *es·*tas *fo·*tos

I don't want to pay the full price.

No quiero pagar el precio   no *kye·*ro pa·*gar* el *pre·*syo
total.   to·*tal*

For more photographic equipment, see the **dictionary**.

---

souvenirs

What is typical of the region?

¿Qué es típico de   ke es *tee·*pee·ko de
la región?   la re·*khyon*

alebrijes m pl   a·le·*bree·*khes
    wood carvings of mythical creatures, crafted mainly in Oaxaca

amate m   a·*ma·*te
    decorated bark paper produced in central Mexico

hamacas f pl   a·*ma·*kas
    hammocks, usually made of cotton or nylon

huaraches m pl   wa·*ra·*ches
    leather sandals available all over Mexico

huipiles m pl   wee·*pee·*les
    traditional tunics worn mostly in the south

jipijapas m pl   khee·pee·*kha·*pas
    Panama-style hats sold in Mérida and Campeche

piñatas f pl   pee·*nya·*tas
    traditional festive dolls filled with candy

post office

el correo

English	Spanish	Pronunciation
I want to send a …	*Quisiera enviar …*	kee·*sye*·ra en·*vyar* …
fax	*un fax*	oon faks
letter	*una carta*	oo·na *kar*·ta
money order	*un giro*	oon *khee*·ro
parcel	*un paquete*	oon pa·*ke*·te
postcard	*una postal*	oo·na pos·*tal*
I want to buy …	*Quisiera comprar …*	kee·*sye*·ra kom·*prar* …
an envelope	*un sobre*	oon *so*·bre
stamps	*unos timbres*	oo·nos *teem*·bres

English	Spanish	Pronunciation
airmail	*correo* m *aéreo*	ko·re·o a·e·re·o
customs declaration	*declaración* f *de aduana*	de·kla·ra·*syon* de a·*dwa*·na
domestic	*nacional*	na·syo·*nal*
express mail	*correo* m *expreso*	ko·re·o ek·*spre*·so
fragile	*frágil*	*fra*·kheel
glue	*pegamento* m	pe·ga·*men*·to
international	*internacional*	een·ter·na·syo·*nal*
mailbox	*buzón* m	boo·*son*
postcode	*código* m *postal*	*ko*·dee·go pos·*tal*
registered mail	*correo* m *certificado*	ko·re·o ser·tee·fee·*ka*·do
regular mail	*correo* m *ordinario*	ko·re·o or·dee·*na*·ryo
sea mail	*vía marítima*	vee·a ma·*ree*·tee·ma

communications

69

a *don*·de lo en·*vee*·a
¿A dónde lo envía? **Where are you sending it?**

lo *kye*·re man·*dar* por ko·*re*·o ser·tee·fee·*ka*·do
¿Lo quiere mandar por **Would you like to send**
correo certificado? **it by registered post?**

por ko·*re*·o ek·*spre*·so o or·dee·*na*·ryo
¿Por correo expreso o **Express post or**
ordinario? **regular post?**

Please send it by air/regular mail to (France).
Por favor, mándelo por vía por fa·*vor* man·de·lo por *vee*·
aérea/terrestre a (Francia). a·*e*·re·a/te·*res*·tre a (*fran*·sya)

It contains ...
Contiene ... kon·*tye*·ne ...

phone

el teléfono

What's your phone number?
¿Cuál es su número de kwal es soo *noo*·me·ro de
teléfono? te·*le*·fo·no

Where's the nearest public phone?
¿Dónde hay un teléfono *don*·de ai oon te·*le*·fo·no
público? *poo*·blee·ko

I want to make a call to (the USA).
Quiero hacer una llamada *kye*·ro a·*ser* oo·na ya·*ma*·da
a (los Estados Unidos). a (los es·*ta*·dos oo·*nee*·dos)

I want to make a reverse charge/collect call to (Singapore).
Quiero hacer una llamada *kye*·ro a·*ser* oo·na ya·*ma*·da
por cobrar a (Singapur). por ko·*brar* a (seen·ga·*poor*)

I want ...	*Quiero ...*	kye·ro ...
to buy a phone card	*comprar una tarjeta telefónica*	kom·*prar oo*·na tar·*khe*·ta te·le·*fo*·nee·ka
to speak for (three) minutes	*hablar por (tres) minutos*	a·*blar* por (tres) mee·*noo*·tos

How much does ... cost?	*¿Cuánto cuesta ...?*	kwan·to kwes·ta ...
a (three)-minute call	*una llamada de (tres) minutos*	*oo*·na ya·*ma*·da de (tres) mee·*noo*·tos
each extra minute	*cada minuto extra*	*ka*·da mee·*noo*·to *ek*·stra

The number is ...
El número es ...   el *noo*·me·ro es ...

What's the area/country code for ...?
¿Cuál es la clave Lada de ...?   kwal es la *kla*·ve *la*·da de ...

It's engaged.
Está llamando.   es·*ta* ya·*man*·do

I've been cut off.
Me colgaron.   me kol·*ga*·ron

The connection's bad.
La conexión es mala.   la ko·nek·*syon* es *ma*·la

Hello. (when making a call)
¡Hola!   *o*·la

It's ... (when introducing yourself)
Habla ...   *a*·bla ...

Is ... there?
¿Está...?   es·*ta* ...

Can I speak to ..., please?
¿Me comunica con..., por favor?   me ko·moo·*nee*·ka kon ... por fa·*vor*

Can I leave a message?
¿Puedo dejar un mensaje?   *pwe*·do de·*khar* oon men·*sa*·khe

What time will he/she be back?
 ¿A qué hora regresa?   a ke o·ra re·gre·sa

Please tell him/her I called.
 Por favor, dile que le llamé.   por fa·vor dee·le ke le ya·me

I'll call back (later).
 Llamaré (más tarde).   ya·ma·re (mas tar·de)

What time should I call?
 ¿A qué hora debería llamar?   a ke o·ra de·be·ree·a ya·mar

My number is …
 Mi número es …   mee noo·me·ro es …

I don't have a contact number.
 No tengo teléfono.   no ten·go te·le·fo·no

listen for …

bwe·no
 ¿Bueno?   Hello! (answering a call)
de par·te de kyen
 ¿De parte de quién?   Who's calling?
kon kyen kye·re a·blar
 *¿Con quién
 quiere hablar?*   Who do you want to
 speak to?
a·o·ree·ta no es·ta
 Ahorita no está.   I'm sorry, he's/she's not here.
see a·kee es·ta
 Sí, aquí está.   Yes, he's/she's here.
no pwe·do o·eer·te
 No puedo oírte.   I can't hear you.
oon mo·men·to
 Un momento.   One moment.
tye·ne el noo·me·ro e·kee·vo·ka·do
 *Tiene el número
 equivocado.*   Sorry, wrong number.

PRACTICAL

72

mobile/cell phone

el teléfono celular

I'd like a/an …	Quisiera …	kee·sye·ra …
adaptor plug	un adaptador	oon a·dap·ta·dor
charger for	un cargador para	oon kar·ga·dor pa·ra
my phone	mi teléfono	mee te·le·fo·no
mobile/cell	rentar un	ren·tar oon
phone for hire	celular	se·loo·lar
prepaid mobile/	un celular con	oon se·loo·lar kon
cell phone	tarjetas	tar·khe·tas
	prepagadas	pre·pa·ga·das
SIM card for	una tarjeta	oo·na tar·khe·ta
your network	SIM para su red	seem pa·ra soo red

What are the rates?
¿Cuáles son las tarifas?   kwa·les son las ta·ree·fas

(Two pesos) per (30) seconds.
(Dos pesos) por (treinta)   (dos pe·sos) por (trayn·ta)
segundos.   se·goon·dos

the internet

el internet

Where's the local Internet cafe?
¿Dónde hay un cafe   don·de ai oon ka·fe
Internet por aquí?   een·ter·net por a·kee

I'd like to …	Quisiera …	kee·sye·ra …
get Internet	usar el	oo·sar el
access	Internet	een·ter·net
check my email	revisar	re·vee·sar
	mi correo	mee ko·re·o
	electrónico	e·lek·tro·nee·ko
use a printer	usar una	oo·sar oo·na
	impresora	eem·pre·so·ra
use a scanner	usar un	oo·sar oon
	escáner	es·ka·ner

communications

73

How much per ...?	¿Cuánto cuesta por ...?	kwan·to kwes·ta por ...
CD	cómpact	kom·pakt
(five) minutes	(cinco) minutos	(seen·ko) mee·noo·tos
hour	hora	o·ra
page	página	pa·khee·na
Do you have ...?	¿Tiene ...?	tye·ne ...
Macs	Macs	maks
PCs	PCs	pe·ses
a Zip drive	una unidad de Zip	oo·na oo·nee·dad de seep

How do I log on?
¿Cómo entro al sistema?   ko·mo en·tro al sees·te·ma

How do I log off?
¿Cómo salgo del sistema?   ko·mo sal·go del sees·te·ma

Can you help me change to English-language preference?
¿Me puede ayudar a   me pwe·de a·yoo·dar a
cambiar la preferencia   kam·byar la pre·fe·ren·sya
al inglés?   al een·gles

Can I burn a CD?
¿Puedo quemar un cómpact?   pwe·do ke·mar oon kom·pakt

I need help with the computer.
Necesito ayuda con la   ne·se·see·to a·yoo·da kon la
computadora.   kom·poo·ta·do·ra

This (computer) isn't working.
Esta (computadora)   es·ta (kom·poo·ta·do·ra)
no funciona.   no foon·syo·na

It's crashed.
Se trabó.   se tra·bo

I've finished.
Ya terminé.   ya ter·mee·ne

For more computer-related terms, see the **dictionary**.

Where can I …?	¿Dónde puedo …?	don·de pwe·do …
I'd like to …	Me gustaría …	me goos·ta·ree·a …
arrange a	hacer una	a·ser oo·na
transfer	transferencia	trans·fe·ren·sya
cash a cheque	cambiar un cheque	kam·byar oon che·ke
change a	cambiar un	kam·byar oon
travellers cheque	cheque de viajero	che·ke de vya·khe·ro
change money	cambiar dinero	kam·byar dee·ne·ro
get a cash	obtener un	ob·te·ner oon
advance	adelanto	a·de·lan·to
use internet	usar la banca	oo·sar la ban·ka
banking	por Internet	por een·ter·net
withdraw money	sacar dinero	sa·kar dee·ne·ro
Where's the nearest …?	¿Dónde está …?	don·de es·ta …
automatic teller machine	el cajero automático más cercano	el ka·khe·ro ow·to·ma·tee·ko mas ser·ka·no
foreign exchange office	la casa de cambio más cercana	la ka·sa de kam·byo mas ser·ka·na

What time does the bank open?
¿A qué hora abre el banco? a ke o·ra a·bre el ban·ko

The automatic teller machine took my card.
El cajero automático el ka·khe·ro ow·to·ma·tee·ko
se tragó mi tarjeta. se tra·go mee tar·khe·ta

I've forgotten my PIN.
Se me olvidó mi NIP. se me ol·vee·do mee neep

Can I use my credit card to withdraw money?
¿Puedo usar mi tarjeta de pwe·do oo·sar mee tar·khe·ta de
crédito para sacar dinero? kre·dee·to pa·ra sa·kar dee·ne·ro

What's the exchange rate?
¿Cuál es el tipo de cambio? kwal es el *tee*·po de *kam*·byo

What's the commission?
¿Cuál es la comisión? kwal es la ko·mee·*syon*

What's the charge for that?
¿Cuánto hay que pagar por éso? *kwan*·to ai ke pa·*gar* por *e*·so

Can I have smaller notes?
¿Me lo puede dar en me lo *pwe*·de dar en
billetes más pequeños? bee·*ye*·tes mas pe·*ke*·nyos

Has my money arrived yet?
¿Ya llegó mi dinero? ya ye·*go* mee dee·*ne*·ro

How long will it take to arrive?
¿Cuánto tiempo tardará *kwan*·to *tyem*·po tar·da·*ra*
en llegar? en ye·*gar*

Where do I sign?
¿Dónde firmo? *don*·de *feer*·mo

For other useful phrases, see **money**, page 35.

---

listen for ...

ai oon pro·*ble*·ma kon soo *kwen*·ta
Hay un problema con **There's a problem**
su cuenta. **with your account.**

feer·me a·*kee*
Firme aquí. **Sign here.**

no po·*de*·mos a·*ser e*·so
No podemos hacer eso. **We can't do that.**

pwe·de es·kree·*beer*·lo
¿Puede escribirlo? **Can you write it down?**

soo ee·den·tee·fee·ka·*syon*/pa·sa·*por*·te
Su identificación/pasaporte. **Your ID/ passport.**

en ...	En ...	In ...
(*seen*·ko)	(*cinco*)	(**five**)
dee·as a·*bee*·les	*días hábiles*	**working days**
(dos) se·*ma*·nas	(*dos*) *semanas*	(**two**) **weeks**

PRACTICAL

76

sightseeing
visitas turísticas

I'd like a/an ...	*Quisiera ...*	kee·*sye*·ra ...
audio set	*una audioguía*	*oo*·na ow·dyo·*gee*·a
catalogue	*un catálogo*	oon ka·*ta*·lo·go
guide (person)	*un guía*	oon *gee*·a
guidebook in English	*una guía turística en inglés*	*oo*·na *gee*·a too·*rees*·tee·ka en een·*gles*
(local) map	*un mapa (de la zona)*	oon *ma*·pa (de la *so*·na)

Do you have information on ... sights?	*¿Tiene información sobre atracciones ...*	*tye*·ne een·for·ma·*syon* *so*·bre a·trak·*syo*·nes ...
cultural	*culturales*	kool·too·*ra*·les
local	*locales*	lo·*ka*·les
religious	*religiosas*	re·lee·*khyo*·sas
unique	*únicas*	*oo*·nee·kas

I'd like to see ...
Me gustaría ver ... — me goos·ta·*ree*·a ver ...

What's that?
¿Qué es eso? — ke es *e*·so

Who made it?
¿Quién lo hizo? — kyen lo *ee*·so

How old is it?
¿De cuándo es? — de *kwan*·do es

Could you take a photograph of me?
¿Me puede tomar una foto? — me *pwe*·de to·*mar* *oo*·na *fo*·to

Can I take a photograph (of you)?
¿Puedo tomar(le) una foto? — *pwe*·do to·*mar*(le) *oo*·na *fo*·to

I'll send you the photograph.
Le mandaré la foto. — le man·da·*re* la *fo*·to

getting in

What time does it open/close?
¿A qué hora abren/cierran?   a ke o·ra a·bren/sye·ran

What's the admission charge?
¿Cuánto cuesta la entrada?   kwan·to kwes·ta la en·tra·da

It costs (20 pesos).
Cuesta (veinte pesos).   kwes·ta (vayn·te pe·sos)

Is there a	*¿Hay descuento*	ai des·kwen·to
discount for …?	*para …?*	pa·ra …
children	*niños*	nee·nyos
families	*familias*	fa·mee·lyas
groups	*grupos*	groo·pos
pensioners	*jubilados*	khoo·bee·la·dos
students	*estudiantes*	es·too·dyan·tes

navel of the moon

The mysterious origins of the word *México* have long been the subject of debate.

One of the most popular theories is that *México* literally means 'navel of the moon' in the indigenous Nahuatl language, derived from *meztli* (moon) and *xictli* (navel). Another theory associates the name with the Nahuatl word *metl* (maguey plant). In the 15th and 16th centuries some clerics tried vainly to establish a link between *México* and the Hebrew word *Mesi* (Messiah). Other theories include 'place of springs' and 'that which kills by an obsidian arrow'.

In 1998, a 'Round Table on the True Meaning of the Word México' was convened in an attempt to lay the issue to rest once and for all. The panel agreed unanimously that the Aztecs who founded Mexico City called themselves *mexítin* (Mexicans) in honour of their leader Mexítli, known affectionately as 'Mexi'. Add the Nahuatl suffix *-co* (place of) and you get *México*: 'Place of the Mexicans'.

tours

Can you recommend a …?	¿Puede recomendar algún …?	pwe·de re·ko·men·dar al·goon …
boat-trip	paseo en lancha	pa·se·o en lan·cha
tour	tour	toor
When's the next …?	¿Cuándo es la próxima …?	kwan·do es la prok·see·ma …
daytrip	excursión de un día	ek·skoor·syon de oon dee·a
excursion	excursión	ek·skoor·syon
Is … included?	¿Incluye …?	een·kloo·ye …
accommodation	alojamiento	a·lo·kha·myen·to
food	comida	ko·mee·da
transport	transporte	trans·por·te

Do I need to take … with me?
¿Necesito llevar …?   ne·se·see·to ye·var …

Can we hire a guide?
¿Podemos contratar un guía?   po·de·mos kon·tra·tar oon gee·a

The guide will pay.
El guía va a pagar.   el gee·a va a pa·gar

The guide has paid.
El guía ya pagó.   el gee·a ya pa·go

How long is the tour?
¿Cuánto dura el tour?   kwan·to doo·ra el toor

What time should I be back?
¿A qué hora tengo que regresar?   a ke o·ra ten·go ke re·gre·sar

Be back here at (five o'clock).
Regrese a (las cinco). re·*gre*·se a (las *seen*·ko)

I'm with them.
Estoy con ellos. es·*toy* kon e·yos

I've lost my group.
He perdido a mi grupo. e per·*dee*·do a mee *groo*·po

local talk

What's (Aguascalientes) like?
¿Cómo es *ko*·mo es
(Aguascalientes)? (a·gwas·ka·*lyen*·tes)

I've been to (Zacatecas).
He estado en (Zacatecas). e es·*ta*·do en (sa·ka·*te*·kas)

There's (not) …	(No) Hay …	(no) ai …
a great restaurant/ hotel	*un buen restaurante/ hotel*	oon bwen res·tow·*ran*·te/ o·*tel*
a lot to see	*mucho que ver*	*moo*·cho ke ver
fabulous nightlife	*una muy buena vida nocturna*	*oo*·na mooy bwe·na *vee*·da nok·*toor*·na
lots of culture	*mucha cultura*	*moo*·cha kool·*too*·ra

There are (no) rip-off merchants.
(No) Hay estafadores. (no) ai es·ta·fa·*do*·res

There are (not) too many tourists.
(No) Hay demasiados (no) ai de·ma·*sya*·dos
turistas. too·*rees*·tas

The best time to go is (December).
La mejor época la me·*khor* e·po·ka
para ir es (en *pa*·ra eer es (en
diciembre). dee·*syem*·bre)

I'm attending a/an ... — *Estoy asistiendo a ...* — es·*toy* a·sees·*tyen*·do a ...

conference	*un congreso*	oon kon·*gre*·so
course	*un curso*	oon *koor*·so
exhibition	*una exhibición*	*oo*·na ek·see·bee·*syon*
meeting	*una reunión*	*oo*·na re·oo·*nyon*
trade fair	*una feria de negocios*	*oo*·na *fe*·rya de ne·*go*·syos
convention	*una convención*	*oo*·na kon·ven·*syon*

I'm with ... — *Estoy con ...* — es·*toy* kon ...

my company	*mi compañía*	mee kom·pa·*nyee*·a
my colleague(s)	*mi(s) colega(s)*	mee(s) ko·*le*·ga(s)
(two) others	*(dos) más*	(dos) mas

I'm alone.
Estoy solo/a. m/f — es·*toy so*·lo/a

I'm staying at (the Hotel Juárez), room (90).
Me estoy alojando en (el Hotel Juárez), habitación (noventa). — me es·*toy* a·lo·*khan*·do en (el o·*tel khwa*·res) a·bee·ta·*syon* (no·*ven*·ta)

I'm here for (two) days/weeks.
Voy a estar (dos) días/ semanas. — voy a es·*tar* (dos) *dee*·as/ se·*ma*·nas

Here's my business card.
Aquí tiene mi tarjeta de presentación. — a·*kee tye*·ne mee tar·*khe*·ta de pre·sen·ta·*syon*

Let me introduce my colleague.
Le/Te presento a mi colega. pol/inf — le/te pre·*sen*·to a mee ko·*le*·ga

I have an appointment with (Mr Alberto Estavillo).
Tengo una cita con (Señor Alberto Estavillo). — *ten*·go *oo*·na *see*·ta kon (se·*nyor* al·*ber*·to es·ta·*vee*·yo)

That went very well.
Estuvo muy bien. es·*too*·vo mooy byen

Shall we go for a drink/meal?
¿Vamos a tomar/comer algo? *va*·mos a to·*mar*/ko·mer al·go

It's on me.
Yo invito. yo een·*vee*·to

Where's the …?	*¿Dónde es …?*	*don*·de es …
business centre	*el centro de conferencias*	el *sen*·tro de kon·fe·*ren*·syas
conference	*el congreso*	el kon·*gre*·so
meeting	*la reunión*	la re·oo·*nyon*
I need …	*Necesito …*	ne·se·*see*·to …
a connection to the Net	*una conexión a Internet*	*oo*·na ko·nek·*syon* a een·ter·*net*
an interpreter	*un intérprete*	oon een·*ter*·pre·te
to make photocopies	*fotocopiar*	fo·to·*ko*·pyar
some space to set up	*espacio para instalarme*	es·*pa*·syo *pa*·ra een·sta·*lar*·me
to send an email	*enviar un correo electrónico*	en·*vyar* oon ko·*re*·o e·lek·*tro*·nee·ko
to send a fax	*enviar un fax*	en·*vyar* oon faks
to use a computer	*usar una computadora*	oo·*sar* oo·na kom·poo·ta·*do*·ra
I'm expecting a …	*Estoy esperando …*	es·*toy* es·pe·*ran*·do …
call	*una llamada*	*oo*·na ya·*ma*·da
fax	*un fax*	oon faks

For equipment you might need at a conference, see the dictionary.

business etiquette

Mexicans have a friendly approach to doing business, and maintaining good relationships with business partners is given the highest priority. Responding to requests with a flat 'no' and throwing documents on the table during a meeting is considered to be highly aggressive business behaviour.

I have a disability.
Soy discapacitado/a. m/f — soy dees·ka·pa·see·*ta*·do/a

I need assistance.
Necesito asistencia. — ne·se·*see*·to a·sees·*ten*·sya

What services do you have for people with a disability?
¿Qué servicios tienen para discapacitados? — ke ser·*vee*·syos *tye*·nen *pa*·ra dees·ka·pa·see·*ta*·dos

I have a hearing aid.
Llevo un aparato para sordera. — *ye*·vo oon a·pa·*ra*·to *pa*·ra sor·*de*·ra

I'm deaf.
Soy sordo/a. m/f — soy *sor*·do/a

Are guide dogs permitted?
¿Se permite la entrada a los perros guía? — se per·*mee*·te la en·*tra*·da a los *pe*·ros *gee*·a

Is there wheelchair access?
¿Hay acceso para la silla de ruedas? — ai ak·*se*·so *pa*·ra la *see*·ya de *rwe*·das

How wide is the entrance?
¿Qué tan ancha es la entrada? — ke tan *an*·cha es la en·*tra*·da

Is there a lift?
¿Hay elevador? — ai e·le·va·*dor*

How many steps are there?
¿Cuántos escalones hay?   kwan·tos es·ka·lo·nes ai

Is there somewhere I can sit down?
¿Hay algún lugar donde me   ai al·goon loo·gar don·de me
pueda sentar?   pwe·da sen·tar

Could you call me a disabled taxi, please?
¿Me puede llamar un taxi   me pwe·de ya·mar oon tak·see
para discapacitados?   pa·ra dees·ka·pa·see·ta·dos

Could you help me cross this street?
¿Me puede ayudar   me pwe·de a·yoo·dar
a cruzar la calle?   a kroo·sar la ka·ye

access for	*acceso* m *para*	ak·se·so pa·ra
the disabled	*discapacitados*	dees·ka·pa·see·ta·dos
Braille library	*biblioteca* f	bee·blyo·te·ka
	Braille	brai·le
guide dog	*perro* m *guía*	pe·ro gee·a
person with	*persona* f	per·so·na
a disability	*discapacitada*	dees·ka·pa·see·ta·da
ramps	*rampas* f pl	ram·pas
space (to move	*espacio* m	es·pa·syo
around)	*(para desplazarse)*	(pa·ra des·pla·sar·se)
wheelchair	*silla* f *de ruedas*	see·ya de rwe·das

X marks the spot

Beware of the letter *x* in Mexican Spanish, which can be pronounced four different ways. In words such as *México* it's pronounced kh (as in the Scottish 'loch') and in words like *expreso* it's pronounced ks. In some words of indigenous origin, such as *mixiotes* and *xcatic* (types of food) it's pronounced sh, but in place names like *Xóchitl* and *Xochicalco* it's spoken as an s. Don't get too confused by this – just check the coloured phonetic guides for the correct pronunciation.

See also **pronunciation**, page 12.

Is there a/an …?	¿Hay …?	ai …
baby change room	una sala para cambiarle el pañal al bebé	oo·na sa·la pa·ra kam·byar·le el pa·nyal al be·be
child-minding service	club para niños	kloob pa·ra nee·nyos
children's menu	menú infantil	me·noo een·fan·teel
creche	guardería	gwar·de·ree·a
(English-speaking) babysitter	niñera (que hable inglés)	nee·nye·ra (ke a·ble een·gles)
family discount	descuento familiar	des·kwen·to fa·mee·lyar
highchair	silla para bebé	see·ya pa·ra be·be
park	un parque	oon par·ke
playground nearby	juegos por aquí	khwe·gos por a·kee
theme park	una feria	oo·na fe·rya
toyshop	una juguetería	oo·na joo·ge·te·ree·a
I need a …	Necesito …	ne·se·see·to …
baby seat	un asiento de seguridad para bebé	oon a·syen·to de se·goo·ree·dad pa·ra be·be
booster seat	un asiento de seguridad para niños	oon a·syen·to de se·goo·ree·dad pa·ra nee·nyos
crib	una cuna	oo·na koo·na
potty	una bacinica	oo·na ba·see·nee·ka
stroller	una carreola	oo·na ka·re·o·la
bottle	una mamila	oo·na ma·mee·la
dummy	un chupón	oon choo·pon
nappies	unos pañales	oo·nos pa·nyal·es

Do you mind if I breast-feed here?
¿Le molesta que dé el pecho aquí? — le mo·les·ta ke de el pe·cho a·kee

Are children allowed?
¿Se admiten niños? — se ad·mee·ten nee·nyos

Is this suitable for (four)-year-old children?
¿Es apto para niños de (cuatro) años? — es ap·to pa·ra nee·nyos de (kwa·tro) a·nyos

kids' talk

When's your birthday?
¿Cuándo es tu cumpleaños? — kwan·do es too koom·ple·a·nyos

Do you go to school or kindergarten?
¿Vas a la primaria o a kinder? — vas a la pree·ma·rya o a keen·der

What grade are you in?
¿En qué grado estás? — en ke gra·do es·tas

Do you like school?
¿Te gusta la escuela? — te goos·ta la es·kwe·la

Do you like sport?
¿Te gusta el deporte? — te goos·ta el de·por·te

What do you do after school?
¿Qué haces después de la escuela? — ke a·ses des·pwes de la es·kwe·la

Do you learn English?
¿Aprendes inglés? — a·pren·des een·gles

I come from very far away.
Vengo de muy lejos. — ven·go de mooy le·khos

Show me how to play.
Dime cómo se juega. — dee·me ko·mo se khwe·ga

Well done!
¡Muy bien! — mooy byen

basics

lo básico

Yes.	*Sí.*	see
No.	*No.*	no
Please.	*Por favor.*	por fa·*vor*
Thank you (very much).	*(Muchas) Gracias.*	(moo·chas) *gra*·syas
You're welcome.	*De nada.*	de *na*·da
Sorry. (regret)	*Lo siento.*	lo *syen*·to
Sorry. (apology)	*Perdón.*	per·*don*
Excuse me. (regret) *Perdón.*		per·*don*
Excuse me. (attention or apology) *Discúlpe.*		dees·*kool*·pe

greetings

saludos

Hi.	*¡Hola!* inf	*o*·la
Hello.	*Buen día.*	bwen *dee*·a
Good day.	*Buen día.*	bwen *dee*·a
Good morning.	*Buenos días.*	*bwe*·nos *dee*·as
Good afternoon. (until about 7pm)	*Buenas tardes.*	*bwe*·nas *tar*·des
Good evening.	*Buenas noches.*	*bwe*·nas *no*·ches
Good night.	*Buenas noches.*	*bwe*·nas *no*·ches
See you later.	*Hasta luego.*	*as*·ta *lwe*·go
Goodbye.	*¡Adiós!*	a·*dyos*
How are you?	*¿Cómo está?* pol	*ko*·mo es·*ta*
	¿Cómo estás? inf	*ko*·mo es·*tas*
	¿Cómo están? pl pol&inf	*ko*·mo es·*tan*
Fine, thanks.	*Bien, gracias.*	byen *gra*·syas

meeting people

87

What's your name?

¿Cómo se llama usted? pol	ko·mo se ya·ma oo·sted
¿Cómo te llamas? inf	ko·mo te ya·mas

My name is …

Me llamo …	me ya·mo …

I'd like to introduce you to …

Le presento a … pol	le pre·sen·to a …
Te presento a … inf	te pre·sen·to a …

I'm pleased to meet you.

Mucho gusto.	moo·cho goos·to

getting friendly

Remember that there are two ways of saying 'you'. When addressing a stranger, an older person or someone in a position of authority, use the polite form *usted* oos·ted. When talking to children or people who are familiar to you, use the informal form *tu* too. In this book we have used the most appropriate form for each phrase, but where you see pol/inf you have both options.

titles & addressing people

títulos & maneras de dirigirse a la gente

The terms *Don* (Sir) and *Doña* (Madam) are sometimes used to address older men and women in rural areas but are rare elsewhere. Use the word *Señor* to show politeness towards a man and *Señora* for a woman. Unless you are talking to a very young girl avoid using *Señorita* altogether, otherwise you may come across as patronising. You might also hear children address their godfather as *padrino* and godmother as *madrina*.

Mr	*Señor*	se·nyor
young man	*Jóven*	kho·ven
Mrs/Ms	*Señora*	se·nyo·ra
Miss/Ms	*Señorita*	se·nyo·ree·ta
Doctor	*Doctor(a)* m/f	dok·tor/dok·to·ra

making conversation

Do you live here?
¿Vive/Vives aquí? pol/inf   *vee*·ve/*vee*·ves a·*kee*

Where are you going?
¿A dónde va/vas? pol/inf   a *don*·de va/vas

What are you doing?
¿Qué hace/haces? pol/inf   ke *a*·se/*a*·ses

Are you waiting (for a bus)?
¿Está/Estás esperando   es·*ta*/es·*tas* es·pe·*ran*·do
(el autobús)? pol/inf   (el ow·to·*boos*)

Can I have a light, please?
¿Tiene/Tienes un   *tye*·ne/*tye*·nes oon
encendedor, por favor? pol/inf   en·sen·de·*dor* por fa·*vor*

What's this called?
¿Cómo se llama ésto?   *ko*·mo se *ya*·ma *es*·to

What a beautiful baby!
¡Qué bebé tan hermoso/a! m/f   ke be·*be* tan er·*mo*·so/a

three amigos

The most common word for friend is *amigo/a* m/f, but
Mexican Spanish has an abundance of fun alternatives.
You may hear people call each other *mano* m or *mana* f, an
abbreviation of *hermano/a* (brother/sister). Close male friends
may call each other *güey* (buddy), while in the north friends
sometimes address each other as *batos* (youngsters). Here are
some other colloquial Mexican words for friend:

cuate m&f	*kwa*·te	(lit: twin)
chavo/a m/f	*cha*·vo/a	(lit: kid)
maestro/a m/f	ma·*es*·tro/a	(lit: master)

This is my …	Éste/a es mi … m/f	es·te/a es mee …
brother	hermano	er·*ma*·no
child	hijo/a m/f	ee·kho/a
colleague	colega m&f	ko·*le*·ga
friend	amigo/a m/f	a·*mee*·go/a
husband	esposo	es·*po*·so
partner (intimate)	pareja m&f	pa·*re*·kha
sister	hermana	er·*ma*·na
wife	esposa	es·*po*·sa

I'm here …	Estoy aquí …	es·toy a·kee …
for a holiday	de vacaciones	de va·ka·*syo*·nes
on business	en viaje de negocios	en *vya*·khe de ne·*go*·syos
to study	estudiando	es·too·*dyan*·do
with my family	con mi familia	kon mee fa·*mee*·lya
with my friends	con mis amigos/as m/f	kon mees a·*mee*·gos/as
with my partner	con mi pareja m&f	kon mee pa·*re*·kha

How long are you here for?
¿Cuánto tiempo va/vas a estar aquí? pol/inf
kwan·to tyem·po va/vas a es·tar a·kee

I'm here for … weeks/days.
Voy a estar …
semanas/días.
*voy a es·tar …
se·ma·nas/dee·as*

Do you like it here?
¿Le/Te gusta este lugar? pol/inf
le/te goos·ta es·te loo·gar

I love it here.
Me encanta este lugar.
me en·kan·ta es·te loo·gar

Hey!	*¡Oye!* inf	o·ye
	¡Oiga! pol	oy·ga
How's things?	*Qué tal?*	ke tal
What's new?	*Qué onda?*	ke on·da
What's up?	*Quihubo?*	kyoo·bo
It's/I'm OK.	*Está/Estoy bien.*	es·ta/es·toy byen
OK.	*Okey.*	o·kay
How cool!	*¡Qué padre!*	ke pa·dre
Great!	*¡Padrísimo!*	pa·dree·see·mo
No problem.	*No hay problema.*	no ai pro·ble·ma
Sure.	*Seguro.*	se·goo·ro
Maybe.	*Tal vez.*	tal ves
No way!	*¡De ninguna manera!*	de neen·goo·na ma·ne·ra
Check this out!	*¡Checa ésto!*	che·ka es·to

nationalities

nacionalidades

Where are you from?
 ¿De dónde es/eres? pol/inf   de don·de es/e·res

I'm from …	*Soy de …*	soy de …
Australia	*Australia*	ow·stra·lya
Japan	*Japón*	kha·pon
the USA	*los Estados Unidos*	los es·ta·dos oo·nee·dos

For more countries, see the **dictionary**.

Are you a *gringo*? In Mexico the word *gringo/a* m/f describes a person from the USA, while elsewhere in Latin America it can refer to any foreigner. Americans needn't be offended by the term, which is rarely derogatory. It can be used to describe anything that has come from over the northern border, whether people, cars or films.

A popular myth is that the term originated during the war between Mexico and the USA (1846–1848). American soldiers, who wore green uniforms, were supposedly taunted with the slogan 'Green, go home!'. The most likely theory though is that *gringo* is derived from the Spanish *griego* meaning 'Greek'.

age

la edad

How old ...?	*¿Cuántos años ...?*	kwan·tos a·nyos ...
are you	*tiene/tienes* pol/inf	tye·ne/tye·nes
is your daughter	*tiene su/tu*	tye·ne soo/too
	hija pol/inf	ee·kha
is your son	*tiene su/tu*	tye·ne soo/too
	hijo pol/inf	ee·kho

I'm ... years old.
Tengo ... años. — ten·go ... a·nyos

He's/She's ... years old.
Tiene ... años. — tye·ne ... a·nyos

Too old!
¡Demasiados! — de·ma·sya·dos

I'm younger than I look.
Soy más joven de lo que parezco. — soy mas kho·ven de lo ke pa·res·ko

For your age, see **numbers & amounts**, page 29.

occupations & studies

What's your occupation?
¿A qué se dedica? pol — a ke se de·*dee*·ka
¿A qué te dedicas? inf — a ke te de·*dee*·kas

I'm a/an ...   *Soy ...*   soy ...
- chef   *chef* m&f   chef
- teacher   *maestro/a* m/f   ma·*es*·tro/a
- writer   *escritor/*   es·kree·*tor*/
     escritora m/f   es·kree·*to*·ra

I work in ...   *Trabajo en ...*   tra·*ba*·kho en ...
- communications   *comunicaciones*   ko·moo·nee·ka·*syo*·nes
- education   *educación*   e·doo·ka·*syon*
- hospitality   *hotelería*   o·te·le·*ree*·a

I'm ...   *Estoy ...*   es·*toy* ...
- retired   *jubilado/a* m/f   khoo·bee·*la*·do/a
- unemployed   *desempleado/a* m/f   des·em·ple·*a*·do/a

I'm self-employed.
Trabajo por mi cuenta. — tra·*ba*·kho por mee *kwen*·ta

What are you studying?
¿Qué estudia/estudias? pol/inf — ke es·*too*·dya/es·*too*·dyas

I'm studying ...   *Estudio ...*   es·*too*·dyo ...
- business   *economía*   e·ko·no·*mee*·a
- history   *historia*   ees·*to*·rya
- languages   *idiomas*   ee·*dyo*·mas

For more occupations and studies, see the **dictionary**.

meeting people

family

Do you have (children)?
¿Tiene/Tienes (hijos)? pol/inf · tye·ne/tye·nes (ee·khos)

I have (a partner).
Tengo (una pareja). · ten·go (oo·na pa·re·kha)

Do you live with (your family)?
¿Vive/Vives con (su/tu familia)? pol/inf · vee·ve/vee·ves kon (soo/too fa·mee·lya)

I live with (my parents).
Vivo con (mis papás). · vee·vo kon (mees pa·pas)

This is (my mother).
Ésta es (mi mamá). · es·ta es (mee ma·ma)

Are you married?
¿Está casado/a? m/f pol · es·ta ka·sa·do/a
¿Estás casado/a? m/f inf · es·tas ka·sa·do/a

I live with someone.
Vivo con alguien. · vee·vo kon al·gyen

I'm ...	Soy ...	soy ...
married	casado/a m/f	ka·sa·do/a
separated	separado/a m/f	se·pa·ra·do/a
single	soltero/a m/f	sol·te·ro/a

For more kinship terms, see the **dictionary**.

farewells

Tomorrow is my last day here.
Mañana es mi último   ma·*nya*·na es mee *ool*·tee·mo
día aquí.   dee·a a·*kee*

Here's my …	*Éste/a es mi …* m/f	es·te/a es mee …
What's your …?	*¿Cuál es tu …?*	kwal es too …
(email) address	*dirección* f	dee·rek·*syon*
	(de email)	(de ee·*mayl*)
fax number	*número* m *de fax*	*noo*·me·ro de faks
mobile number	*número* m *de*	*noo*·me·ro de
	celular	se·loo·*lar*
work number	*número* m *del*	*noo*·me·ro del
	trabajo	tra·*ba*·kho

If you ever visit	*Si algún día*	see al·*goon* dee·a
(Australia) …	*visitas*	vee·*see*·tas
	(Australia) …	(ow·*stra*·lya) …
come and	*ven a*	ven a
visit us	*visitarnos*	vee·see·*tar*·nos
you can stay	*te puedes quedar*	te *pwe*·des ke·*dar*
with me	*conmigo*	kon·*mee*·go

I'll send you copies of the photos.
Te mandaré copias   te man·da·*re* ko·pyas
de las fotos.   de las *fo*·tos

Keep in touch!
¡Mantente en contacto!   man·*ten*·te en kon·*tak*·to

It's been great meeting you.
Ha sido un placer   a *see*·do oon pla·*ser*
conocerte.   ko·no·*ser*·te

I'm going to miss you!
¡Te voy a extrañar!   te voy a ek·stra·*nyar*

For addresses, see also **directions**, page 49.

Americans with a Mexican background often choose to identify themselves as *chicanos* – or *chicanas* for women – a label derived from the word *mexicano* (formally pronounced me·shee·*ka*·no). Though originally a derogatory term, today the word *chicano* denotes an empowered Mexican-American cultural identity.

The rise of *chicano* identity politics in the USA has led to a greater recognition of Chicano Spanish as a unique form of Mexican Spanish. *Chicanos* may use older words that have disappeared from 'standard' Mexican and European Spanish such as *semos* for *somos* (we are), as well as new words influenced by English such as *cookiar* (cook). Here are a few common chicanoisms:

Chicano Spanish	'Standard' Mexican Spanish	English
ansina	*así*	like this
dispués	*después*	after
leyer	*leer*	read
muncho	*mucho*	much/a lot
naiden	*nadie*	nobody
nejecitar	*necesitar*	need
ónde	*dónde*	where
parkiar	*estacionar*	park
pos	*pués*	since
prebar	*probar*	try
watchar	*mirar*	watch

common interests

intereses en común

What do you do in your spare time?
¿Qué te gusta hacer en tu tiempo libre?
ke te *goos*·ta a·*ser* en too *tyem*·po lee·bre

Do you like …?	*¿Te gusta …?*	te *goos*·ta …
I (don't) like …	*(No) Me gusta …*	(no) me *goos*·ta …
cooking	*cocinar*	ko·see·*nar*
dancing	*bailar*	bai·*lar*
films	*el cine*	el *see*·ne
gardening	*la jardinería*	la khar·dee·ne·*ree*·a
reading	*la lectura*	la lek·*too*·ra
socialising	*hacer vida social*	a·*ser* vee·da so·*syal*
travelling	*viajar*	vya·*khar*

For more hobbies and sports, see **sports**, page 125, and the dictionary.

if you please

In Spanish, in order to say you like something, you say *me gusta* (lit: me it-pleases). If it's a plural noun, use *me gustan* (lit: me they-please).

I like dancing.
Me gusta bailar.
me *goos*·ta bai·*lar*

I like this song.
Me gusta ésta canción.
me *goos*·ta es·ta kan·*syon*

I like tacos.
Me gustan los tacos.
me *goos*·tan los *ta*·kos

music

Do you like to …?	*Te gusta …?*	te *goos*·ta …
dance	*bailar*	bai·*lar*
go to concerts	*ir a conciertos*	eer a kon·*syer*·tos
listen to music	*escuchar*	es·koo·*char*
	música	*moo*·see·ka
play an	*tocar un*	to·*kar* oon
instrument	*instrumento*	een·stroo·*men*·to
sing	*cantar*	kan·*tar*

What bands do you like?
 ¿Qué grupos te gustan?   ke *groo*·pos te *goos*·tan

What music do you like?
 ¿Qué música te gusta?   ke *moo*·see·ka te *goos*·ta

classical music	*música* f	*moo*·see·ka
	clásica	*kla*·see·ka
electronic music	*música* f	*moo*·see·ka
	electrónica	e·lek·*tro*·nee·ka
jazz	*jazz* m	yas
metal	*metal* m	me·*tal*
pop	*música* f *pop*	*moo*·see·ka pop
punk	*música* f *punk*	*moo*·see·ka ponk
merengue	*merengue* m	me·*ren*·ge
music in Spanish	*música* f *en*	*moo*·see·ka en
	español	es·pa·*nyol*
rock	*rock* m	rok
R & B	*rhythm and blues* m	*ree*·dem and bloos
salsa	*salsa* f	*sal*·sa
traditional music	*música* f	*moo*·see·ka
	tradicional	tra·dee·syo·*nal*
world music	*música* f	*moo*·see·ka
	folklórica	fol·*klo*·ree·ka

Planning to go to a concert? See **buying tickets**, page 38 and **going out**, page 109.

From latin rhythms blaring from bus stereos to wandering *mariachis* and live *salsa* bands, music is absolutely every-where in Mexico. Here are some unique styles to listen for:

corridos   ko·*ree*·dos
  narrative ballads influenced by polka and waltz styles

huapango   wa·*pan*·go
  a fast, indigenous dance-song from the Huastec region

música tropical   moo·see·ka tro·pee·*kal*
  slow-paced rhythmic music of Caribbean origin including
  danzón (Cuba) and *cumbia* (Colombia)

norteño   nor·*ten*·yo
  country ballad and dance music from northern Mexico

ranchera   ran·*che*·ra
  very cheesy country-style music

son   son
  a folk fusion of African, Spanish and indigenous music
  styles, combining guitar, violin and voice

trova   *tro*·va
  poetic troubadour-style folk music

cinema & theatre

el cine & el teatro

I feel like going	*Tengo ganas*	ten·go *ga*·nas
to a ...	*de ir a ver una ...*	de eer a ver *oo*·na ...
comedy	*comedia*	ko·*me*·dya
film	*película*	pe·*lee*·koo·la
play	*obra de teatro*	o·bra de te·*a*·tro

What's showing at the cinema/theatre tonight?
 ¿Qué dan en el cine/teatro   ke dan en el *see*·ne/te·*a*·tro
 esta noche?   *es*·ta *no*·che

Is it in English/Spanish?
 ¿Es en inglés/español?   es en een·*gles*/es·pan·*nyol*

Does it have subtitles?
 ¿Tiene subtítulos?   *tye*·ne soob·*tee*·too·los

Have you seen …?
 ¿Has visto …?   as *vees*·to …

Who's in it?
 ¿Quién actúa?   kyen ak·*too*·a

It stars …
 Actúa(n) … sg/pl   ak·*too*·a(n) …

Did you like the film?
 ¿Te gustó la película?   te goos·*to* la pe·*lee*·koo·la

I thought it was …	*Pienso que fue …*	*pyen*·so ke fwe …
excellent	*excelente*	ek·se·*len*·te
OK	*regular*	re·goo·*lar*
long	*largo/a* m/f	*lar*·go/a
very bad	*malísimo/a* m/f	ma·*lee*·see·mo/a

animated films	*dibujos* m pl	dee·*boo*·khos
	animados	a·nee·*ma*·dos
comedy	*comedia* f	ko·*me*·dya
documentaries	*documentales* m pl	do·koo·men·*ta*·les
drama	*drama* m	*dra*·ma
film noir	*cine* m *negro*	*see*·ne *ne*·gro
(Mexican) cinema	*cine* m	*see*·ne
	(mexicano)	(me·khee·*ka*·no)
horror movies	*películas* f pl	pe·*lee*·koo·las
	de terror	de te·*ror*
sci-fi	*películas* f pl	pe·*lee*·koo·las
	de ciencia ficción	de *syen*·sya feek·*syon*
short films	*cortos* m pl	*kor*·tos
thrillers	*películas* f pl	pe·*lee*·koo·las
	de suspenso	de soos·*pen*·so

reading

What kind of books do you read?
¿Qué tipo de libros lees?   ke *tee*·po de *lee*·bros *le*·es

Which (Mexican) author do you recommend?
¿Qué autor (mexicano)   ke ow·*tor* (me·khee·*ka*·no)
me recomiendas?   me re·ko·*myen*·das

Have you read anything by (Carlos Fuentes)?
¿Has leído a (Carlos Fuentes)?   as le·*ee*·do a (*kar*·los *fwen*·tes)

Have you read (Our Word is Our Weapon)?
¿Has leído (Nuestra arma   as le·*ee*·do (*nwes*·tra *ar*·ma
es nuestra palabra)?   es *nwes*·tra pa·*la*·bra)

novel ideas

Literature is considered an important part of Mexican culture and the nation has a very lively literary scene. Much of the activity centres on Mexico City, the location of choice for literary greats such as the Colombian emigre Gabriel García Marquéz. You may already be familiar with Laura Esquivel's *Como agua para chocolate* (*Like Water for Chocolate*) which has been adapted as a film.

Good bookshops will stock English translations of famous modern authors such as Carlos Fuentes, Rosario Castellanos, Mariano Azuela and Nobel Prize winner Octavio Paz. Newer Mexican writers to look out for include Jorge Volpi, Pedro Ángel Palou and Ignacio Padilla.

interests

On this trip I'm reading …
En este viaje estoy   en *es*·te *vya*·khe es·*toy*
leyendo …   le·*yen*·do …

I'd recommend …
Te recomiendo a …   te re·ko·*myen*·do a …

Where can I exchange books?
¿Dónde puedo   *don*·de *pwe*·do
intercambiar libros?   een·ter·kam·*byar lee*·bros

body language

Be aware of sending the wrong signals with your body language. In Mexico, women are expected to initiate handshakes with men, but will greet other women with a kiss on the cheek or a pat on the forearm. Conversations take place at a close physical distance and male acquaintances often hug each other when meeting.

When paying for something, place the cash or credit card directly into the hand of the person you're dealing with, even if you're in a restaurant. Leaving payment on the counter can be interpreted as a sign that you don't respect the person enough to have contact with them.

feelings

los sentimientos

Feelings are described with either nouns or adjectives: the nouns use 'have' in Spanish (eg, 'I have hunger') and the adjectives use 'be' (like in English).

I'm (not) …	(No) Estoy …	(no) es·toy …
Are you …?	¿Está/Estás …? pol/inf	es·ta/es·tas …
bored	aburrido/a m/f	a·boo·ree·do/a
happy	feliz	fe·lees
sick	enfermo/a m/f	en·fer·mo/a

I'm (not) …	(No) Tengo …	(no) ten·go …
Are you …?	¿Tiene/Tienes …? pol/inf	tye·ne/tye·nes …
cold	frío	free·o
hungry	hambre	am·bre
sleepy	sueño	swe·nyo
thirsty	sed	sed

For more feelings, see the **dictionary**.

mixed emotions

a little
 un poco — oon po·ko

I'm a little sad.
 Estoy un poco triste. — es·toy oon po·ko trees·te

quite
 bastante — bas·tan·te

I'm quite disappointed.
 Estoy bastante
 decepcionado/a. m/f — es·toy bas·tan·te
 de·sep·syo·na·do/a

very
 muy — mooy

I'm very happy.
 Estoy muy feliz. — es·toy mooy fe·lees

opinions

Did you like it?
¿Le/Te gustó? pol/inf   le/te goos·to

What did you think of it?
¿Qué pensó/pensaste   ke pen·so/pen·sas·te
de eso? pol/inf   de e·so

I thought it was …	*Pienso que fue …*	*pyen·so ke fwe …*
It's …	*Es …*	*es …*
absurd	*absurdo/a* m/f	ab·soor·do/a
beautiful	*hermoso/a* m/f	er·mo·so/a
bizarre	*extraño/a* m/f	ek·stra·nyo/a
crap	*una porquería*	oo·na por·ke·ree·a
crazy	*loco/a* m/f	lo·ko/a
cute	*bonito/a* m/f	bo·nee·to/a
entertaining	*entretenido/a* m/f	en·tre·te·nee·do/a
excellent	*excelente*	ek·se·len·te
full-on	*extremo/a* m/f	ek·stre·mo/a
horrible	*horrible*	o·ree·ble
incomprehen-sible	*incompren-sible*	een·kom·pren-see·ble

---

revolutionary acronyms

Mexican politics is peppered with acronyms. Look for some of the following in newspaper headlines and street graffiti:

EZLN   *Ejército Zapatista de Liberación Nacional*
(Zapatista National Liberation Army)

FZLN   *Frente Zapatista de Liberación Nacional*
(Zapatista National Liberation Front)

PAN   *Partido Acción Nacional*
(National Action Party)

PDPR   *Partido Democrático Popular Revolucionario*
(People's Revolutionary Democratic Party)

PRD   *Partido de la Revolución Democrática*
(Democratic Revolution Party)

PRI   *Partido Revolucionario Institucional*
(Institutional Revolutionary Party)

politics & social issues

While Mexicans are very critical of their leaders, they can also be fiercely patriotic at the same time. Visitors should try to pick the mood, and ask questions before offering opinions. Mexican history, art and culture are fruitful subjects of conversation. As a rule, avoid topics such as the Mexican-American war and illegal immigration.

Who do you vote for?
¿Por quién vota/votas? pol/inf   por kyen *vo*·ta/*vo*·tas

I support the	*Apoyo al*	a·*po*·yo al
... party.	*partido …*	par·*tee*·do …
I'm a member	*Soy miembro del*	soy *myem*·bro del
of the ... party.	*partido …*	par·*tee*·do …
communist	*Comunista*	ko·moo·*nees*·ta
conservative	*Conservador*	kon·ser·va·*dor*
green	*Verde*	*ver*·de
liberal	*Progresista*	pro·gre·*sees*·ta
(progressive)		
labour	*Laborista*	la·bo·*rees*·ta
social democratic	*Socialdemócrata*	so·syal·de·*mo*·kra·ta
socialist	*Socialista*	so·sya·*lees*·ta

I (don't) agree with …
(No) estoy de acuerdo con …   (no) es·*toy* de a·*kwer*·do kon …

Are you against …?
¿Está/Estás en   es·*ta*/es·*tas* en
contra de …? pol/inf   *kon*·tra de …

Are you in favour of …?
¿Está/Estás a favor de …? pol/inf   es·*ta*/es·*tas* a fa·*vor* de …

How do people feel about …?
¿Cómo se siente la gente   *ko*·mo se *syen*·te la *khen*·te
acerca de …?   a·*ser*·ka de …

In my country we are concerned about …
En mi país nos   en mi pa·*ees* nos
preocupamos por …   pre·o·koo·*pa*·mos por …

abortion	*aborto* m	a·*bor*·to
animal rights	*derechos* m pl	de·*re*·chos
	de animales	de a·nee·*ma*·les
corruption	*corrupción* f	ko·roop·*syon*
crime	*crimen* m	*kree*·men
discrimination	*discriminación* f	dees·kree·mee·na·*syon*
drugs	*drogas* f pl	*dro*·gas
the economy	*economía* f	e·ko·no·*mee*·a
education	*educación* f	e·doo·ka·*syon*
exploitation	*explotación* f	ek·splo·ta·*syon*
the environment	*medio* m	*me*·dyo
	ambiente	am·*byen*·te
equal opportunity	*igualdad* f	ee·gwal·*dad*
	de oportunidades	de o·por·too·nee·*da*
euthanasia	*eutanasia* f	e·oo·ta·*na*·sya
globalisation	*globalización* f	glo·ba·lee·sa·*syon*
human rights	*derechos* m pl	de·*re*·chos
	humanos	oo·*ma*·nos
indigenous rights	*derechos* m pl	de·*re*·chos
	de indígenas	de een·*dee*·khe·nas
immigration	*inmigración* f	een·mee·gra·*syon*
inequality	*desigualdad* f	des·ee·gwal·*dad*
machismo	*machismo* m	ma·*chees*·mo
party politics	*políticas* f pl	po·*lee*·tee·kas
	de partido	de par·*tee*·do
poverty	*pobreza* f	po·*bre*·sa
privatisation	*privatización* f	pree·va·tee·sa·*syon*
racism	*racismo* m	ra·*sees*·mo
sexism	*sexismo* m	sek·*sees*·mo
social welfare	*seguridad* f	se·goo·ree·*dad*
	social	so·*syal*
terrorism	*terrorismo* m	te·ro·*rees*·mo
the war in …	*la guerra* f en …	la *ge*·ra en …
unemployment	*desempleo* m	des·em·*ple*·o
violence	*violencia* f	vyo·*len*·sya

the environment

Is there a/an (environmental) problem here?

¿Aquí hay problemas con (el medio ambiente)?

a·*kee* ai pro·*ble*·mas kon (el *me*·dyo am·*byen*·te)

biodegradable	*biodegradable*	byo·de·gra·*da*·ble
conservation	*conservación* f *del medio ambiente*	kon·ser·va·*syon* del *me*·dyo am·*byen*·te
deforestation	*deforestación* f	de·fo·res·ta·*syon*
drought	*sequía* f	se·*kee*·a
ecosystem	*ecosistema* m	e·ko·sees·*te*·ma
genetically modified crops/foods	*cultivos/ alimentos* m pl *transgénicos*	kool·*tee*·vos/ a·lee·*men*·tos trans·*khe*·nee·kos
irrigation	*irrigación* f	ee·ree·ga·*syon*
ozone layer	*capa* f *de ozono*	*ka*·pa de o·*so*·no
pesticides	*pesticidas* m pl	pes·tee·*see*·das
pollution	*contaminación* f	kon·ta·mee·na·*syon*
recyclable	*reciclable*	re·see·*kla*·ble
recycling programme	*programas* m pl *de reciclaje*	pro·*gra*·mas de re·see·*kla*·khe
water supply	*suministro* m *de agua*	soo·mee·*nees*·tro de *a*·gwa
Is this ... protected?	*¿Está protegido/a éste/a ...?* m/f	es·*ta* pro·te·*khee*·do/a *es*·te /a ...
forest	*bosque* m	*bos*·ke
park	*parque* m	*par*·ke
species	*especie* f	es·*pe*·sye

local talk

Are you pulling my leg?	¿Me estás vacilando?	me es·*tas* va·see·*lan*·do
How about that?	¿Qué tal?	ke tal
How interesting!	¡Qué interesante!	ke een·te·re·*san*·te
Just joking.	Estoy bromeando.	es·*toy* bro·me·*an*·do
Listen (to this)!	¡Escucha (esto)!	es·*koo*·cha (es·to)
Look!	¡Mira!	*mee*·ra
Of course!	¡Por supuesto!	por soo·*pwes*·to
Really?	¿De veras?	de *ve*·ras
That's great!	¡Está padrísimo!	es·*ta* pa·*dree*·see·mo
That's incredible!	¡Es increíble!	es een·kre·*ee*·ble
You bet!	¡Ya lo creo!	ya lo *kre*·o
You don't say!	¡No me digas!	no me *dee*·gas

where to go

a dónde ir

What's there to do in the evenings?
¿Qué se puede hacer en las noches?
ke se *pwe*·de a·*ser* en las *no*·ches

What's on …?	*¿Qué hay …?*	ke ai …
locally	*en la zona*	en la *so*·na
this weekend	*este fin de semana*	*es*·te feen de se·*ma*·na
today	*hoy*	oy
tonight	*esta noche*	*es*·ta *no*·che

Is there a local … guide?	*¿Hay una guía de … de la zona?*	ai *oo*·na *gee*·a de … de la *so*·na
entertainment	*entretenimiento*	en·tre·te·nee·*myen*·to
film	*cines*	*see*·nes
gay	*los lugares gay*	los loo·*ga*·res gay
music	*de música*	de *moo*·see·ka

Where are the …?	*¿Dónde hay …?*	*don*·de ai …
bars	*bares*	*ba*·res
cafes	*cafeterías*	ka·fe·te·*ree*·as
clubs	*discos*	*dees*·kos
gay venues	*lugares gay*	loo·*ga*·res gay
places to eat	*lugares donde comer*	loo·*ga*·res *don*·de ko·*mer*
pubs	*bares*	*ba*·res

I feel like going to ...	Tengo ganas de ir ...	ten·go ga·nas de eer ...
a cafe	a una cafetería	a oo·na ka·fe·te·ree·a
a concert	a un concierto	a oon kon·syer·to
the movies	al cine	al see·ne
a party	a una fiesta	a oo·na fyes·ta
a restaurant	a un restaurante	a oon res·tow·ran·te
the theatre	al teatro	al te·a·tro

Where can we go (salsa) dancing?

¿Dónde podemos ir a bailar (salsa)?

don·de po·de·mos eer a bai·lar (sal·sa)

What's the cover charge?

¿Cuánto cuesta el cover?

kwan·to kwes·ta el ko·ver

It's free.

Es gratis.

es gra·tees

three mexicans walk into a bar ...

From rowdy rum-soaked saloons to cosy and romantic lounge-bars, Mexico has it all.

antro an·tro
bar or nightclub, formerly used to describe a dive

bar bar
a place for drinking and talking, rather than dancing or listening to live music

cantina kan·tee·na
a uniquely Mexican establishment (often recognisable by Wild-West style swinging doors) where tequila, mezcal, beer, rum and brandy are the order of the day – some cantinas are exclusively men-only zones, while others are more relaxed.

peña pen·ya
a place to go for either a drink or a meal, usually with live romantic Mexican music

invitations

What are you doing …?	¿Qué vas a hacer …?	ke vas a a·ser …
right now	ahorita	a·o·ree·ta
this evening	esta noche	es·ta no·che
this weekend	este fin de semana	es·te feen de se·ma·na
tomorrow	mañana	ma·nya·na
Would you like to go …?	¿Te gustaría …?	te goos·ta·ree·a …
dancing	ir a bailar	eer a bai·lar
out somewhere	salir a algún lado	sa·leer a al·goon la·do
I feel like going for a …	Me gustaría ir a …	me goos·ta·ree·a eer a …
coffee	tomar un café	to·mar oon ka·fe
drink	tomar algo	to·mar al·go
meal	comer	ko·mer
walk	caminar	ka·mee·nar

My round.
Yo invito. — yo een·vee·to

Do you know a good restaurant?
¿Conoces algún buen restaurante? — ko·no·ses al·goon bwen res·tow·ran·te

Do you want to come to the (Café Tacuba) concert with me?
¿Quieres venir conmigo al concierto (de Café Tacuba)? — kye·res ve·neer kon·mee·go al kon·syer·to (de ka·fe ta·koo·ba)

We're having a party.
Vamos a hacer una fiesta. — va·mos a a·ser oo·na fyes·ta

You should come.
¿Por qué no vienes? — por ke no vye·nes

responding to invitations

Sure!
¡Claro que sí, gracias!   kla·ro ke see gra·syas

Yes, I'd love to.
Sí, me encantaría.   see me en·kan·ta·ree·a

Where shall we go?
¿En dónde vamos?   en don·de va·mos

Thanks, but I'm afraid I can't.
Gracias, pero no puedo.   gra·syas pe·ro no pwe·do

What about tomorrow?
¿Qué tal mañana?   ke tal ma·nya·na

Sorry, I can't sing/dance.
Perdón, no sé cantar/bailar.   per·don no se kan·tar/bai·lar

arranging to meet

What time shall we meet?
¿A qué hora nos vemos?   a ke o·ra nos ve·mos

Where will we meet?
¿Dónde nos vemos?   don·de nos ve·mos

Let's meet …   *Nos vemos …*   nos ve·mos …
   at (eight o'clock)   *a (las ocho)*   a (las o·cho)
   at the (entrance)   *en la (entrada)*   en la (entrada)

I'll pick you up.
  Paso por tí. pa·so por tee

I'll be coming later.
  Te alcanzo más tarde. te al·kan·so mas tar·de

Where will you be?
  ¿Dónde vas a estar? don·de vas a es·tar

If I'm not there by (nine), don't wait for me.
  Si no llego a las (nueve), see no ye·go a las (nwe·ve)
  no me esperes. no me es·pe·res

OK!
  ¡OK! o·kay

I'll see you then.
  Nos vemos. nos ve·mos

See you later.
  Hasta luego. as·ta lwe·go

See you tomorrow.
  Hasta mañana. as·ta ma·nya·na

I'm looking forward to it.
  Tengo muchas ganas de ir. ten·go moo·chas ga·nas de eer

Sorry I'm late.
  Perdón por llegar tarde. per·don por ye·gar tar·de

Never mind.
  No te preocupes. no te pre·o·koo·pes

---

timing isn't everything

Being late for an appointment isn't the end of the world in Mexico. In situations where punctuality is important, make sure you add *en punto* – meaning 'exactly' – after arranging a time to meet. Family obligations always take precedence over social or business meetings, and if you're invited to a party it's expected that you'll arrive between thirty minutes to an hour later than the specified time.

drugs

I don't take drugs.
No consumo drogas.   no kon·*soo*·mo *dro*·gas

I have … occasionally.
Consumo …   kon·*soo*·mo …
de vez en cuando.   de ves en *kwan*·do

Do you want to have a smoke?
¿Nos fumamos un churro?   nos foo·*ma*·mos oon *choo*·ro

I'm high.
Estoy pacheco/a. m/f   es·*toy* pa·*che*·ko/a

smoking the devil

Slang words for marijuana include *mota* (lit: fleck) or *hierba* (lit: grass). A joint is called a *churro* (lit: fritter) or a *gallo* (lit: rooster). If someone wants to suggest having a smoke they may ask *¿Le quemamos las patas al diablo?*, which can be translated as 'Shall we burn the devil's paws?'

asking someone out

Would you like to do something (tonight)?

¿Quieres hacer algo (esta noche)?
kye·res a·ser al·go
(es·ta no·che)

Yes, I'd love to.

Sí, me encantaría.
see me en·kan·ta·ree·a

No, I'm afraid I can't.

Gracias, pero no puedo.
gra·syas pe·ro no pwe·do

Not if you were the last person on Earth!

¡Ni aunque fueras la última persona en el mundo!
nee own·ke fwe·ras la ool·tee·ma
per·so·na en el moon·do

local talk

He's (a) …	*Él …*	el es …
She's (a) …	*Ella es …*	e·ya es …
bitch	*una perra*	oo·na pe·ra
hot	*caliente*	ka·lyen·te
hot girl	*cachonda*	ka·chon·da
hot guy	*cachondo*	ka·chon·do
gorgeous	*guapísimo/a* m/f	gwa·pee·see·mo/a
prick	*un cabrón*	oon ka·bron
slut	*una puta*	oo·na poo·ta

What a babe! (about a man)

¡Que tipo tan bueno!
ke tee·po tan bwe·no

What a babe! (about a woman)

¡Que vieja tan buena!
ke vye·kha tan bwe·na

He/She gets around.

Se va a la cama con cualquiera.
se va a la ka·ma kon
kwal·kye·ra

pick-up lines

Would you like a drink?
¿Te invito una copa? — te een·vee·to oo·na ko·pa

What star sign are you?
¿Cuál es tu signo? — kwal es too seeg·no

Shall we get some fresh air?
¿Vamos afuera? — va·mos a·fwe·ra

Do you study or do you work?
¿Estudias o trabajas? — es·too·dyas o tra·ba·jas

You mustn't come here much, because I would have noticed you sooner.
No debes venir muy seguido porque me habría fijado en tí antes. — no de·bes ve·neer mooy se·gee·do por·ke me a·bree·a fee·kha·do en tee an·tes

Do you have a light?
¿Tienes encendedor? — tye·nes en·sen·de·dor

You have (a) beautiful …	*Tienes …*	tye·nes …
body	*un muy buen cuerpo*	oon mooy bwen kwer·po
eyes	*unos ojos preciosos*	oo·nos o·khos pre·syo·sos
hands	*unas manos preciosas*	oo·nas ma·nos pre·syo·sas
laugh	*una risa preciosa*	oo·na ree·sa pre·syo·sa
personality	*una gran personalidad*	oo·na gran per·so·na·lee·dad

rejections

I'm here with my boyfriend/girlfriend.
Estoy aquí con mi novio/a.   es·toy a·kee kon mee no·vyo/a

I have a boyfriend/girlfriend.
Tengo novio/a.   ten·go no·vyo/a

Excuse me, I have to go now.
Lo siento, pero me tengo   lo syen·to pe·ro me ten·go
que ir.   ke eer

I'm not interested.
No estoy interesado/a. m/f   no es·toy een·te·re·sa·do/a

Hey, I'm not interested in talking to you.
Mira, no me interesa   mee·ra no me een·te·re·sa
hablar contigo.   ab·lar kon·tee·go

Your ego is out of control.
Tu ego está fuera de   too e·go es·ta fwe·ra de
control.   kon·trol

Leave me alone!
Déjame en paz.   de·kha·me en pas

Piss off!
¡Vete a la mierda!   ve·te a la myer·da

getting closer

You're very nice.
Eres muy simpático/a. m/f   e·res mooy seem·pa·tee·ko/a

You're very attractive.
Eres muy atractivo/a. m/f   e·res mooy a·trak·tee·vo/a

You're great.
Eres genial.   e·res khe·nyal

I like you very much.
Me gustas mucho.   me goos·tas moo·cho

Do you like me too?
  ¿Yo te gusto?   yo te *goos*·to

I'm interested in you.
  Me interesas.   me een·te·*re*·sas

Can I kiss you?
  ¿Te puedo besar?   te *pwe*·do be·*sar*

Will you take me home?
  ¿Me acompañas a mi casa? me a·kom·*pa*·nyas a mee *ka*·sa

Do you want to come inside for a while?
  ¿Quieres pasar un rato?   *kye*·res pa·*sar* oon *ra*·to

sticky situations

The adjective *cachondo/a* m/f has two different meanings depending on which form of the verb 'to be' is used. For example:

*Juan **es** cachondo*	**but**	*Juan **está** cachondo*
means 'Juan is a babe'.		means 'Juan is horny'.
(the verb *ser*)		(the verb *estar*)

sex

sexo

I want to make love to you.
  Quiero hacerte el amor.   *kye*·ro a·*ser*·te el a·*mor*

Do you have a condom?
  ¿Tienes un condón?   *tye*·nes oon kon·*don*

Let's use a condom.
  Usemos un condón.   oo·*se*·mos oon kon·*don*

I won't do it without protection.
  No lo haré sin protección. no lo a·*re* seen pro·tek·*syon*

I think we should stop now.
  Pienso que deberíamos   *pyen*·so ke de·be·*ree*·a·mos
  parar.   pa·*rar*

Let's go to bed!	¡Vamos a la cama!	va·mos a la ka·ma
Kiss me!	¡Bésame!	be·sa·me
I want you.	Te deseo.	te de·se·o
Take this off.	Quítate ésto.	kee·ta·te es·to
Do you like this?	¿Te gusta éstos?	te goos·ta es·to
I (don't) like that.	Esto (no) me gusta.	es·to (no) me goos·ta
Touch me here.	Tócame aquí.	to·ka·me a·kee
Oh my God!	¡Ay dios!	ai dyos
Oh yeah!	¡Sí, sí!	see see
That's great.	¡Eso es genial!	e·so es khe·nyal
Easy tiger!	¡Tranquilo!	tran·kee·lo
Please stop!	¡Para!	pa·ra
Please don't stop!	¡No pares!	no pa·res
harder	más fuerte	mas fwer·te
faster	más rápido	mas ra·pee·do
softer	más suave	mas swa·ve
slower	más despacio	mas des·pa·syo

That was amazing.
   Eso fue increíble.   e·so fwe een·kre·ee·ble

It's my first time.
   Es mi primera vez.   es mee pree·me·ra ves

I can't get it up – sorry.
   Lo siento, no se me para.   lo syen·to no se me pa·ra

Don't worry, I'll do it myself.
   No te preocupes, yo lo hago.   no te pre·o·koo·pes yo lo a·go

It helps to have a sense of humour.
   Ayuda tener sentido del   a·yoo·da te·ner sen·tee·do del
   humor.   oo·mor

Can I meet you tomorrow?
   ¿Puedo verte mañana?   pwe·do ver·te ma·nya·na

Can I stay over?
   ¿Puedo quedarme?   pwe·do ke·dar·me

When can I see you again?
   ¿Cuándo nos vemos   kwan·do nos ve·mos
   de nuevo?   de nwe·vo

love

I'm in love with you.
Estoy enamorado/a de tí. m/f es·*toy* e·na·mo·*ra*·do/a de tee

I love you.
Te amo. te *a*·mo

I think we're good together.
Creo que hacemos buena kre·o ke a·*se*·mos *bwe*·na
pareja. pa·*re*·kha

problems

Are you seeing someone else?
¿Me estás engañando con me es·*tas* en·ga·*nyan*·do kon
alguien? al·gyen

He's just a friend.
Es un amigo, nada más. es oon a·*mee*·go *na*·da mas

She's just a friend.
Es una amiga, nada más. es *oo*·na a·*mee*·ga *na*·da mas

We'll work it out.
Lo resolveremos. lo re·sol·ve·*re*·mos

I want to end the relationship.
Quiero que terminemos. kye·ro ke ter·mee·*ne*·mos

I never want to see you again.
No quiero volver a verte. no kye·ro vol·ver a ver·te

I want to stay friends.
Quiero que quedemos kye·ro ke ke·*de*·mos
como amigos. ko·mo a·*mee*·gos

---

are you horny?

If someone suspects that their partner is cheating on them,
they may ask *¿Me está poniendo los cuernos?* which roughly
means 'Are you putting horns on my head?'

religion

la religión

What's your religion?
¿Cuál es su/tu religión? pol/inf   kwal es soo/too re·lee·khyon

I (don't) believe in God.
(No) Creo en Dios.   (no) kre·o en dyos

I'm (not) ...	*(No) Soy ...*	(no) soy ...
agnostic	*agnóstico/a* m/f	ag·nos·tee·ko/a
atheist	*ateo/a* m/f	a·te·o/a
Buddhist	*budista*	boo·dees·ta
Catholic	*católico/a* m/f	ka·to·lee·ko/a
Christian	*cristiano/a* m/f	krees·tya·no/a
Hindu	*hindú*	een·doo
Jewish	*judío/a* m/f	khoo·dee·o/a
Muslim	*musulmán/*	moo·sool·man/
	musulmana m/f	moo·sool·ma·na
practising	*practicante*	prak·tee·kan·te
protestant	*protestante*	pro·tes·tan·te
religious	*religioso/a* m/f	re·lee·khyo·so/a

I'd like to go to (the) ...	*Me gustaría ir a ...*	me goos·ta·ree·a ...
church	*la iglesia*	la ee·gle·sya
mosque	*la mezquita*	la mes·kee·ta
synagogue	*la sinagoga*	la see·na·go·ga
temple	*el templo*	el tem·plo

Can I ... here?	*¿Puedo ... aquí?*	pwe·do ... a·kee
Where can I ...?	*¿Dónde puedo ...?*	don·de pwe·do ...
attend mass	*ir a misa*	eer a mee·sa
make confession (in English)	*confesarme (en inglés)*	kon·fe·sar·me (en een·gles)
pray	*rezar*	re·sar
receive communion	*comulgar*	ko·mool·gar

cultural differences

Is this a local or national custom?

¿Es una costumbre local   es *oo*·na kos·*toom*·bre lo·*kal*
o nacional?   o na·syo·*nal*

I'm not used to this.

No estoy acostumbrado/a   no es·*toy* a·kos·toom·*bra*·do/a
a ésto. m/f   a *es*·to

I don't mind watching, but I'd rather not join in.

No me importa mirar,   no me eem·*por*·ta mee·*rar*
pero prefiero no participar. *pe*·ro pre·*fye*·ro no par·tee·see·*par*

I'll try it.

Lo probaré.   lo pro·ba·*re*

Sorry, I didn't mean to say/do something wrong.

Perdón, lo dice/hice   per·*don* lo *dee*·se/*ee*·se
sin querer.   seen ke·*rer*

I'm sorry, it's	*Perdón, pero eso*	per·*don* *pe*·ro *e*·so
against my …	*va en contra de …*	va en *kon*·tra de …
beliefs	*mis creencias*	mees kre·*en*·syas
culture	*mi cultura*	mee kool·*too*·ra
religion	*mi religión*	mee re·lee·*khyon*

This is (very) …	*Esto es (muy) …*	*es*·to es (mooy) …
different	*diferente*	dee·fe·*ren*·te
fun	*divertido*	dee·ver·*tee*·do
interesting	*interesante*	een·te·re·*san*·te

When's the museum open?
¿A qué hora abre el museo?   a ke *o*·ra *a*·bre el moo·*se*·o

When's the gallery open?
¿A qué hora abre la galería?   a ke *o*·ra *a*·bre la ga·le·*ree*·a

What kind of art are you interested in?
¿Qué tipo de arte le/te   ke *tee*·po de *ar*·te le/te
interesa? **pol/inf**   een·te·*re*·sa

What's in the collection?
¿Qué hay en la colección?   ke ai en la ko·lek·*syon*

It's a (cartoon) exhibition.
Hay una exposición de   ai *oo*·na ek·spo·see·*syon* de
(historieta).   (ees·to·*rye*·ta)

What do you think of (Frida Kahlo)?
¿Qué piensa/piensas de   ke *pyen*·sa/*pyen*·sas de
(Frida Kahlo)? **pol/inf**   (*free*·da ka·lo)

I'm interested in (Mexican muralism).
Me interesa (el muralismo   me een·te·*re*·sa (el moo·ra·*lees*·mo
mexicano).   me·khee·*ka*·no)

I like the works of (José Guadalupe Posada).
Me gusta la obra de (José   me *goos*·ta la *o*·bra de (kho·se
Guadalupe Posada).   gwa·da·*loo*·pe po·sa·da)

... art	*arte* m ...	*ar*·te ...
abstract	*abstracto*	ab·*strak*·to
Aztec	*Azteca*	as·*te*·ka
colonial	*colonial*	ko·lo·*nyal*
contemporary	*contemporáneo*	kon·tem·po·*ra*·ne·o
Mayan	*maya*	*ma*·ya
Mexican	*mexicano*	me·khee·*ka*·no
Modernist	*modernista*	mo·der·*nees*·ta
prehispanic	*prehispánico*	pre·ees·*pa*·nee·ko
religious	*religioso*	re·lee·*khyo*·so
revolutionary	*revolucionario*	re·vo·loo·syo·*na*·ryo

artist	artista m&f	ar·tees·ta
architecture	arquitectura f	ar·kee·tek·too·ra
artwork	obra f de arte	o·bra de ar·te
canvas	tela f	te·la
curator	curador m	koo·ra·dor
design	diseño m	dee·se·nyo
etching	grabado m	gra·ba·do
handicraft	artesanía f	ar·te·sa·nee·a
installation	instalación f	een·sta·la·syon
opening	inauguración f	ee·now·goo·ra·syon
painter	pintor/pintora m/f	peen·tor/peen·to·ra
painting (canvas)	cuadro m	kwa·dro
painting (art)	pintura f	peen·too·ra
period	periodo m	pe·ryo·do
print	impresión f	eem·pre·syon
sculptor	escultor/ escultora m/f	es·kool·tor/ es·kool·to·ra
sculpture	escultura f	es·kool·too·ra
statue	estatua f	es·ta·twa
studio	estudio m	es·too·dyo
style	estilo m	es·tee·lo
technique	técnica f	tek·nee·ka

sporting interests

los intereses deportivos

Do you like (sport)?
¿Te gustan los deportes?　te goos·tan los de·por·tes

Yes, very much.
Sí, mucho.　see moo·cho

Not really.
En realidad, no mucho.　en re·a·lee·dad no moo·cho

I like watching it.
Me gusta ver.　me goos·ta ver

What sport do you play?
¿Qué deporte practicas?　ke de·por·te prak·tee·kas

What sport do you follow?
¿A qué deporte eres　a ke de·por·te e·res
aficionado/a? m/f　a·fee·syo·na·do/a

I play (basketball).
Practico (el balconcesto).　prak·tee·ko (el ba·lon·ses·to)

I follow (soccer).
Soy aficionado/a al (fútbol). m/f　soy a·fee·syo·na·do/a al (foot·bol)

Who's your favourite sportsperson?
¿Quién es tu deportista　kyen es too de·por·tees·ta
favorito/a? m/f　fa·vo·ree·to/a

Who's your favourite team?
¿Cuál es tu equipo favorito?　kwal es too e·kee·po fa·vo·ree·to

For more sports, see the **dictionary**.

going to a game

Would you like to go to a (soccer) match?
¿Te gustaría ir a un   te goos·ta·*ree*·a eer a oon
partido (de fútbol)?   par·*tee*·do (de *foot*·bol)

Who are you supporting?
¿A qué equipo te vas?   a ke e·*kee*·po te vas

Who's playing?
¿Quién juega?   kyen *khwe*·ga

Who's winning?
¿Quién va ganando?   kyen va ga·*nan*·do

How much time is left?
¿Cuánto tiempo queda   *kwan*·to *tyem*·po *ke*·da
(de partido)?   (de par·*tee*·do)

What's the score?
¿Cómo van?   *ko*·mo van

It's a draw.
Es un empate.   es oon em·*pa*·te

What was the final score?
¿Cómo terminó el partido?   *ko*·mo ter·mee·*no* el par·*tee*·do

It was a draw.
Fue un empate.   fwe oon em·*pa*·te

That was a ... game!	*¡Fue un partido ...!*	fwe oon par·*tee*·do ...
bad	*malo*	*ma*·lo
boring	*aburridísimo*	a·boo·ree·*dee*·see·mo
great	*buenísimo*	bwe·*nee*·see·mo

sports talk

What a ...!	*¡Qué ...!*	ke ...
goal	*gol*	gol
hit	*tiro*	*tee*·ro
kick	*chute*	*choo*·te
pass	*pase*	*pa*·se

playing sport

Do you want to play?
¿Quieres jugar?
kye·res khoo·gar

Can I join in?
¿Puedo jugar?
pwe·do khoo·gar

Yes, that'd be great.
Sí, me encantaría.
see me en·kan·ta·ree·a

Not at the moment, thanks.
Ahorita no, gracias.
a·o·ree·ta no gra·syas

I have an injury.
Estoy lastimado/a. m/f
es·toy las·tee·ma·do/a

Where's the best place to jog around here?
¿Cuál es el mejor sitio kwal es el me·khor see·tyo
para correr por aquí cerca? pa·ra ko·rer por a·kee ser·ka

Where's the nearest …?	*¿Dónde queda …?*	don·de ke·da …
gym	*el gimnasio más cercano*	el kheem·na·syo mas ser·ka·no
park	*el parque más cercano*	el par·ke mas ser·ka·no
sports club	*el club deportivo más cercano*	el kloob de·por·tee·vo mas ser·ka·no
swimming pool	*la alberca más cercana*	la al·ber·ka mas ser·ka·na
tennis court	*la cancha de tenis más cercana*	la kan·cha de te·nees mas ser·ka·na

What's the charge per …?	*¿Cúanto cobran por …?*	kwan·to ko·bran por …
day	*día*	dee·a
game	*juego*	khwe·go
hour	*hora*	o·ra
visit	*visita*	vee·see·ta

Can I hire a …?	¿Puedo	pwe·do
	rentar una …?	ren·tar oo·na …
ball	pelota	pe·lo·ta
court	cancha	kan·cha
racquet	raqueta	ra·ke·ta

Do I have to be a member to attend?

¿Hay que ser socio/a ai ke ser so·syo/a
para entrar? m/f pa·ra en·trar

Is there a women-only pool?

¿Hay alguna alberca sólo ai al·goo·na al·ber·ka so·lo
para mujeres? pa·ra moo·khe·res

Where are the changing rooms?

¿Dónde están los vestidores? don·de es·tan los ves·tee·do·res

Can I have a locker?

¿Puedo usar un casillero? pwe·do oo·sar oon ka·see·ye·ro

a sporting chance

Some visitors might find Mexico's traditional sports to be a little gruesome, but whatever your opinion, local sports are a cultural experience to remember. Look for posters advertising the following:

corridas de toros ko·ree·das de to·ros
bullfighting, especially popular in major towns

pelota mixteca pe·lo·ta meek·ste·ka
a five-a-side ball game reconstructed from a pre-Hispanic version that often ended with human sacrifice

lucha libre loo·cha lee·bre
theatrical free-style Mexican wrestling in which both competitors are masked

peleas de gallos pe·le·as de ga·yos
cockfights – two roosters fight to the death using deadly blades attached to their feet

diving

el buceo

I'd like to …	Me gustaría …	me goos·ta·ree·a …
explore wrecks	explorar naufragios	ek·splo·rar now·fra·khyos
go scuba diving	hacer buceo libre	a·ser boo·se·o lee·bre
go snorkelling	esnorquelear	es·nor·ke·le·ar
hire diving gear	rentar equipo de buceo	ren·tar e·kee·po de boo·se·o
hire snorkelling gear	rentar equipo para esnorkelear	ren·tar e·kee·po pa·ra es·nor·ke·le·ar
join a diving tour	unirme a un tour de buceo	oo·neer·me a oon toor de boo·se·o
learn to dive	aprender a bucear	a·pren·der a boo·se·ar

Where are some good diving sites?
¿Dónde hay buenos lugares para bucear?   don·de ai bwe·nos loo·ga·res pa·ra boo·se·ar

Are there jellyfish?
¿Hay aguasmalas?   ai a·gwas·ma·las

Where can I hire (flippers)?
¿Dónde puedo rentar (aletas)?   don·de pwe·do ren·tar (a·le·tas)

extreme sports

los deportes extremos

Are you sure this is safe?
¿De verdad que ésto es seguro?   de ver·dad ke es·to es se·goo·ro

Is the equipment secure?
¿Es seguro el equipo?   es se·goo·ro el e·kee·po

This is insane!
¡Esto es una locura!   es·to es oo·na lo·koo·ra

abseiling	*rappel* m	ra·*pel*
bungy-jumping	*bungy-jump* m	*bon*·yee yomp
caving	*espeleología* f	es·pe·le·o·lo·*khee*·a
game fishing	*pesca* f *deportiva*	*pes*·ka de·por·*tee*·va
mountain biking	*ciclismo* m de *montaña*	see·*klees*·mo de mon·*ta*·nya
parasailing	*esquí* m *acuático con paracaídas*	es·*kee* a·*kwa*·tee·ko kon pa·ra·ka·*ee*·das
rock-climbing	*escalada* f en *roca*	es·ka·*la*·da en *ro*·ka
skydiving	*paracaidismo* m	pa·ra·ka·ee·*dees*·mo
white-water rafting	*descenso* m de *ríos*	de·*sen*·so de *ree*·os

For more words and phrases you might need while hiking or trekking, see **outdoors**, page 133, and **camping**, page 58.

fishing

la pesca

Do I need a fishing permit?
¿Necesito una licencia para pescar?
ne·se·*see*·to *oo*·na lee·*sen*·sya *pa*·ra pes·*kar*

Do you do fishing tours?
¿Hay tours de pesca?
ai toors de *pes*·ka

Where are the good spots (for fishing)?
¿Dónde hay buenos lugares (para pescar)?
don·de ai *bwe*·nos loo·*ga*·res (*pa*·ra pes·*kar*)

What's the best bait?
¿Cuál es la mejor carnada?
kwal es la me·*khor* kar·*na*·da

Are they biting?
¿Están picando?
es·*tan* pee·*kan*·do

What kind of fish are you landing?
¿Qué peces estás sacando?
ke *pe*·ses es·*tas* sa·*kan*·do

How much does it weigh?
¿Cuánto pesa?
kwan·to *pe*·sa

bait	*carnada* f	kar·*na*·da
handline	*línea* f *de mano*	*lee*·ne·a de *ma*·no
hooks	*anzuelos* m pl	an·*swe*·los
flare	*luz* f *de bengala*	loos de ben·*ga*·la
float	*flotador* m	flo·ta·*dor*
lifejacket	*chaleco* m	cha·*le*·ko
	salvavidas	sal·va·*vee*·das
lures	*señuelos* m pl	se·*nywe*·los
rod	*caña* f *de pescar*	*ka*·nya de pes·*kar*
sinkers	*plomadas* f pl	plo·*ma*·das

soccer

Who plays for (the Pumas)?
*¿Quién juega en
(los Pumas)?*
kyen *khwe*·ga en
(los *poo*·mas)

He's a great (player).
Es un gran (jugador).
es oon gran (khoo·ga·*dor*)

He/She played brilliantly in the match against (Venezuela).
*Jugó excelente en el
partido contra
(Venezuela).*
khoo·*go* ek·se·*len*·te en el
par·*tee*·do *kon*·tra
(ve·ne·*swe*·la)

Which team is at the top of the league?
*¿Qué equipo está primero
en la liga?*
ke e·*kee*·po es·*ta* pree·*me*·ro
en la *lee*·ga

What a terrible team!
¡Qué equipo tan malo!
ke e·*kee*·po tan *ma*·lo

ball	*balón* m	ba·*lon*
corner (kick)	*tiro* m *de esquina*	*tee*·ro de es·*kee*·na
free kick	*tiro* m *libre*	*tee*·ro *lee*·bre
goal	*gol* m	gol
goal (place)	*portería* f	por·te·*ree*·a
goalkeeper	*portero* m	por·*te*·ro
mid-fielder	*mediocampista* m	me·dyo·kam·*pees*·ta
offside	*fuera de lugar*	*fwe*·ra de loo·*gar*
penalty	*penalty* m	pe·nal·tee
red card	*tarjeta* f *roja*	tar·*khe*·ta *ro*·kha
striker	*delantero* m	de·lan·*te*·ro
yellow card	*tarjeta* f *amarilla*	tar·*khe*·ta a·ma·*ree*·ya

Off to see a match? Check out **going to a game**, page 126.

tennis

el tenis

Would you like to play tennis?
  ¿Quieres jugar tenis?   kye·res khoo·*gar* te·nees

Can we play at night?
  ¿Podemos jugar de noche?   po·*de*·mos khoo·*gar* de *no*·che

ace	*saque* m *as*	*sa*·ke as
advantage	*ventaja* f	ven·*ta*·kha
fault	*falta* f	*fal*·ta
game, set,	*juego, set y*	*khwe*·go set ee
match	*partido* m	par·*tee*·do
play doubles	*jugar dobles*	khoo·*gar* *do*·bles
serve	*saque* m	*sa*·ke
set	*set* m	set
tennis balls	*pelotas* f pl *de tenis*	pe·*lo*·tas de *te*·nees
tennis court	*cancha* f *de tenis*	*kan*·cha de *te*·nees

hiking

el excursionismo

Where can I ...?	¿Dónde puedo ...?	don·de pwe·do ...
buy supplies	comprar	kom·prar
	provisiones	pro·vee·syo·nes
find out about	encontrar	en·kon·trar
hiking trails	información	een·for·ma·syon
	sobre rutas	so·bre roo·tas
	para	pa·ra
	excursionismo	ek·skoor·syo·nees·mo
find someone	encontrar a	en·kon·trar a
who knows	alguien que	al·gyen ke
this area	conozca la zona	ko·nos·ka la so·na
get a map	obtener un mapa	ob·te·ner oon ma·pa
hire hiking gear	rentar equipo	ren·tar e·kee·po
	para	pa·ra
	excursionismo	ek·skoor·syo·nees·mo
Do we need to	¿Necesitamos	ne·se·see·ta·mos
take ...?	llevar ...?	ye·var ...
bedding	algo en que	al·go en ke
	dormir	dor·meer
food	comida	ko·mee·da
water	agua	a·gwa
Which is the ...	¿Cuál es la ruta	kwal es la roo·ta
route?	más ...?	mas ...
easiest	fácil	fa·seel
longest	larga	lar·ga
shortest	corta	kor·ta
Is the track ...?	¿El sendero está ...?	el sen·de·ro es·ta ...
(well-)marked	(bien) marcado	(byen) mar·ka·do
open	abierto	a·byer·to

How high is the climb?
¿A qué altura se escala?   a ke al·*too*·ra se es·*ka*·la

How long is the hike?
¿Qué tan larga es la caminata?   ke tan *lar*·ga es la ka·mee·*na*·ta

How long is the trail?
¿Qué tan larga es la ruta?   ke tan *lar*·ga es la *roo*·ta

Is the track scenic?
¿Es escénico el sendero?   es e·*se*·nee·ko el sen·*de*·ro

Do we need a guide?
¿Necesitamos un guía?   ne·se·see·*ta*·mos oon *gee*·a

Are there guided treks?
¿Hay escaladas guiadas?   ai es·ka·*la*·das gee·*a*·das

Is it safe?
¿Es seguro?   es se·*goo*·ro

Is there a hut there?
¿Hay alguna cabaña?   ai al·*goo*·na ka·*ba*·nya

When does it get dark?
¿A qué hora oscurece?   a ke *o*·ra os·koo·*re*·se

Where have you come from?
¿De dónde vienes/vienen? sg/pl   de *don*·de *vye*·nes/*vye*·nen

How long did it take?
¿Cuánto tardaste?   *kwan*·to tar·*das*·te

Does this path go to (Morelia)?
¿Este camino va a (Morelia)?   *es*·te ka·*mee*·no va a (mo·*re*·lya)

Can we go through here?
¿Podemos atravesar   po·*de*·mos a·tra·ve·*sar*
por aquí?   por a·*kee*

Is the water OK to drink?
¿Se puede tomar el agua?   se *pwe*·de to·*mar* el *a*·gwa

I'm lost.
Estoy perdido/a. m/f   es·*toy* per·*dee*·do/a

Where's …?	¿Dónde …?	don·de …
a camping site	hay un lugar para acampar	ai oon loo·gar pa·ra a·kam·par
the nearest village	está pueblo más cercano	es·ta el pwe·blo mas ser·ka·no

Where are the …?	¿Dónde hay …?	don·de ai …
showers	regaderas	re·ga·de·ras
toilets	sanitarios	sa·nee·ta·ryos

beach

la playa

Where's the … beach?	¿Dónde está la playa …?	don·de es·ta la pla·ya …
best	más padre	mas pa·dre
nearest	más cercana	mas ser·ka·na
nudist	nudista	noo·dees·ta

Is it safe to … here?	¿Es seguro … aquí?	es se·goo·ro … a·kee
dive	echarse clavados	e·char·se kla·va·dos
scuba dive	bucear	boo·se·ar
swim	nadar	na·dar

What time is … tide?	¿A qué hora es la marea …?	a ke o·ra es la ma·re·a …
high	alta	al·ta
low	baja	ba·kha

listen for …

e·res mo·de·lo
¿Eres modelo? — **Are you a model?**

es pe·lee·gro·so
¡Es peligroso! — **It's dangerous!**

kwee·da·do kon la ko·ryen·te
Cuidado con la corriente. — **Be careful of the undertow.**

How much for a/an ...?	¿Cuánto cuesta rentar una ...?	kwan·to kwes·ta ren·tar oo·na ...
chair	silla	see·ya
hut	palapa	pa·la·pa
umbrella	sombrilla	som·bree·ya

Are there any ...?	¿Hay ...?	ai ...
reefs	arrecifes	a·re·see·fes
rips	corrientes	ko·ryen·tes
water hazards	peligros en el agua	pe·lee·gros en el a·gwa

signs

Prohibido Nadar	pro·ee·bee·do na·dar	No Swimming

weather

el clima

What's the weather like?
¿Cómo está el clima?   ko·mo es·ta el klee·ma

(Today) It's raining.
(Hoy) Llueve.   (oy) ywe·ve

(Tomorrow) It will be raining.
(Mañana) Lloverá.   (ma·nya·na) yo·ve·ra

(Today) It's ... Will it be ... tomorrow?	Hoy está ... ¿Estará ... mañana?	oy es·ta ... es·ta·ra ... ma·nya·na
cloudy	nublado	noo·bla·do
sunny	soleado	so·le·a·do
warm	cálido	ka·lee·do
windy	ventoso	ven·to·so

(Today) It's ... Will it be ... tomorrow?	(Hoy) hace ... Mañana hará ...?	(oy) a·se ... ma·nya·na a·ra ...
cold	frío	free·o
hot	calor	ka·lor

Where can I buy ...?	¿Dónde puedo comprar un ...?	don·de pwe·do kom·prar oon ...
an umbrella	paraguas	pa·ra·gwas
a rain jacket	impermeable	eem·per·me·a·ble
dry season	época f de secas	e·po·ka de se·kas
hail	granizo m	gra·nee·so
rainy season	época f de lluvias	e·po·ka de yoo·vyas
storm	tormenta f	tor·men·ta
sun	sol m	sol

flora & fauna

What ... is that?	¿Qué ... es ése/a? m/f	ke ... es e·se/a
animal	animal m	a·nee·mal
flower	flor f	flor
plant	planta f	plan·ta
tree	árbol m	ar·bol
Is it ...?	¿Es ...?	es ...
common	común	ko·moon
dangerous	peligroso/a m/f	pe·lee·gro·so/a
endangered	en peligro de extinción	en pe·lee·gro de ek·steen·syon
poisonous	venenoso/a m/f	ve·ne·no·so/a
protected	protegido/a m/f	pro·te·khee·do/a

What's it used for?
¿Para qué se usa? pa·ra ke se oo·sa

Can you eat it?
¿Se puede comer? se pwe·de ko·mer

From the raucous howler monkeys to scorpions and vampire bats, Mexico ranks as one of the most biologically diverse countries in the world. Whether you're trekking across the northern deserts or exploring the southern jungles, ask a local what you're looking at.

What animal is that?

¿Qué animal es ése?		ke a·nee·*mal* es e·se

anteater	oso m hormiguero	o·so or·mee·*ge*·ro
armadillo	armadillo m	ar·ma·*dee*·yo
buzzard	zopilote m	so·pee·*lo*·te
eagle	águila f	a·gee·la
hawk	halcón m	al·*kon*
howler monkey	mono m aullador	mo·no ow·ya·*dor*
iguana	iguana f	ee·*gwa*·na
macaw	guacamayo m	gwa·ka·*ma*·yo
ocelot	ocelote m	o·se·*lo*·te
rabbit	conejo m	ko·*ne*·kho
raccoon	mapache m	ma·*pa*·che
skunk	zorrillo m	so·*ree*·yo
scorpion	escorpión m	es·kor·*pyon*
snake	serpiente f	ser·*pyen*·te
spider monkey	mono m araña	mo·no a·*ra*·nya
tapir	tapir m	ta·*peer*
toucan	tucán m	too·*kan*
vampire bat	vampiro m	vam·*pee*·ro

```
                PV# 0073841
                CASH              8.70
                TOTAL             8.70
WASHINGTON  8.900% T              .71
            SUBTOTAL             7.99
01 1740594959                    7.99
REF 8.3/1.12 71  5:47:14
SALE    1928  103  3841  05-10-0
```

BORDERS.

Returns to Borders Stores:

Merchandise presented for return, including sale or marked-down items, must be accompanied by the original Borders store receipt. Returns must be completed within 30 days of purchase. The purchase price will be refunded in the medium of purchase (cash, credit card, or gift card). Items purchased by check may be returned for cash after 10 business days.

Merchandise unaccompanied by the original Borders store receipt, or presented for return beyond 30 days from date of purchase, must be carried by Borders at the time of the return. The lowest price offered for the item during the 12-month period prior to the return will be refunded via a gift card.

Opened videos, discs, and cassettes may only be exchanged for replacement copies of the original item.

Periodicals, newspapers, and out-of-print, collectible and pre-owned items may not be returned.

Returned merchandise must be in saleable condition.

key language

breakfast	*desayuno* m	de·sa·*yoo*·no
dinner	*cena* f	*se*·na
drink	*beber*	be·*ber*
eat	*comer*	ko·*mer*
lunch	*comida* f	ko·*mee*·da
snack	*botana* f	bo·*ta*·na

I'm starving!
　　¡Me muero de hambre!　　me *mwe*·ro de *am*·bre

tacos to go

Fresh tacos are cheap, tasty and absolutely everywhere.
Don't leave without trying these three favourites:

tacos al pastor　　*ta*·kos al pas·*tor*
　　tacos with thinly-sliced meat, pineapple, onions and coriander

tacos de carne asada　　*ta*·kos de *kar*·ne a·*sa*·da
　　tacos with marinated minced steak, fresh onions and coriander

tacos de carnitas　　*ta*·kos de kar·*nee*·tas
　　tacos with finely-diced pork,onions and coriander

finding a place to eat

Can you recommend a …	*¿Me puede recomendar …?*	me *pwe*·de re·ko·men·*dar* …
bar	*un bar*	oon bar
cafe	*un café*	oon ka·*fe*
coffee bar	*una cafetería*	*oo*·na ka·fe·te·*ree*·a
restaurant	*un restaurante*	oon res·tow·*ran*·te

Where would you go for …?	¿Dónde se puede …?	don·de se pwe·de …
a celebration	festejar	fes·te·khar
a cheap meal	comer barato	ko·mer ba·ra·to.
local specialities	comer comida típica	ko·mer ko·mee·da tee·pee·ka

listen for …

a·kee tye·ne
Aquí tiene.
Here you go!

don·de le goos·ta·ree·a sen·tar·se
¿Dónde le gustaría sentarse?
Where would you like to sit?

es·ta·mos ye·nos
Estamos llenos.
We're fully booked.

ke de·se·a or·de·nar
¿Qué desea ordenar?
What can I get for you?

ko·mo lo kye·re pre·pa·ra·do
¿Cómo lo quiere preparado?
How would you like that cooked?

kye·re to·mar al·go myen·tras es·pe·ra
¿Quiere tomar algo mientras espera?
Would you like a drink while you wait?

le goos·ta …
¿Le gusta …?
Do you like …?

le re·ko·myen·do …
Le recomiendo …
I suggest the …

no te·ne·mos me·sas
No tenemos mesas.
We have no tables.

oon mo·men·tee·to
Un momentito.
One moment.

ya se·ra·mos
Ya cerramos.
We're closed.

I'd like to reserve a table for ...	Quisiera reservar una mesa para ...	kee·sye·ra re·ser·var oo·na me·sa pa·ra ...
(two) people	(dos) personas	(dos) per·so·nas
(eight) o'clock	a las (ocho)	a las (o·cho)

Are you still serving food?
¿Siguen sirviendo comida? see·gen seer·vyen·do ko·mee·da

How long is the wait?
¿Cuánto hay que esperar? kwan·to ai ke es·pe·rar

I'd like ..., please.	Quisiera ..., por favor.	kee·sye·ra ... por fa·vor
a table for (five)	una mesa para (cinco)	oo·na me·sa pa·ra (seen·ko)
the menu	el menú	el me·noo
the drink list	la carta de bebidas	la kar·ta de be·bee·das
the (non-smoking) section	el área de (no) fumar	el a·re·a de (no) foo·mar

Do you have ...?	¿Tienen ...?	tye·nen ...
children's meals	menú infantil	me·noo een·fan·teel
a menu in English	un menú en inglés	oon me·noo en een·gles

at the restaurant

en el restaurante

I'd like the menu, please.
Quisiera el menú, por favor. kee·sye·ra el me·noo por fa·vor

Is it self-serve?
¿Es autoservicio? es ow·to·ser·vee·syo

We're just having drinks.
Sólo queremos tomar algo. so·lo ke·re·mos to·mar al·go

What would you recommend?
¿Qué recomienda? ke re·ko·myen·da

I'll have what they're having.
Quiero lo mismo que ellos.
kye·ro lo mees·mo ke e·yos

What's in that dish?
¿Qué tiene ese platillo?
ke tye·ne e·se pla·tee·yo

Does it take long to prepare?
*¿Se tarda mucho en
prepararlo?*
se tar·da moo·cho en
pre·pa·rar·lo

Are these complimentary?
¿Éstos son de cortesía?
es·tos son de kor·te·see·a

I'd like a local speciality.
*Quisiera un platillo
típico.*
kee·sye·ra oon pla·tee·yo
tee·pee·ko

I'd like a meal fit for a king.
*Quisiera comer como
un rey.*
kee·sye·ra ko·mer ko·mo
oon ray

Is service included in the bill?
*¿La cuenta incluye el
cubierto?*
la kwen·ta een·kloo·ye el
koo·byer·to

ashtray
cenicero m
see·nee·se·ro

spoon
cuchara f
koo·cha·ra

fork
tenedor m
te·ne·dor

plate
plato m
pla·to

knife
cuchillo m
koo·chee·yo

wineglass
copa f *de vino*
ko·pa de vee·no

glass
vaso m
va·so

table
mesa f
me·sa

botanas	bo·*ta*·nas	appetisers
comida	ko·*mee*·da	set meals
corrida	ko·*ree*·da	
ensaladas	en·sa·*la*·das	salads
entradas	en·*tra*·das	entrees
guarniciones	gwar·nee·*syo*·nes	side dishes
platillo	pla·*tee*·yo	main course
principal	preen·see·*pal*	
postre	*pos*·tre	desserts
sopas	*so*·pas	soups
aguas frescas	*a*·gwas *fres*·kas	fruit drinks
de frutas	de *froo*·tas	
aperitivos	a·pe·ree·*tee*·vos	aperitifs
bebidas	be·*bee*·das	drinks
cervezas	ser·*ve*·sas	beers
digestivos	dee·khes·*tee*·vos	digestifs
licores	lee·*ko*·res	spirits
refrescos	re·*fres*·kos	soft drinks
vinos blancos	*vee*·nos *blan*·kos	white wines
vinos dulces	*vee*·nos *dool*·ses	dessert wines
vinos espumosos	*vee*·nos es·poo·*mo*·sos	sparkling wines
vinos tintos	*vee*·nos *teen*·tos	red wines

For more words you might see on the menu, see the **culinary reader** page 157.

Please bring us ...	*Por favor, nos trae ...*	por fa·*vor* nos *tra*·e ...
the bill	*la cuenta*	la *kwen*·ta
a knife	*un cuchillo*	oon koo·*chee*·yo
a serviette	*una servilleta*	*oo*·na ser·vee·*ye*·ta
a spoon	*una cuchara*	*oo*·na koo·*cha*·ra

Is there (any chilli sauce)?
¿Hay (salsa picante)?   ai (*sal*·sa pee·*kan*·te)

talking food

That was delicious!
¡Estaba delicioso!
es·ta·ba de·lee·syo·so

My compliments to the chef.
Mis felicitaciones al chef.
mees fe·lee·see·ta·syo·nes al chef

I'm full.
Estoy satisfecho/a. m/f
es·toy sa·tees·fe·cho/a

I love …	*Me encanta …*	me en·kan·ta …
this dish	*este platillo*	es·te pla·tee·yo
the local cuisine	*la comida típica*	la ko·mee·da tee·pee·ka

This is …	*Esto está …*	es·to es·ta …
burnt	*quemado*	ke·ma·do
(too) cold	*(muy) frío*	(mooy) free·o
(too) hot	*(muy) caliente*	(mooy) kal·yen·te
spicy	*picante*	pee·kan·te
superb	*exquisito*	es·kee·see·to

Tex-Mex teaser

If you were expecting crunchy tacos you'll be disappointed and don't order a burrito unless you're after a little donkey. Some foods that you may have thought were Mexican – like fajitas, burritos and nachos – are actually all from Texas. Some say these dishes are a pale imitation of Mexican food, while others claim Tex-Mex cuisine belongs in a class of its own. As a former state of Mexico, Texas certainly maintains strong cultural influences from further south, but homesick Texans should order *tacos dorados* (deep-fried tacos) if they need a bit of crunch.

breakfast

el desayuno

What's a typical (Mexican) breakfast?

¿Cómo es un típico		ko·mo es oon *tee*·pee·ko
desayuno (mexicano)?		de·sa·*yoo*·no (me·khee·*ka*·no)

bacon	*tocino* m	to·*see*·no
beans	*frijoles* m pl	free·*kho*·les
bread	*pan* m	pan
butter	*mantequilla* f	man·te·*kee*·ya
cereal	*cereal* m	se·re·*al*
(hot/cold)	*chocolate* m	cho·ko·*la*·te
chocolate	*(caliente/frío)*	(ka·*lyen*·te/*free*·o)
coffee	*café* m	ka·*fe*
fruit	*fruta* f	*froo*·ta
hot corn drink	*atole* m	a·*to*·le
eggs	*huevos* m pl	*we*·vos
fried eggs	*huevos* m pl	*we*·vos
	estrellados	es·tre·*ya*·dos
Mexican-style	*huevos* m pl	*we*·vos
eggs	*a la mexicana*	a la me·khee·*ka*·na
scrambled eggs	*huevos* m pl *revueltos*	*we*·vos re·*vwel*·tos
jam	*mermelada* f	mer·me·*la*·da
milk	*leche* f	*le*·che
orange juice	*jugo* m de	*khoo*·go de
	naranja	na·*ran*·kha
sauce	*salsa* f	*sal*·sa
sweet bread	*pan* m *dulce*	pan *dool*·se
stuffed corn dough	*tamales* m pl	ta·*ma*·les
tea	*té* m	te
toast	*pan* m *tostado*	pan tos·*ta*·do
tortillas	*tortillas* f pl	tor·*tee*·yas
cornflour	*tortillas* f pl	tor·*tee*·yas
tortillas	*de maíz*	de ma·*ees*
cheese tortillas	*quesadillas* f pl	ke·sa·*dee*·yas

See **self-catering**, page 151, and the **culinary reader**, page 157, for more breakfast foods.

methods of preparation

I'd like it …	Lo quiero …	lo kye·ro …
I don't want it …	No lo quiero …	no lo kye·ro …
boiled	hervido/a m/f	er·vee·do/a
broiled	asado/a a la parrilla m/f	a·sa·do/a a la pa·ree·ya
deep-fried	sumergido/a en aceite m/f	soo·mer·khee·do/a en a·say·te
fried	frito/a m/f	free·to/a
grilled	a la parrilla	a la pa·ree·ya
medium	término medio	ter·mee·no me·dyo
rare	roja	ro·kha
re-heated	recalentado/a m/f	re·ka·len·ta·do/a
steamed	al vapor	al va·por
well-done	bien cocido/a m/f	byen ko·see·do/a
with the dressing on the side	con el aderezo aparte	kon el a·de·re·so a·par·te
without (chilli)	sin (chile)	seen (chee·le)

in the bar

Excuse me!
¡Oiga!   oy·ga

I'm next.
¡Sigo yo!   see·go yo

I'll have (a tequila).
Quiero (una tequila).   kye·ro (oo·na te·kee·la)

Same again, please.
Otro igual, por favor.   o·tro eeg·wal por fa·vor

No ice, please.
Sin hielo, por favor.   seen ye·lo por fa·vor

I'll buy you a drink.
Te invito una copa.   te een·vee·to oo·na ko·pa

What would you like?
¿Qué quieres tomar?　　　ke *kye*·res to·*mar*

It's my round.
Yo invito esta ronda.　　　yo een·*vee*·to *es*·ta *ron*·da

You can get the next one.
Tu invitas la que sigue.　　too een·*vee*·tas la ke *see*·ge

Do you serve meals here?
¿Sirven comidas aquí?　　*seer*·ven ko·*mee*·das a·*kee*

nonalcoholic drinks

(cup of) tea	*(un) té* m	(oon) te
(cup of) coffee	*(un) café* m	(oon) ka·*fe*
... with (milk)	*... con (leche)*	... kon (*le*·che)
... without (sugar)	*... sin (azúcar)*	... seen (a·*soo*·kar)
juice	*jugo* m	*khoo*·go
lemonade	*limonada* f	lee·mo·*na*·da
milkshake	*malteada* f	mal·te·*a*·da
orangeade	*naranjada* f	na·ran·*kha*·da
soft drink (general)	*refresco* m	re·*fres*·ko
soft drink (northern Mexico)	*soda* f	*so*·da
... water	*agua* f ...	*a*·gwa ...
boiled	*hervida*	er·*vee*·da
jamaica	*de jamaica*	de kha·*may*·ka
mineral	*mineral*	mee·ne·*ral*
rice	*de horchata*	de or·*cha*·ta
sparkling	*con gas*	kon gas
still	*sin gas*	seen gas
tamarind	*de tamarindo*	de ta·ma·*reen*·do

eating out

147

alcoholic drinks

beer	*cerveza* f	ser·*ve*·sa
champagne	*champán* m	cham·*pan*
cocktail	*coctel* m	kok·*tel*
gin	*ginebra* f	khee·*ne*·bra
rum	*ron* m	ron
vodka	*vodka* m	*vod*·ka
whisky	*whisky* m	*wees*·kee

the spirit of Mexico

I would like a shot of …
   Quisiera un shot de …   kee·*sye*·ra oon shot de …

mezcal   mes·*kal*
   liquor distilled from agave

posh   posh
   cane liquor flavoured with herbs

pulque   *pool*·ke
   alcohol made from fermented agave sap

rompope   rom·*po*·pe
   eggnog with cane alcohol and cinnamon

tepache   te·*pa*·che
   alcohol made from fermented pineapple rinds

tequila   te·*kee*·la
   popular spirit distilled from the maguey plant

a bottle/glass	*una botella/copa*	oo·na bo·*te*·ya/ko·pa
of … wine	*de vino …*	de *vee*·no …
dessert	*dulce*	*dool*·se
red	*tinto*	*teen*·to
rose	*rosado*	ro·*sa*·do
sparkling	*espumoso*	es·poo·*mo*·so
white	*blanco*	*blan*·ko

a ... of beer	... de cerveza	... de ser·ve·sa
glass	un tarro	oon ta·ro
jug	una jarra	oo·na kha·ra
large bottle (940ml)	una caguama	oo·na ka·gwa·ma
small bottle (325ml)	una botella	oo·na bo·te·ya

one too many?

Cheers!
¡Salud!   sa·lood

Thanks, but I don't feel like it.
Gracias, pero no se me   gra·syas pe·ro no se me
antoja.   an·to·kha

I don't drink alcohol.
No bebo.   no be·bo

I'm tired, I'd better go home.
Estoy cansado/a, mejor   es·toy kan·sa·do/a me·khor
me voy a mi casa. m/f   me voy a mee ka·sa

Where's the toilet?
¿Dónde está el baño?   don·de es·ta el ba·nyo

This is hitting the spot.
Me lo estoy pasando   me lo es·toy pa·san·do
muy bien.   mooy byen

I'm feeling drunk.
Se me está subiendo   se me es·ta soo·byen·do
mucho.   moo·cho

I feel fantastic!
¡Me siento muy bien!   me syen·to mooy byen

I really, really love you.
Te quiero muchísimo.   te *kye*·ro moo·*chee*·see·mo

I think I've had one too many.
Creo que he tomado   *kre*·o ke e to·*ma*·do
demasiado.   de·ma·*sya*·do

Can you call a taxi for me?
¿Me puedes pedir   me *pwe*·des pe·*deer*
un taxi?   oon *tak*·see

I don't think you should drive.
No creo que debas manejar.   no *kre*·o ke *de*·bas ma·ne·*khar*

I'm pissed.
Estoy borracho/a. m/f   es·*toy* bo·*ra*·cho/a

I feel ill.
Me siento mal.   me *syen*·to mal

the best seat in the house

Nature calls by many names in Mexico. Toilets are widely known as *baños*, while public toilets may also advertise themselves as *sanitarios* or *servicios*. An unexpected bout of 'Montezuma's revenge' – a bowel condition afflicting those still adjusting to spicy food – can leave you charging for the door. Before rushing in blindly, take a moment to consider your best option:

Caballeros	ka·ba·*ye*·ros	Gentlemen
Damas	*da*·mas	Ladies
Hombres	*om*·bres	Men
Mujeres	moo·*khe*·res	Women
Señores	sen·*yo*·res	Sirs
Señoras	sen·*yo*·ras	Madams

key language

		lenguaje básico
cooked	*cocido/a* m/f	ko·*see*·do/a
dried	*seco/a* m/f	*se*·ko/a
fresh	*fresco/a* m/f	*fres*·ko/a
frozen	*congelado/a* m/f	kon·khe·*la*·do/a
raw	*crudo/a* m/f	*kroo*·do/a

market munchies

The mouthwatering aroma of fresh food in a Mexican market can really work up your appetite. For a cheap local meal in a rowdy atmosphere, grab a seat at a *comedor* (lit: eatery) usually found in the centre of the market.

buying food

comprando comida

How much?
¿Cuánto? · *kwan*·to

How much does it cost?
¿Cuánto cuesta? · *kwan*·to *kwes*·ta

How much is (a kilo of cheese)?
¿Cuánto vale · *kwan*·to *va*·le
(un kilo de queso)? · (oon *kee*·lo de *ke*·so)

What's the local speciality?
¿Cuál es la especialidad · kwal es la es·pe·sya·lee·*dad*
de la zona? · de la *so*·na

What's that?
¿Qué es eso? · ke es *e*·so

Can I taste it?
¿Puedo probarlo/a? m/f · *pwe*·do pro·*bar*·lo/a

Can I have a bag, please?
¿Me da una bolsa, por favor?   me da *oo*·na *bol*·sa por fa·*vor*

I'd like …	*Quisiera …*	kee·*sye*·ra …
(100) grams	*(cien) gramos*	(syen) *gra*·mos
a kilo	*un kilo*	oon *kee*·lo
(two) kilos	*(dos) kilos*	(dos) *kee*·los
a bottle	*una botella*	*oo*·na bo·*te*·ya
a dozen	*una docena*	*oo*·na do·*sen*·a
a jar	*un jarra*	oon *kha*·ra
a packet	*un paquete*	oon pa·*ke*·te
a piece	*una pieza*	*oo*·na *pye*·sa
(three) pieces	*(tres) piezas*	(tres) *pye*·sas
a slice	*una rebanada*	*oo*·na re·ba·*na*·da
(six) slices	*(seis) rebanadas*	(says) re·ba·*na*·das
a tin	*una lata*	*oo*·na *la*·ta
that one	*ése/a* m/f	e·se/a
this one	*ésto*	es·to
a bit more	*un poco más*	oon *po*·ko mas
less	*menos*	*me*·nos

That's enough, thanks.		
Así está bien, gracias.		a·*see* es·*ta* byen *gra*·syas

Do you have …?	*¿Tiene …?*	*tye*·ne …
anything cheaper	*algo más barato*	*al*·go mas ba·*ra*·to
any other kinds	*otros tipos*	*o*·tros *tee*·pos

Where can I find the … section?	*¿Dónde está la sección de …?*	*don*·de es·*ta* la sek·*syon* de …
dairy	*lácteos*	*lak*·te·os
fish and seafood	*pescados y mariscos*	pes·*ka*·dos ee ma·*rees*·kos
frozen goods	*productos congelados*	pro·*dook*·tos kon·khe·*la*·dos
fruit and vegetable	*frutas y verduras*	*froo*·tas ee ver·*doo*·ras
meat	*carnes*	*kar*·nes
poultry	*aves*	*a*·ves

listen for …

al·go mas	
¿Algo más?	**Anything else?**
en ke le *pwe*·do ser·*veer*	
¿En qué le puedo servir?	**Can I help you?**
e·se es (*mo*·le)	
Ese es (mole).	**That's (mole).**
ke de·*se*·a	
¿Qué desea?	**What would you like?**
no *ten*·go	
No tengo.	**I don't have any.**
se ter·mee·*no*	
Se terminó	**There's none left.**
son (*seen*·ko *pe*·sos)	
Son (cinco pesos).	**That's (five pesos).**

cooking utensils

Could I please borrow (a corkscrew)?
   ¿Me puede prestar (un   me *pwe*·de pres·*tar* (oon
   sacacorchos)?   sa·ka·*kor*·chos)

Where's (a frying pan)?
   ¿Dónde hay (un sartén)?   *don*·de ai (oon sar·*ten*)

bottle opener	*destapador* m	des·ta·pa·*dor*
bowl	*refractario* m	re·frak·*ta*·ryo
can opener	*abrelatas* m	a·bre·*la*·tas
chopping board	*tabla* f *para picar*	*ta*·bla pa·ra pee·*kar*
cup	*taza* f	*ta*·sa
corkscrew	*sacacorchos* m	sa·ka·*kor*·chos
fork	*tenedor* m	te·ne·*dor*
fridge	*refrigerador* m	re·free·khe·ra·*dor*
frying pan	*sartén* m	sar·*ten*
glass	*vaso* m	*va*·so
knife	*cuchillo* m	koo·*chee*·yo
oven	*horno* m	*or*·no
plate	*plato* m	*pla*·to
saucepan	*olla* f	*o*·ya
spatula	*espátula* f	es·*pa*·too·la
spoon	*cuchara* f	koo·*cha*·ra
toaster	*tostador* m	tos·ta·*dor*
tongs	*pinzas* f pl	*peen*·sas

vegetarian & special meals
comidas vegetarianas & platos especiales

ordering food

Is there a (vegetarian) restaurant near here?

| *¿Hay un restaurante* | ai oon res·tow·*ran*·te |
| *(vegetariano) por aquí?* | (ve·khe·ta·*rya*·no) por a·*kee* |

I'm (vegan).

| *Soy (vegetariano/a* | soy (ve·khe·ta·*rya*·no/a |
| *estricto/a).* **m/f** | es·*treek*·to/a) |

I don't eat (meat).

| *No como (carne).* | no *ko*·mo (*kar*·ne) |

Is it cooked in/with (oil)?

| *¿Está cocinado en/* | e·*sta* ko·see·*na*·do en/ |
| *con (aceite)?* | con (a·*say*·te) |

Do you	*¿Tienen*	*tye*·nen
have … food?	*comida …?*	ko·*mee*·da …
halal	*halal*	kha·*lal*
kosher	*kosher*	*ko*·sher
vegetarian	*vegetariana*	ve·khe·ta·*rya*·na

Is this …?	*¿Esto es …?*	*es*·to es …
decaffeinated	*descafeinado*	des·ka·fay·*na*·do
free of animal	*sin productos*	seen pro·*dook*·tos
produce	*animales*	a·nee·*ma*·les
free range	*de corral*	de ko·*ral*
genetically	*transgénico*	trans·*khe*·nee·ko
modified		
gluten-free	*sin gluten*	seen *gloo*·ten
low-fat	*bajo en grasas*	*ba*·kho en *gra*·sas
low in sugar	*bajo en azúcar*	*ba*·kho en a·*soo*·kar
organic	*orgánico*	or·*ga*·nee·ko
salt-free	*sin sal*	seen sal

Could you	¿Me puede	me *pwe*·de
prepare a meal	*preparar una*	pre·pa·*rar* oo·na
without …?	*comida sin …?*	ko·*mee*·da seen …
butter	*mantequilla*	man·te·*kee*·ya
eggs	*huevos*	*we*·vos
fish	*pescado*	pes·*ka*·do
meat/fish stock	*consomé de*	kon·so·*me* de
	carne/pescado	*kar*·ne/pes·*ka*·do
pork	*cerdo*	*ser*·do
poultry	*aves*	*a*·ves
(red) meat	*carne (roja)*	*kar*·ne (ro·kha)

listen for …

le pre·goon·ta·re al ko·see·ne·ro
Le preguntaré al cocinero. **I'll check with the cook.**

pwe·de ko·mer …
¿Puede comer …? **Can you eat …?**

to·do tye·ne (kar·ne)
Todo tiene (carne). **It all has (meat) in it.**

special diets & allergies

dietas especiales & alergias

I'm on a special diet.
Estoy a dieta especial. es·*toy* a *dye*·ta es·pe·*syal*

I'm allergic to …	*Soy alérgico/a …* m/f	soy a·*ler*·khee·ko/a …
dairy produce	*a los productos*	a los pro·*dook*·tos
	lácteos	*lak*·te·os
eggs	*a los huevos*	a los *we*·vos
gelatin	*a la gelatina*	a la khe·la·*tee*·na
gluten	*al gluten*	al *gloo*·ten
MSG	*al glutamato*	al gloo·ta·*ma*·to
	monosódico	mo·no·so·dee·ko
nuts	*a las nueces*	a las *nwe*·ses
peanuts	*a los cacahuates*	a los ka·ka·*khwa*·tes
seafood	*a los mariscos*	a los ma·*rees*·kos
shellfish	*a los moluscos*	a los mo·*loos*·kos

For a more detailed version of this glossary, see Lonely Planet's *World Food Mexico*.

A

abulón ⓜ a·boo·*lon* abalone

aceite ⓜ a·*say*·te oil
— **de girasol** de khee·ra·*sol* sunflower oil
— **de oliva** de o·*lee*·va olive oil
— **vegetal** ve·khe·*tal* vegetable oil

aceituna ⓕ a·say·*too*·na olive
— **negra** ne·gra black olive
— **verde** ver·de green olive

acitrón ⓜ a·see·*tron* cactus prepared as a candy but also used in savoury dishes

acocil ⓜ a·ko·*seel* small red shrimp

achiote ⓜ a·*chyo*·te red, musky-flavoured spice used as a colouring agent in **mole** & other foods (also called **annatto**)

adobo ⓜ a·*do*·bo paste of garlic, vinegar, herbs & chillies – used as a sauce, marinade or pickling agent

agave ⓜ a·*ga*·ve American aloe, also known as 'century plant' – source of alcoholic beverages such as **pulque**, **mezcal** & **tequila**
— **azul** a·*sool* blue agave – used to produce **tequila** & **mezcal**

agua ⓕ a·gwa water
— **caliente** ka·*lyen*·te hot water
— **con gas** kon gas soda water • carbonated water
— **de horchata** de or·*cha*·ta rice water
— **de jamaica** de kha·*mai*·ka drink made by steeping dried hibiscus flowers in warm water – served chilled
— **de la llave** de la *ya*·ve tap water
— **de manantial** de ma·nan·*tyal* spring water
— **embotellada** em·bo·te·ya·da bottled water
— **fresca** *fres*·ka fruit-flavoured water
— **fría** *free*·a cold water
— **mineral** mee·ne·*ral* mineral water
— **purificada** poo·ree·fee·*ka*·da purified water
— **quina** *kee*·na tonic water
— **sin gas** seen gas still water
— **tónica** *to*·nee·ka tonic water

aguacate ⓜ a·gwa·*ka*·te avocado

aguamiel ⓜ a·gwa·*myel* agave juice

aguardiente ⓜ a·gwar·*dyen*·te sugar cane alcohol

ajo ⓜ a·kho garlic

ajonjolí ⓜ a·khon·kho·*lee* sesame seeds

albahaca ⓕ al·*ba*·ka sweet basil

albóndigas ⓕ pl al·*bon*·dee·gas meatballs

alcachofa ⓕ al·ka·*cho*·fa artichoke

alcaparras ⓕ pl al·ka·*pa*·ras capers

alegrías ⓕ pl a·le·*gree*·as traditional sweet made from amaranth seeds & molasses

alfajor ⓜ **de coco** al·fa·*khor* de ko·ko pastry filled with jam & sprinkled with grated coconut

algodón ⓜ **de azúcar** al·go·*don* de a·soo·kar fairy floss • cotton candy

alimentos ⓜ pl a·lee·*men*·tos food

almeja ⓕ al·*me*·kha clam • scallop

almendra ⓕ al·*men*·dra almond

almuerzo ⓜ al·*mwer*·so brunch, also translated as 'lunch' – a late-morning snack typically consisting of a quick plate of **tacos** or a sandwich

alubia ⓕ a·*loo*·bya haricot bean

amaranto ⓜ a·ma·*ran*·to amaranth – a native plant similar to spinach

anchoa ⓕ an·*cho*·a anchovy

anguila ⓕ an·*gee*·la eel

anís ⓜ a·*nees* anise • aniseed (used in desserts, liqueurs & breads)

annatto a·*na*·to see **achiote**

antojitos ⓜ pl an·to·*khee*·tos *'little whimsies'* – small portions of classic Mexican dishes, such as **quesadillas**, **sopes** & **tostadas**, served as snack food for street eating or as appetisers

añejo/a ⓜ/ⓕ a·*nye*·kho/a *'aged'* – used to describe certain cheeses, meat & **tequila**

apio ⓜ *a*·pyo celery

arándano ⓜ a·*ran*·da·no bilberry
— **agrio** *a*·gryo cranberry

arenque ⓜ a·*ren*·ke herring • kipper

arroz ⓜ a·*ros* rice
— **a la Mexicana** a la me·khee·*ka*·na *'Mexican rice'* – may be coloured red with tomatoes & cooked with diced carrots & peas
— **a la poblana** a la po·*bla*·na pilaf with **chile poblano**, corn & melted cheese
— **con leche** kon *le*·che rice pudding
— **de grano corto** de *gra*·no *kor*·to short-grain rice
— **glutinoso** gloo·tee·*no*·so glutinous rice
— **integral** een·te·*gral* brown rice
— **salvaje** sal·*va*·khe wild rice
— **verde** *ver*·de green rice, made with **chile poblano**

asadero ⓜ a·sa·*de*·ro white cheese used in **quesadillas**

atole ⓜ a·*to*·le thin porridge or gruel of maize flour or cornflour, usually served hot for breakfast
— **de chocolate** de cho·ko·*la*·te chocolate **atole**
— **de fresa** de *fre*·sa strawberry **atole**
— **de nuez** de nwes nut **atole**
— **de vainilla** de vai·*nee*·ya vanilla **atole**

atún ⓜ a·*toon* tuna

avellana ⓕ a·ve·*ya*·na hazelnut

avena ⓕ a·*ve*·na rolled oats – a breakfast staple usually served with milk

azafrán ⓜ a·sa·*fran* saffron

azúcar ⓜ a·*soo*·kar sugar
— **blanca** *blan*·ka white sugar
— **morena** mo·*re*·na brown sugar

B

bacalao ⓜ ba·ka·*la*·o cod – usually dried

balché ⓜ bal·*che* Mayan alcoholic drink made from the fermented bark of the balché tree

banderillas ⓕ pl ban·de·*ree*·yas long flaky pastries

barbacoa ⓕ bar·ba·*ko*·a Mexican-style barbecue – a lamb, goat or chicken is steamed with vegetables, then baked in the ground

bebida ⓕ be·*bee*·da drink
— **alcohólica** al·ko·*lee*·ka alcoholic drink

berenjena ⓕ be·ren·*khe*·na aubergine • eggplant

betabel ⓜ be·ta·*bel* beet • beetroot

birria ⓕ *bee*·rya soupy stew made with meat (usually goat) in a tomato-based broth

blanquillos ⓜ pl blan·*kee*·yos eggs (also **huevos**)

bolillo ⓜ bo·*lee*·yo large, French-style roll, served with most meals

borrego ⓜ bo·*re*·go lamb (see also **cordero**)

botana ⓕ bo·*ta*·na appetiser

botella ⓕ bo·*te*·ya bottle

brocheta ⓕ bro·*che*·ta skewer • kebab

brócoli ⓜ *bro*·ko·lee broccoli

buey ⓜ bway ox

buñuelo ⓜ boo·*nywe*·lo tortilla-sized fritter sprinkled with sugar & cinnamon

C

cabra ⓕ *ka*·bra goat

cabrito ⓜ ka·*bree*·to milk-fed kid rubbed with butter or oil & seasoned with salt, pepper & lime, then roasted whole on a spit

cacahuates ⓜ pl ka·ka·*wa*·tes peanuts
— **japoneses** kha·po·*ne*·ses Japanese-style peanuts, covered with a crunchy coating

cacao ⓜ ka·*ka*·o cocoa

café ⓜ ka-*fe* cafe • coffee
— **con leche** kon *le*-che coffee with milk
— **de olla** de o-ya coffee flavoured with cinnamon & sweetened with **piloncillo**
— **expresso** ek-*spre*-so espresso coffee

cajeta ⓕ ka-*khe*-ta goat's milk caramel

calabacita ⓕ ka-la-ba-*see*-ta zucchini • courgette • vegetable marrow

calabaza ⓕ ka-la-*ba*-sa pumpkin • squash

calamar ⓜ ka-la-*mar* squid

calaveras ⓕ pl ka-la-*ve*-ras confectionery skulls eaten to celebrate the Day of the Dead (2 November)
— **de azúcar** de a-*soo*-kar skulls made from sugar
— **de chocolate** de cho-ko-*la*-te skulls made from chocolate

caldo ⓜ *kal*-do broth
— **tlalpeño** tlal-*pe*-nyo vegetable soup
— **xóchitl** so-*cheetl* fiery hot soup with serrano peppers on top

camarón ⓜ ka-ma-*ron* prawn • shrimp
— **para pelar** pa-ra pe-*lar* whole shrimp boiled in a very weak broth, milled & then served with lime

camote ⓜ ka-*mo*-te sweet potato

canela ⓕ ka-*ne*-la cinnamon

cangrejo ⓜ kan-*gre*-kho crab (also **jaiba**)
— **moro** *mo*-ro stone crab

caña ⓕ **de azúcar** *ka*-nya de a-*soo*-kar sugar cane

capeado ⓜ ka-pe-*a*-do fried, battered meat or vegetables

capirotada ⓕ ka-pee-ro-*ta*-da Mexican-style bread pudding

capulines ⓜ pl ka-poo-*lee*-nes black cherries

cardo ⓜ *kar*-do cardoon (vegetable similar to an artichoke)

carne ⓕ *kar*-ne meat
— **asada** a-*sa*-da thinly cut, broiled tenderloin or steak, usually served with sliced onion & grilled sweet pepper strips, rice, beans & **guacamole**

— **a la Tampiqueña** a la tam-pee-*ke*-nya plate piled with a small piece of meat, **chile poblano**, a **taco** or **enchilada**, beans, **guacamole** & shredded lettuce
— **de cerdo** de *ser*-do pork
— **de res** de res beef
— **de vaca** de *va*-ka beef
— **para asar** pa-ra a-*sar* brisket
— **para taquear** pa-ra ta-ke-*ar* meat for use in **tacos**

carnero ⓜ kar-*ne*-ro mutton

carnitas ⓕ pl kar-*nee*-tas slow-simmered chunks of seasoned pork served on **tortillas** with salsa, chopped onion & fresh coriander

cáscara ⓕ *kas*-ka-ra rind • shell • husk

castaña ⓕ kas-*ta*-nya chestnut

caza ⓕ *ca*-sa game (animals)

cebada ⓕ se-*ba*-da barley

cebolla ⓕ se-*bo*-ya onion
— **blanca** *blan*-ka white onion
— **de Cambray** de kam-*bray* spring onion
— **morada** mo-*ra*-da red onion • Spanish onion

cena ⓕ *se*-na supper • dinner

cerdo ⓜ *ser*-do pig • pork

cereal ⓜ se-re-*al* cereal

cerveza ⓕ ser-*ve*-sa beer
— **amarga** a-*mar*-ga bitter
— **clara** *kla*-ra blonde beer • light beer
— **de barril** de ba-*reel* draught beer
— **oscura** os-*koo*-ra stout

ceviche ⓜ se-*vee*-che cocktail with fish, shrimp, oysters or crab, mixed with onion, coriander & tomato

cidra ⓕ *see*-dra cider

cilantro ⓜ see-*lan*-tro coriander • cilantro

ciruela ⓕ see-*rwe*-la plum
— **pasa** *pa*-sa prune

clayuda ⓕ kla-*yoo*-da large, crisp **tortilla** (also spelled **tlayuda**)

cocada ⓕ ko-*ka*-da traditional candy made with coconut, eggs, milk, almonds & sugar

coco ⓜ *ko*-ko coconut

coctel ⓜ kok-*tel* cocktail
— **de camarón** de ka-ma-*ron* shrimp cocktail

cochinita ① **pibil** ko-chee-*nee*-ta pee-*beel* pork cooked with *achiote*, red onions & orange juice

codorniz ① ko-dor-*nees* quail

col ① kol cabbage

cola ① *ko*-la tail

coles ① pl **de Bruselas** *ko*-les de broo-se-las Brussels sprouts

coliflor ① ko-lee-*flor* cauliflower

comida ① ko-*mee*-da food · lunch (the biggest meal of the day, taken between 1pm – 4pm)

comino ① ko-*mee*-no cumin

conchas ① pl **de vainilla** *kon*-chas de vay-*nee*-ya mini loaves topped with vanilla icing

conchas ① pl **de chocolate** *kon*-chas de cho-ko-*la*-te mini loaves topped with chocolate icing

conejillo ① **de indias** ko-ne-*khee*-yo de *een*-dyas guinea pig

conejo ① ko-*ne*-kho rabbit

consomé kal-do meat broth · stock
  — **de camarón** de ka-ma-*ron* prawn soup
  — **de pollo** de *po*-yo chicken broth · soup with chicken, vegetables & sometimes rice & chickpeas
  — **de res** de res beef & vegetable soup

corazón ① ko-ra-*son* heart

cordero ① kor-*de*-ro lamb · mutton

corundas ① pl ko-*roon*-das little **tamales**

costillas ① pl kos-*tee*-yas ribs

crema ① *kre*-ma cream
  — **ácida** *a*-see-da sour cream
  — **batida** ba-*tee*-da whipping cream
  — **chantilly** chan-*tee*-yee chantilly
  — **espesa** es-*pe*-sa clotted cream

crepas ① pl *kre*-pas crepes

croqueta ① kro-*ke*-ta croquette

Cuba ① **libre** *koo*-ba *lee*-bre rum & cola (also simply called Cuba)

cubierta ① koo-*byer*-ta topping

cubiertos ① pl koo-*byer*-tos cutlery

cuerno ① *kwer*-no croissant

cuitlacoche ① kwee-tla-*ko*-che black corn fungus (also **huitlacoche**)

culebra ① koo-*le*-bra snake

cúrcuma ① *koor*-koo-ma turmeric

CH

chabacano ① cha-ba-*ka*-no apricot

chalote ① cha-*lo*-te shallot onion

chalupas ① pl cha-*loo*-pas small **tortillas** made with cornflour, chilli, beans & cheese

chamorro ① cha-*mo*-ro leg of pork marinated in **adobo** then oven-roasted at a very low heat

champiñones ① pl cham-pee-*nyo*-nes mushrooms

champurrado ① cham-poo-*ra*-do similar to **atole** but made with chocolate, water & cornflour

chapulín ① cha-poo-*leen* grasshopper

charal ① cha-*ral* sardine-like fish

chaya ① *cha*-ya type of spinach

chayote ① cha-*yo*-te popular type of squash that was once the staple of the Aztecs & Maya – usually stuffed & baked or used raw in salad

chícharo ① chee-*cha*-ro pea
  — **seco** *se*-ko green split pea
  — **verde** *ver*-de snap pea

chicharra ① chee-*cha*-ra cricket (insect)

chicharrones ① pl chee-cha-*ro*-nes deep-fried pork rinds, usually sold by street vendors with a topping · flour-based fried snack

chilaquiles ① pl chee-la-*kee*-les crisp **tortillas** topped with chicken, onion, cream, fresh cheese & **salsa** – this popular breakfast choice is sometimes made with scrambled eggs & **chorizo**

chile ① *chee*-le chilli – a huge variety of fresh & dried chillies is available at Mexican markets, sometimes pickled & sold in bottles
  — **ancho** *an*-cho 'broad chilli' – so named for its size & shape, this chilli has wrinkled, reddish-brown skin & is the most common form of dried **chile poblano**
  — **cayena** ka-*ye*-na cayenne
  — **chipotles** chee-*pot*-les smoke-dried version of **chile jalapeño**
  — **dulce en adobo** *dool*-se en a-*do*-bo sweet, non-spicy pickled chilli

— **en nogada** en no·ga·da *a green chile poblano stuffed with a stew of beef & fruits, topped with **nogada** & decorated with pomegranate seeds*

— **guajillo** gwa·khee·yo *very hot, dried chilli, almost black in colour*

— **habanero** a·ba·ne·ro *extremely hot type of chilli*

— **jalapeño** kha·la·pe·nyo *Jalapeno pepper, often eaten in pickled form*

— **mulato** moo·la·to *dried **chile poblano** – its almost-black colour means it can be substituted for **chilhuacle negro** in the dish **mole negro***

— **pasilla** pa·see·ya *dark, dried & very spicy chile used in **mole** and marinades*

— **poblano** po·bla·no *medium-green to purple-black chilli, sometimes dried to produce **chile ancho** & **chile mulato** – this mildly hot, arrow-shaped chilli is also used for making stuffed peppers*

— **relleno** re·ye·no *green **chile poblano** stuffed with cheese, covered in egg batter & fried*

— **serrano** se·ra·no *fiery green chilli used in **moles** & **salsa***

hilhuacle ⓜ **negro** cheel·wa·kle ne·gro *very dark, spicy strain of **chilhuacle**, a chilli about the shape & size of a small bell pepper*

hilpachole ⓜ **de Jaiba** cheel·pa·cho·le de khai·ba *a soup made with crab*

hirimoya ⓕ chee·ree·mo·ya *custard apple • cherimoya*

hocolate ⓜ **oaxaqueño** cho·ko·la·te wa·kha·ke·nyo *chocolate from Oaxaca mixed with hot milk*

hongos ⓜ pl **zamoranos** chon·gos sa·mo·ra·nos *popular dessert of curdled milk, sugar, cinnamon & egg yolks*

horiqueso ⓜ cho·ree·ke·so *chorizo & melted cheese*

horizo ⓜ cho·ree·so *spicy pork sausage, fried with eggs as breakfast, or cooked with potatoes as a filling for **tacos***

huletas ⓕ choo·le·tas *chops*

— **de cerdo** de ser·do *pork chops*

— **de res** de res *small beef steaks*

hurro ⓜ choo·ro *long doughnut covered with sugar*

D

dátiles ⓜ pl da·tee·les *dates*

desayuno ⓜ de·sa·yoo·no *breakfast – Mexicans usually eat eggs or meat for breakfast, including one or more staples such as **tortillas**, beans, chillies & **atole***

diente ⓜ **de ajo** dyen·te de a·kho *clove of garlic*

dona ⓕ do·na *doughnut*

dulce ⓕ dool·se *sweet • candy*

durazno ⓜ doo·ras·no *peach*

E

elote ⓜ e·lo·te *maize • corn*

— **tierno** tyer·no *sweet corn*

empanada ⓕ em·pa·na·da *pastry turnover with a savoury meat & vegetable filling, baked or fried, or filled with fruit & served as a dessert*

encebollado en·se·bo·ya·do *served with onion*

encurtidos ⓜ pl en·koor·tee·dos *table condiment consisting of a bowl of chillies marinated in vinegar, combined with onions, carrots & other vegetables*

enchiladas ⓕ pl en·chee·la·das *meat or cheese wrapped in **tortillas** & smothered in red or green salsa, cream & melted cheese*

— **adobadas** a·do·ba·das *beef or chicken **enchiladas** in adobo sauce*

— **queretanas** ke·re·ta·nas *fresh **enchiladas** topped with shredded lettuce & other raw vegetables*

— **rojas** ro·khas *meat or cheese **enchiladas** with a red **chile ancho** sauce, the most popular **enchiladas** on menus*

— **suizas** swee·sas *mild & creamy Swiss-style **enchiladas** filled with chicken or cheese, served with creamy green tomato sauce*

— **verdes** ver·des *served with a delicate green **tomatillo** sauce*

endivia ① en-*dee*-vya *endive*

enebro ⓜ e-*ne*-bro *juniper*

eneldo ⓜ e-*nel*-do *dill*

enfrijolado/a ⓜ/① en-free-kho-*la*-do/a *describes anything cooked in a bean sauce, most commonly corn* **tortillas** *in a smooth black bean sauce & topped with thinly sliced onions, cream & crumbled cheese*

enmolado/a ⓜ/① en-mo-*la*-do/a *describes anything cooked in a* **mole** *sauce*

ensalada ① en-sa-*la*-da *salad*
— **César** *se*-sar *Caesar salad, named after its inventor César Cardini, an Italian immigrant to Mexico*
— **de verduras** de ver-*doo*-ras *salad of cooked vegetables, a mix of fresh vegetables, or a combination of the two*
— **mixta** *meek*-sta *mix of lettuce, red tomatoes, cucumber, peas, avocado & fresh onion rings*

entrada ① en-*tra*-da *entree*

entremés ⓜ en-tre-*mes* *appetiser*

epazote ⓜ e-pa-*so*-te *wormseed, a pungent herb similar to coriander, used in sauces, beans &* **quesadillas**

escabeche ⓜ es-ka-*be*-che *a brine used as a pickling agent or as a fish marinade*

escamoles ⓜ es-ka-*mo*-les *ant eggs, a delicacy that looks like rice – usually sauteed in butter & wine, served as an accompaniment to meat or with* **tortillas***, avocado & salad*

espárragos ⓜ pl es-*pa*-ra-gos *asparagus*

especias ① pl es-*pe*-syas *spices*

espinaca ① es-pee-*na*-ka *spinach*

esquites ⓜ pl es-*kee*-tes *fresh corn grains boiled with butter,* **epazote** *& onions, served with fresh lime juice, chilli powder & grated cheese*

estofado ⓜ es-to-*fa*-do *stew • a Oaxacan* **mole** *served over chicken or pork, prepared with tomatoes, almonds, bread, raisins, cloves & ground* **chile guajillo**

estragón ⓜ es-tra-*gon* *tarragon*

esturión ⓜ es-too-*ryon* *sturgeon*

F

faisán ⓜ fay-*san* *pheasant*

filete ⓜ fee-*le*-te **a la Mexicana** a la me-khee-*ka*-na *grilled white fish with a tomato-based sauce*

flan ⓜ flan *a caramel egg custard flavoured with vanilla & covered in a syrupy topping*
— **napolitano** na-po-lee-*ta*-no *whiter & thicker than the custard-style flan, sometimes flavoured with liqueur*

flautas ① pl *flow*-tas *tube-shaped* **tacos** *topped with chicken meat, deep-fried & served with cream, cheese & green or red sauce*

flor ① **de calabaza** flor de ka-la-*ba*-sa *large squash flowers used in soups & other dishes*

frambuesa ① fram-*bwe*-sa *raspberry*

fresa ① *fre*-sa *strawberry*

fideos ⓜ fee-*de*-os *noodles*

frijoles ⓜ pl free-*kho*-les *beans, of which nearly 100 varieties are included in the Mexican cuisine*
— **borrachos** bo-*ra*-chos *'drunken beans', made as* **frijoles charros** *but flavoured with flat beer*
— **charros** *cha*-ros *'cowboy beans' – pork rind, fried tomatoes, onion & coriander, served as a soup*
— **molidos** mo-*lee*-dos *ground beans*
— **negros** *ne*-gros *'black beans' – served mashed & refried, pureed as a soup or whole, usually seasoned with* **epazote**
— **refritos** re-*free*-tos *mashed beans fried in lard or vegetable oil*

frutas ① pl *froo*-tas *fruits*
— **cristalizadas** krees-ta-lee-*sa*-das *different fruits cooked with sugar & water until crunchy*
— **secas** *se*-kas *dried fruit*

G

galleta ① ga-*ye*-ta *biscuit • cookie • cracker*

gallina ① ga-*yee*-na *hen*

ganso ⓜ *gan*-so *goose*

garbanzo ⓜ gar-*ban*-so *chickpea*

gelatina ① khe-la-*tee*-na *gelatin*

germen ⓜ **de trigo** *kher*-men de *tree*-go *wheat germ*

germinado ⓜ **de soya** kher-mee-*na*-do de *so*-ya *bean sprout*

ginebra ① khee-*ne*-bra *gin*

gorditas ① pl gor-*dee*-tas *thick corn tortillas fried then filled with beef, chicken or pork, then topped with cheese & lettuce*

granada ① gra-*na*-da *grenadine • pomegranate*

grasa ① *gra*-sa *dietary fat*

grosella ① gro-*se*-ya *currant*

guacamole ⓜ gwa-ka-*mo*-le *mashed avocado mixed with lemon or lime juice, onion & chilli*

guaraches ⓜ pl gwa-*ra*-ches *tortilla shells piled high with chorizo, meat, potato, coriander & chilli salsa*

guarnición ① gwar-nee-*syon* *garnish*

guisado ⓜ gee-*sa*-do *stew*

guiso ⓜ *gee*-so *stew*

gusano ⓜ goo-*sa*-no *worm*

gusanos ⓜ pl **de maguey** goo-*sa*-nos de ma-*gay* *worms that live in maguey – they're usually placed in the bottom of the bottle as a sign that you've bought true* **mezcal**

— **con salsa borracha** kon *sal*-sa bo-*ra*-cha *a dish of* **maguey** *worms fried in oil & accompanied by a sauce of roasted* **chile pasilla**, *garlic, onion, cheese &* **pulque**

H

haba ① *a*-ba *broad bean*

habanero ⓜ a-ba-*ne*-ro *extremely spicy type of chilli*

hamburguesa ① am-boor-*ge*-sa *hamburger*

helado ⓜ e-*la*-do *ice cream*

hielo ⓜ *ye*-lo *ice*

hígado ⓜ *ee*-ga-do *liver*

— **encebollado** en-se-bo-*ya*-do *liver with onions*

higo ⓜ *ee*-go *fig*

hinojo ⓜ ee-*no*-kho *fennel*

hojas ① pl *o*-khas *leaves (banana, avocado, corn or* **maguey***) used in cooking for subtle flavouring, to wrap food for steaming & to line or cover earthenware pots*

— **de laurel** de *low*-rel *bay leaves*

— **de plátano** de *pla*-ta-no *banana leaves*

— **santas** *san*-tas *large anise-flavoured leaves*

huachinango ⓜ wa-chee-*nan*-go *red snapper*

— **a la Veracruzana** a la ve-ra-kroo-*sa*-na *specialty of the port city of Veracruz where fresh red snapper is broiled in a lightly spiced sauce of tomato, onion & green olives*

huarache ⓜ wa-*ra*-che *flat & oval tortilla with beans and/or meat, topped with cream, cheese & a variety of sauces – a common street food*

huatape ⓜ **tamaulipeco** wa-*ta*-pe ta-mow-lee-*pe*-ko *green prawn soup thickened with corn dough*

huauzontle ⓜ wow-*son*-tle *green vegetable whose buds are dipped in flour & fried*

huevos ⓜ pl *hwe*-vos *eggs*

— **entomatados** en-to-ma-*ta*-dos *eggs in a tomato sauce*

— **estrellados** es-tre-*ya*-dos *fried eggs*

— **fritos** *free*-tos *fried eggs*

— **revueltos** re-*vwel*-tos *scrambled eggs*

— **rancheros** ran-*che*-ros *eggs on tortillas, topped with chilli sauce*

— **tibios** *tee*-byos *soft-boiled eggs*

huitlacoche ⓜ weet-la-*ko*-che *black fungus that grows on young corn during the rainy season, used in crepes,* **quesadillas** *& soups*

I

iguana ① ee-*gwa*-na *iguana – some species are protected and should not be eaten*

J

jabalí m kha-ba-*lee* boar
jabón m kha-*bon* soap
jaiba f *khay*-ba crab
— **de río** de *ree*-o crayfish
jalapeño m kha-la-*pe*-nyo hot green chilli from Jalapa
jamón m kha-*mon* ham
jengibre m khen-*khee*-bre ginger
jerez m khe-*res* sherry
jícama f *khee*-ka-ma crunchy, sweet turnip • potato-like tuber often sold by street vendors, sliced & garnished with red chilli powder, salt & fresh lime juice
jitomates m pl khee-to-*ma*-tes red tomatoes, specifically plum or roma
— **cereza** se-*re*-sa cherry tomatoes
— **deshidratados** des-ee-dra-*ta*-dos sun-dried tomatoes
jugo m *khoo*-go juice
— **de fruta** de *froo*-ta fruit juice
— **fresco** *fres*-ko freshly squeezed juice

L

langosta f lan-*gos*-ta lobster
laurel m low-*rel* bay leaf
lavanda f la-*van*-da lavender
leche f *le*-che milk
— **descremada** des-kre-*ma*-da skimmed milk
— **entera** en-*te*-ra full cream milk
lengua f *len*-gwa tongue
lenguado m len-*gwa*-do sole (fish)
lentejas f pl len-*te*-khas brown lentils
— **rojas** *ro*-khas red lentils
— **verdes** *ver*-des green lentils
levadura f le-va-*doo*-ra yeast
licor m lee-*kor* liqueur
licores m pl lee-*ko*-res spirits
lichi m *lee*-chee lychee
liebre f *lye*-bre hare
lima f *lee*-ma lime
limón m lee-*mon* lemon
— **agrio** a-*gryo* bitter lemon
— **sin semilla** seen se-*mee*-ya seedless lemon
limonada f lee-mo-*na*-da lemonade

M

lomo m *lo*-mo loin • rump • shoulder
longaniza f lon-ga-*nee*-sa dried speciality pork sausage
lonche m *lon*-che sandwich made with a long bun – in Guadalajara most of the bread is scooped out of the middle to make way for a filling of meat, cheese, avocado & mayonnaise or cream
lucio m *loo*-syo pike (fish)

M

macadamia f ma-ka-*da*-mya macadamia
machaca f ma-*cha*-ka meat grinder • sheets of dried beef or beef jerky
machacado m ma-cha-*ka*-do dried meat
maguey m ma-*gay* any of the various American agave plants, used to make alcoholic beverages such as **pulque** and **tequila**
maíz m ma-*ees* corn • maize
— **molido** mo-*lee*-do de-husked dried maize kernels with the germ removed, usually softened in boiling water
malta f *mal*-ta malt
malteada f mal-te-*a*-da milkshake
mamey m ma-*may* rough brown fruit with bitter yellow inner skin & orangey flesh, often used to make smoothies, gelatin, ice cream & mousses
mantequilla f man-te-*kee*-ya butter
manzana f man-*sa*-na apple
maracuyá m ma-ra-koo-*ya* passion fruit
margarina f mar-ga-*ree*-na margarine
Margarita f mar-ga-*ree*-ta cocktail made with **tequila**, lime juice, Cointreau & crushed ice, served in a chilled glass with salt on the rim
mariscos m pl ma-*rees*-kos seafood • shellfish
masa f *ma*-sa ground, cooked corn mixed with slaked lime and made into a dough or batter used for making **tortillas**
— **de harina de maíz** de a-*ree*-na de ma-*ees* cornflour
— **de harina de trigo** de a-*ree*-na de *tree*-go wheat flour
maseca f ma-*se*-ka type of cornflour used in **tortillas** & **tamales**

mayonesa ⓕ ma-yo-*ne*-sa *mayonnaise*

mazapán ⓜ ma-sa-*pan* marzipan

medio *me*-dyo *half • medium cooked*

médula ⓕ *me*-doo-la *bone marrow, also called* **tuétano**

mejillón ⓜ me-khee-*yon* *mussel*

mejorana ⓕ me-kho-*ra*-na *marjoram*

melón ⓜ me-*lon* *melon • cantaloupe*

membrillo ⓜ mem-*bree*-yo *quince*

menta ⓕ *men*-ta *peppermint • mint*

menudo ⓜ me-*noo*-do *tripe stew – a popular hangover remedy with an acquired taste*

merienda ⓕ me-*ryen*-da *the equivalent of English afternoon tea*

merluza ⓕ mer-*loo*-sa *hake*

mermelada ⓕ mer-me-*la*-da *fruit jam • jelly • marmalade*

mezcal ⓜ mes-*kal* *distilled liquor made from agave – a worm is usually placed in the bottle*

miel ⓕ myel *honey*

migajas ⓕ pl mee-*ga*-khas *crumbs*

mijo ⓜ *mee*-kho *millet*

milanesa ⓕ mee-la-*ne*-sa *pork, beef or chicken schnitzel – inferior cuts of beef are pounded to a thin slab, then fried in an egg & bread batter, served with mayonnaise & fresh limes & accompanied by rice, beans & salad*

mixiotes ⓜ pl mee-*shyo*-tes *lamb, chicken or rabbit meat wrapped in a thin layer of* **maguey** *leaves & steamed in a rich broth, then served with a mild green sauce, sliced avocado &* **tortillas**

modongo ⓜ **jarocho** mon-*don*-go kha-*ro*-cho *rich, stew-like dish with ham, tripe, pork, chickpeas, coriander &* **tortillas**

mojarra ⓕ **a la veracruzana** mo-*kha*-ra a la ve-ra-kroo-*sa*-na *spicy baked perch in a tomato, onion & green olive salsa*

mole ⓜ *mo*-le *the quintessential Mexican sauce, made using a variety of chillies, herbs, spices & chocolate*

— **almendrado** al-men-*dra*-do *a mole made mainly with almonds*

— **coloradito** ko-lo-ra-*dee*-to *a Oaxacan* **mole** *made with chillies, sesame seeds, almonds, raisins, bananas & spices, ladled over chicken*

— **de olla** de *o*-ya *type of* **mole** *prepared with pork, lamb or smoked meat, cactus fruit &* **epazote**

— **de xico** de *khee*-ko *a slightly sweet* **mole**

— **naolinco** na-o-*leen*-ko *a spicy* **mole**

— **negro** *ne*-gro *a dark* **mole**

— **poblano** po-*bla*-no *type of* **mole** *made from deseeded & pureed chillies, onion, coriander, anise, cinnamon, garlic, toasted peanuts, almonds & sweetened chocolate*

mollejas ⓕ pl mo-*ye*-khas *giblets*

molletes ⓜ pl mo-*ye*-tes *savoury, filled bread roll spread with refried beans & melted cheese & topped with fresh* **salsa**

mondongo ⓜ mon-*don*-go *a kind of stew with several regional variations*

mora ⓕ *mo*-ra *mulberry*

moronga ⓕ mo-*ron*-ga *black pudding*

mostaza ⓕ mos-*ta*-sa *mustard*

N

nabo ⓜ *na*-bo *turnip*

naranja ⓕ na-*ran*-kha *orange*

— **agria** *a*-grya *bitter orange used in marinades & sauces*

— **china** ⓕ *chee*-na *kumquat*

nieves ⓕ pl *nye*-ves *sherbets made with fruits or other ingredients such as* **tequila,** *avocado, shrimp, roseships or sweet corn*

nixtamal ⓜ neek-sta-*mal* *mixture of corn & lime used in tortilla dough (see* **masa**)

nogada ⓕ no-*ga*-da *walnut or walnut sauce*

nogal no-*gal* *walnut tree*

nopal ⓜ no-*pal* *prickly pear cactus – the cactus pads (leaves) are cut into strips & boiled as a vegetable or added to scrambled eggs*

nudillo ⓜ noo-*dee*-yo *knuckle*

nueva cocina ⓕ **mexicana** *nwe-va ko-see-na me-khee-ka-na* 'new Mexican cuisine' – a movement among some chefs to combine traditional ingredients with contemporary preparations & presentations

nuez ⓕ *nwes* nut
— **de Castilla** *de kas-tee-ya* walnut
— **del Brasil** *del bra-seel* brazil nut
— **de la India** *de la een-dya* cashew
— **moscada** *mos-ka-da* nutmeg
— **pacana** *pa-ka-na* pecan

O

obleas ⓕ pl *o-ble-as* coloured wafers filled with raw brown sugar syrup & decorated with toasted pumpkin seeds

octli ⓜ *ok-tlee* alcoholic drink made from a combination of juices from different agave plants

olivo ⓜ *o-lee-vo* olive tree

oporto ⓜ *o-por-to* port

ostra ⓕ *os-tra* oyster

oveja ⓕ *o-ve-kha* sheep

P

palanquetas ⓕ pl *pa-lan-ke-tas* traditional candy made with peanuts or pumpkin seeds conformed in rectangular or round shapes using caramelised sugar

paleta ⓕ *pa-le-ta* lollipop • Popsicle • icy pole
— **de agua** *de a-gwa* icy pole made with water & fruit juice
— **de leche** *de le-che* icy pole made with milk & fruits or other ingredient such as vanilla, chocolate or nuts

palomitas ⓕ pl **de maíz** *pa-lo-mee-tas de ma-ees* pop corn

pan ⓜ *pan* bread
— **árabe** *a-ra-be* pita bread
— **de muerto** *de mwer-to* heavy bread used as an offering on the Day of the Dead (2 November)
— **de yema** *de ye-ma* yellow, rich & heavy bread made with egg yolks
— **dulce** *dool-se* sweet bread

— **duro** *doo-ro* stale bread
— **tostado** *tos-ta-do* toasted bread

panuchos ⓜ pl *pa-noo-chos* finger food taken as an appetiser, these are bean-stuffed **tortillas**, fried crisp then topped with a tower of shredded turkey or chicken, tomato, lettuce & onions

papas ⓕ pl *pa-pas* potatoes
— **a la francesa** *a la fran-se-sa* chips • French fries

papadzules ⓜ pl *pa-pad-soo-les* fresh corn **tortillas** wrapped around a filling of chopped hard-boiled eggs then covered with sauce made from pumpkin seed & **epazote**

papitas ⓕ pl **del monte** *pa-pee-tas del mon-te* wild potatoes

paprika ⓕ *pap-ree-ka* paprika

parillada ⓕ *pa-ree-ya-da* flame-grilled meat platter

pasa ⓕ **(de uva)** *pa-sa (de oo-va)* raisin

pastel ⓜ *pas-tel* pastry • cake
— **de tres leches** *de tres le-ches* cake made with evaporated milk, condensed milk & evaporated cream

pastelería ⓕ *pas-te-le-ree-a* cake shop

pastelito ⓜ *pas-te-lee-to* pastry

patas ⓕ pl *pa-tas* hooves

pato ⓜ *pa-to* duck

pavo ⓜ *pa-vo* turkey

pechuga ⓕ *pe-choo-ga* breast
— **de pollo** *de po-yo* chicken breast

pepinillo ⓜ *pe-pee-nee-yo* gherkin

pepino ⓜ *pe-pee-no* cucumber

pepitoria ⓕ *pe-pee-to-rya* traditional candy made with coloured **obleas**

pera ⓕ *pe-ra* pear

perejil ⓜ *pe-re-kheel* parsley

pescadería ⓕ *pes-ka-de-ree-a* fishmonger

pescado ⓜ *pes-ka-do* fish

pibil ⓜ *pee-beel* sauce made with **achiote**, bitter orange juice, garlic, salt & pepper, used as a marinade for chicken or pork

picadillo ⓜ *pee-ka-dee-yo* mincemeat cooked with tomatoes, almonds, raisins & vegetables

pierna ⓕ *pyer-na* leg

piloncillo ⓜ *pee-lon-see-yo* raw brown sugar

pimentón ⓜ pee·men·ton *cayenne • red pepper • paprika*

pimienta ⓕ pee·myen·ta *black pepper*
— **de cayena** de ka·ye·na *cayenne pepper*
— **entera** en·te·ra *ground pepper*
— **inglesa** een·gle·sa *allspice*
— **negra** ne·gra *black pepper*
— **recién molida** re·syen mo·lee·da *freshly ground black pepper*
— **verde** ver·de *green pepper*

pinole ⓜ pee·no·le *flour made with a mixture of toasted corn & amaranth seeds*

piña ⓕ pee·nya *pineapple*

piñatas ⓕ pl pee·nya·tas *balloons or animal-shaped dolls made with clay or papier mache, filled with sweets, fruits, peanuts & toys*

piñón ⓜ pee·nyon *pine nut*

pipián verde ⓜ pee·pyan ver·de *a type of mole made with ground spices & pumpkin or squash seeds, green tomatoes, peanuts – served over pork or chicken*

pistaches ⓜ pl pees·ta·ches *pistachios*

plátano ⓜ pla·ta·no *banana • plantain*
— **dominico** do·mee·nee·ko *small & very sweet banana*
— **macho** ma·cho *large banana, fried & served with sour cream & sugar*

poc chuc ⓜ pok chook *thin slice of pork, cooked on a grill & served on a sizzling plate with a bitter orange sauce & chopped onions*

pollo ⓜ po·yo *chicken*
— **a la pibil** a la pee·beel *chicken marinated in pibil sauce*
— **frito** free·to *fried chicken*
— **rostisado** ros·tee·sa·do *roast chicken*

ponche ⓜ pon·che de froo·tas *fruit punch prepared during Christmas festivities made with guava, tejocotes, sugar cane, cinnamon, raisins, cloves & raw sugar*
— **con piquete** kon pee·ke·te *fruit punch with a shot of tequila or rum*

postre ⓜ pos·tre *dessert*

pozole ⓜ po·so·le *thick soup made of corn, chicken or pork, lettuce & slices of radish, traditionally eaten at Christmas*
— **blanco** blan·ko *corn soup prepared with stock but without chillies*
— **rojo** ro·kho *corn soup made with chilli*
— **verde** ver·de *corn soup made with green chillies & toasted pumpkin seeds*

puchero ⓜ poo·che·ro *stew made of chicken & vegetables*

puerro ⓜ pwe·ro *leek*

pulpo ⓜ pool·po *octopus*
— **en su tinta** en soo teen·ta *octopus in its own ink*

pulque ⓜ pool·ke *white, thick, sweet alcoholic drink made from the fermented sap of agave plants, especially the maguey*

Q

queretanas ⓕ pl ke·re·ta·nas *Queretaro-style enchiladas topped with shredded lettuce & other raw vegetables*

quesadillas ⓕ pl ke·sa·dee·yas *flour or corn tortillas with a savoury cheese filling • corn dough filled with different toppings such as mushrooms, mashed potatoes, huitlacoche & rajas*

quesillo ⓜ ke·see·yo *stringy goat's milk cheese from Oaxaca*

queso ⓜ ke·so *cheese*
— **añejo** a·nye·kho *hard, aged cheese with a sharp flavour similar to Parmesan*
— **Chihuahua** chee·wa·wa *creamy yellow cheese often used in quesadillas*
— **crema** kre·ma *cream cheese*
— **fresco** fres·ko *cheese made from cow's milk*
— **fundido** foon·dee·do *cheese fondue*
— **manchego** man·che·go *although this cheese is originally from La Mancha in Spain, it's a popular cheese in Mexico & used in many recipes*
— **Oaxaca** wa·kha·ka *Oaxacan cheese, made from goat's milk (see quesillo)*
— **parmesano** par·me·sa·no *Parmesan cheese*

R

rábano ⓜ *ra·ba·no* radish
— **picante** pee·kan·te horseradish

rabo ⓜ *ra·bo* tail

rajas ⓕ pl *ra·khas* slices of chilli
— **con crema** kon *kre·ma* a dish made with chile poblano & sour cream
— **en escabeche** en es·ka·be·che pickled chillies

rana ⓕ *ra·na* frog

ranchera ⓕ *ran·che·ra* sauce made with chillies, tomatoes, onions, coriander – used for eggs or **enchiladas**

raspados ⓜ pl *ras·pa·dos* 'scrapings' – flavoured ice with fruit juice, sold by pushcart vendors as a refreshing treat

rebanada ⓕ *re·ba·na·da* a slice

regaliz ⓜ *re·ga·lees* liquorice

refresco ⓜ *re·fres·ko* soft drink

relleno ⓜ *re·ye·no* stuffing
— **negro** *ne·gro* green pepper, **chiles anchos** & **achiote**, served over shredded turkey & a hard-boiled egg

relleno/a ⓜ/ⓕ *re·ye·no/a* stuffed

reposado ⓜ *re·po·sa·do* an alcoholic drink such as **tequila** that has been aged two to 12 months

requesón ⓜ *re·ke·son* cottage cheese

res ⓕ res beef

riñón ⓜ *ree·nyon* kidney

robalo ⓜ *ro·ba·lo* sea bass

romero ⓜ *ro·me·ro* rosemary

ron ⓜ ron rum

rosca ⓕ **de reyes** *ros·ka* de *re·yes* eaten on Epiphany (6 January), this large, wreath-shaped pastry has a small china doll representing Christ, baked into it – whoever gets the piece with the doll in it throws a party on Candlemas Day (2 February)

S

sal ⓕ sal salt

salbutes ⓜ pl *sal·boo·tes* fried crisp **tortillas** topped with a tower of shredded turkey or chicken, tomato, lettuce & onions

salchicha ⓕ *sal·chee·cha* frankfurter
— **de coctel** de kok·tel small cocktail sausage
— **de Viena** de *vye·na* sausages used for hot dogs

salsa ⓕ *sal·sa* a spicy, tomato-based sauce
— **a la veracruzana** a la ve·ra·kroo·sa·na sauce of tomato, onion & green olives
— **bandera** ban·de·ra 'flag sauce' – named for the red of the tomato, the white of the onion & the green of the chilli
— **borracha** bo·ra·cha 'drunken sauce' – made from roasted **chile pasilla**, garlic, onion, cheese & **pulque**
— **de tomatillos** sauce with green chillies, onion & coriander
— **picante** pee·kan·te hot sauce
— **roja** *ro·*kha red sauce made with plum tomatoes, onions, garlic & salt
— **tártara** tar·ta·ra tartare sauce
— **verde** ver·de green sauce made with **tomatillos**, green chillies, onion & coriander

sandía ⓕ san·dee·a watermelon – a symbol of Mexico (the red, white & green correspond to the colours of the Mexican flag)

sangría ⓕ san·gree·a refreshing cold drink of Spanish origin made with red wine, lemonade & sliced fresh fruit

sangrita ⓕ san·gree·ta bright red, thickish mixture of crushed tomatoes (or tomato juice), orange juice, grenadine, chilli & salt – served chilled with a shot of **tequila**

sardina ⓕ sar·dee·na sardine

semilla ⓕ se·mee·ya seed
— **de ajonjolí** de a·khon·kho·lee sesame seed
— **de amapola** de a·ma·po·la poppy seed
— **de apio** de *a·*pyo celery seed
— **de hinojo** de ee·no·kho fennel seed

semita ⓕ se·mee·ta round & flat sweet bread

semillas ⓕ pl **de alcaravea** se·mee·yas de al·ka·ra·ve·a caraway seeds

sémola ⓕ se·mo·la semolina

sesos ⓜ pl se·sos brains

sidra ⓕ see·dra cider

sopa ① so·pa *soup • chowder*

— **de coco** de *ko·ko coconut soup*

— **de lima** de *lee·ma lime soup*

— **de nopales** de *no·pa·les soup with cactus leaves*

— **de tortilla** de *tor·tee·ya chicken broth-based soup featuring strips of leftover corn* **tortillas**

— **seca** *se·ka 'dry soup' – a rice, pasta or tortilla-based dish*

sope ① so·pe *thick cornflour* **tortilla** *stuffed with refried beans, served with chicken or other meat with lettuce & cream on the top*

T

tablillas ① pl **de chocolate** ta·*blee·*yas de cho·ko·*la·*te *blocks of chocolate*

tacos ⑩ pl *ta·kos folded corn* **tortillas** *filled with meat, beans & other ingredients*

— **al pastor** al pas·*tor tacos with meat cut from a roasting spit, served with fresh pineapple, onions, coriander & salsa*

— **árabe** *a·ra·be tacos made with slightly thicker wheat bread (pita bread)*

— **de carne asada** de *kar·*ne a·*sa·*da *tacos with minced beef*

— **de carnitas** de kar·*nee·*tas *tacos with finely chopped pork*

— **de pollo** de *po·*yo *chicken tacos*

— **dorados** do·*ra·*dos *deep fried tacos*

tallo ⑩ *ta·*yo *shank*

tamales ⑩ pl ta·*ma·*les *corn dough stuffed with meat,* **mole**, *green or red salsa, fruit or nothing at all, usually wrapped in banana leaves, sometimes in corn husks & then steamed*

tamarindo ⑩ ta·ma·*reen·*do *tamarind, a fruit used for making* **aguas**, **nieves** & *desserts*

taquería ① ta·ke·*ree·*a *place that specialises in serving* **tacos**

taquito ⑩ ta·*kee·*to *a small* **tortilla** *wrapped around meat or chicken*

té ⑩ *te tea*

— **de hierbabuena** de yer·ba·*bwe·*na *peppermint tea*

— **de limón** de lee·*mon lemongrass tea*

— **de manzanilla** de man·sa·*nee·*ya *chamomile tea*

— **de menta** de *men·*ta *mint tea*

— **descafeinado** des·ka·fay·*na·*do *decaffeinated tea*

— **negro** *ne·*gro *black tea*

tejate ⑩ te·*kha·*te *Oaxacan recipe for chocolate that includes* **mamey** *seeds, cacao flowers & corn dough*

tejocote ⑩ te·kho·*ko·*te *hawthorn*

telera ① te·*le·*ra *French-style roll used to make* **tortas**

tepache ⑩ te·*pa·*che *alcoholic drink made from fermented pineapple*

tequila ① te·*kee·*la *classic Mexican spirit distilled from the* **maguey** *plant, also known as the blue agave plant*

ternera ① ter·*ne·*ra *veal*

tescalate ⑩ tes·ka·*la·*te *type of chocolate popular in Chiapas, made by grinding the cacao beans with toasted corn &* **achiote**

tlayuda ① tla·*yoo·*da *large, crisp* **tortilla** *topped with Oaxacan cheese, tomatoes & beans, also called* **clayuda**

tocino ⑩ to·*see·*no *bacon*

— **de lomo** de *lo·*mo *bacon (off the back)*

tomate verde to·*ma·*te *ver·*de *see* **tomatillo**

tomatillo ⑩ to·ma·*tee·*yo *small green native tomato wrapped in a brownish papery husk – used for salsas (also known as* **tomate verde***)*

tomillo ⑩ to·*mee·*yo *thyme*

tonronja ⑩ to·*ron·*kha *grapefruit*

to'owloche ⑩ tow·*lo·*che *'wrapped in corn leaves' – Mayan* **tamal** *made by home chefs & served to people in the street on festival days*

toro ⑩ *to·*ro *bull*

torta ① *tor·*ta *sandwich made with crusty bread*

tortillas ① tor·*tee·*yas *ubiquitous round flatbread made with corn or wheat flour, a staple in the Mexican diet for thousands of years – used in making* **tacos**, **chalupas**, **huaraches**, **sopes** & **tostadas**

— **de maíz** de ma·*ees corn* **tortillas**

— **de trigo** de *tree·*go *wheat* **tortillas**

— **yucatecas** yoo·ka·*te·*kas *see* **papadzules**

tortillería ① tor·tee·ye·*ree*·a *bakery in which Mexicans buy their* **tortillas** *by the kilo (if they don't make it themselves at home)*
tostadas ① pl tos·*ta*·das *fried corn tortillas*
totopos ⑩ pl to·*to*·pos *deep-fried wedges of stale corn* **tortillas**
trigo ⑩ *tree*·go *wheat*
— **integral** een·te·*gral* *whole-grain wheat*
— **sarraceno** ⑩ sa·ra·se·no *buckwheat*
tripa ① *tree*·pa *tripe*
trucha ① *troo*·cha *trout*
tuna ① *too*·na *prickly pear • cactus fruit*
tuétano ⑩ *twe*·ta·no *marrow*
turrón ⑩ too·*ron* *nougat*

U

uchepos ⑩ pl oo·*che*·pos *corn dough, wrapped in corn husks, steamed & served with fresh cream*
uvas ① pl *oo*·vas *grapes*

V

vainilla ① vay·*nee*·ya *vanilla*
vajilla ① va·*khee*·ya *crockery • china*
venado ⑩ ve·*na*·do *venison • deer*
verdulería ① ver·doo·le·*ree*·a *greengrocer*
verduras ① pl ver·*doo*·ras *mixed greens*
vinagre ⑩ vee·*na*·gre *vinegar*
— **balsámico** bal·*sa*·mee·ko *balsamic vinegar*

vino ⑩ *vee*·no *wine*
— **afrutado** a·froo·*ta*·do *fruity wine*
— **blanco** *blan*·ko *white wine*
— **de la casa** de la *ka*·sa *house wine*
— **dulce** *dool*·se *sweet wine*
— **espumoso** es·poo·*mo*·so *sparkling wine*
— **ligeramente dulce** lee·khe·ra·*men*·te *dool*·se *lightly sweet wine*
— **muy seco** mooy *se*·ko *very dry wine*
— **nacional** na·syo·*nal* *domestic wine*
— **seco** *se*·ko *dry wine*
— **semi-seco** *se*·mee *se*·ko *semi-dry wine*
— **tinto** *teen*·to *red wine*
vuelve a la vida ⑩ *vwel*·ve a la *vee*·da *'go back to life' – seafood cocktail in a tomato salsa*

W

whiskey ⑩ *wees*·kee *whiskey*
— **canadiense** ka·na·*dyen*·se *rye whiskey*
— **de centeno** de sen·*te*·no *bourbon whiskey*

X

xcatik ⑩ shka·*teek* *kind of chilli found in Yucatán state*
xtabentún ⑩ shta·ben·*toon* *Mayan liqueur made from native xtabentún flowers*

Z

zanahoria ① sa·na·o·*rya* *carrot*

emergencies

emergencias

Help!	¡Socorro!	so·ko·ro
Stop!	¡Pare!	pa·re
Go away!	¡Váyase!	va·ya·se
Thief!	¡Ladrón!	la·dron
Fire!	¡Fuego!	fwe·go
Watch out!	¡Cuidado!	kwee·da·do

Call the police!
¡Llame a la policía!   ya·me a la po·lee·see·a

Call a doctor!
¡Llame a un médico!   ya·me a oon me·dee·ko

Call an ambulance!
¡Llame a una ambulancia!   ya·me a oo·na am·boo·lan·sya

It's an emergency.
Es una emergencia.   es oo·na e·mer·khen·sya

Could you help me, please?
¿Me puede ayudar, por favor?   me pwe·de a·yoo·dar por fa·vor

I have to use the telephone.
Necesito usar el teléfono.   ne·se·see·to oo·sar el te·le·fo·no

We've had a (traffic) accident.
Tuvimos un accidente   too·vee·mos oon ak·see·den·te
(de tráfico).   (de tra·fee·ko)

I'm lost.
Estoy perdido/a. m/f   es·toy per·dee·do/a

Where are the toilets?
¿Dónde están los baños?   don·de es·tan los ba·nyos

Is it safe ...?	¿Es seguro ...?	es se·*goo*·ro ...
at night	*de noche*	de *no*·che
for foreigners	*para los*	*pa*·ra los
	extranjeros	ek·stran·*khe*·ros
for gay	*para viajeros*	*pa*·ra vya·*khe*·ros
travellers	*gay*	gay
for women	*para viajeras*	*pa*·ra vya·*khe*·ras
travellers		
to go alone	*para ir solo/a* m/f	*pa*·ra eer *so*·lo/a
to hitch	*pedir aventón*	pe·*deer* a·ven·*ton*

police

Where's the police station?
¿Dónde está la estación   *don*·de es·*ta* la es·ta·*syon*
de policía?   de po·lee·*see*·a

I want to report an offence.
Quiero denunciar un   *kye*·ro de·noon·*syar* oon
delito.   de·*lee*·to

I've lost (my wallet).
Perdí (mi cartera).   per·*dee* (mee kar·*te*·ra)

My ... was	Mi ... fue	mee ... fwe
stolen.	*robado/a.* m/f	ro·*ba*·do/a
backpack	*mochila* f	mo·*chee*·la
money	*dinero* m	dee·*ne*·ro

My ... were	Mis ... fueron	mees ... *fwe*·ron
stolen.	*robados/as.* m/f pl	ro·*ba*·dos/as
bags	*maletas* f pl	ma·*le*·tas
tickets	*boletos* m pl	bo·*le*·tos

He/She tried to ...	Él/Élla intentó ... m/f	el/e·ya een·ten·*to* ...
assault	*asaltarme*	a·sal·*tar*·me
rape	*violarme*	vyo·*lar*·me
rob	*robarme*	ro·*bar*·me

I've been robbed.
Me han robado. me an ro·*ba*·do

He's/She's been assaulted.
Lo/La asaltaron. m/f lo/la a·sal·*ta*·ron

I've been raped.
Me violaron. m&f me vyo·*la*·ron

He's/She's been raped.
Lo/La violaron. m/f lo/la vyo·*la*·ron

I want to contact my consulate/embassy.
Quiero ponerme en *kye*·ro po·*ner*·me en
contacto con mi kon·*tak*·to kon mee
consulado/embajada. kon·soo·*la*·do/em·ba·*kha*·da

Can I call someone ?
¿Puedo llamar a alguien? *pwe*·do ya·*mar* a *al*·gyen

Can I call a lawyer?
¿Puedo llamar a un *pwe*·do ya·*mar* a oon
abogado? a·bo·*ga*·do

Can I have a lawyer who speaks English?
Quisiera un abogado que kee·*sye*·ra oon a·bo·*ga*·do ke
hable inglés. *a*·ble een·*gles*

Can we pay an on-the-spot fine?
¿Podemos pagar una po·*de*·mos pa·*gar* oo·na
multa de contado? *mool*·ta de kon·*ta*·do

This drug is for personal use.
Esta droga es para uso *es*·ta *dro*·ga es *pa*·ra oo·so
personal. per·so·*nal*

I have a prescription for this drug.
Tengo receta para esta *ten*·go re·*se*·ta *pa*·ra *es*·ta
medicina. me·dee·*see*·na

I (don't) understand.
(No) Entiendo. (no) en·*tyen*·do

What am I accused of?
¿De qué me acusan? de ke me a·*koo*·san

I'm sorry.
Lo siento. lo *syen*·to

I didn't realise I was doing anything wrong.

| No sabía que estaba | no sa·bee·a ke es·ta·ba |
| haciendo algo mal. | a·syen·do al·go mal |

I didn't do it.

| No lo hice. | no lo ee·se |

I'm innocent.

| Soy inocente. | soy ee·no·sen·te |

the police may say …

You'll be charged with …	Será acusado/a de … m/f	se·ra a·koo·sa·do/a de …
He'll/She'll be charged with …	Él/Ella será acusado/a de … m/f	el/e·ya se·ra a·koo·sa·do/a de …
anti-government activity	actividades contra el gobierno	ak·tee·vee·da·des kon·tra el go·byer·no
assault	agresión	a·gre·syon
disturbing the peace	alterar el orden público	al·te·rar el or·den poo·blee·ko
indecent behaviour	faltas a la moral	fal·tas a la mo·ral
overstaying your visa	quedarse más tiempo de lo que permite la visa	ke·dar·se mas tyem·po de lo ke per·mee·te la vee·sa
possession (of illegal substances)	posesión (de sustancias ilegales)	po·se·syon (de soos·tan·syas ee·le·ga·les)
shoplifting	robo	ro·bo
speeding	exceso de velocidad	ek·se·so de ve·lo·see·dad
theft	robo	ro·bo

doctor

el médico

Where's the nearest ...?	¿Dónde está ... más cercano/a? m/f	don·de es·ta ... mas ser·ka·no/a
(night) chemist	la farmacia f (de guardia)	la far·ma·sya (de gwar·dya)
dentist	el dentista m	el den·tees·ta
doctor	el médico m	el me·dee·ko
hospital	el hospital m	el os·pee·tal
medical centre	la clínica f	la klee·nee·ka
optometrist	el optometrista m	el op·to·me·trees·ta

I need a doctor (who speaks English).
Necesito un doctor (que hable inglés).
ne·se·see·to oon dok·tor (ke a·ble een·gles)

Could I see a female doctor?
¿Puede revisarme una doctora?
pwe·de re·vee·sar·me oo·na dok·to·ra

Can the doctor come here?
¿Puede visitarme el doctor?
pwe·de vee·see·tar·me el dok·tor

I've been against ...	Estoy vacunado/a contra ... m/f	es·toy va·koo·na·do/a kon·tra ...
He's/She's been vaccinated against ...	Está vacunado/a contra ... m/f	es·ta va·koo·na·do/a kon·tra ...
hepatitis A/B/C	hepatitis A/B/C	e·pa·tee·tees a/be/se
tetanus	tétanos	te·ta·nos
typhoid	tifoidea	tee·foy·de·a

I need new ...	Necesito ... nuevos.	ne·se·see·to ... nwe·vos
contact lenses	lentes de contacto	len·tes de kon·tak·to
glasses	lentes	len·tes

I've run out of my medication.
Se me terminaron mis   se me ter·mee·*na*·ron mees
medicinas.   me·dee·*see*·nas

This is my usual medicine.
Esta es mi medicina   es·te es mee me·dee·*see*·na
habitual.   a·bee·*twal*

Can I have a receipt for my insurance?
¿Puede darme un recibo   *pwe*·de *dar*·me oon re·*see*·bo
para mi seguro médico?   *pa*·ra mee se·*goo*·ro *me*·dee·ko

I don't want a blood transfusion.
No quiero que me hagan   no *kye*·ro ke me *a*·gan
una transfusión de sangre.   *oo*·na trans·foo·*syon* de *san*·gre

Please use a new syringe.
Por favor, use una   por fa·*vor* *oo*·se *oo*·na
jeringa nueva.   khe·*reen*·ga *nwe*·va

I have my own syringe.
Tengo mi propia jeringa.   *ten*·go mee *pro*·pya khe·*reen*·ga

symptoms & conditions

los síntomas & las condiciones

I'm sick.
Estoy enfermo/a. m/f   es·*toy* en·*fer*·mo/a

My friend is sick.
Mi amigo/a está   mee a·*mee*·go/a es·*ta*
enfermo/a. m/f   en·*fer*·mo/a

It hurts here.
Me duele aquí.   me *dwe*·le a·*kee*

I've been injured.
He sido lastimado/a. m/f   e *see*·do las·tee·*ma*·do/a

I've been vomiting.
He estado vomitando.   e es·*ta*·do vo·mee·*tan*·do

I'm dehydrated.
Estoy deshidratado/a. m/f   es·*toy* des·ee·dra·*ta*·do/a

I'm all hot and cold.
Tengo escalofríos.   *ten*·go es·ka·lo·*free*·os

I can't sleep.
No puedo dormir.   no *pwe*·do dor·*meer*

Where does it hurt?
¿Dónde le duele?   don·de le dwe·le

How long have you been like this?
¿Desde cuándo se   des·de kwan·do se
siente así?   syen·te a·see

Have you had this before?
¿Ha tenido ésto antes?   a te·nee·do es·to an·tes

Have you had unprotected sex?
¿Ha tenido relaciones   a te·nee·do re·la·syo·nes
sexuales sin   sek·swa·les seen
protección?   pro·tek·syon

Are you on medication?
¿Está tomando algún   es·ta to·man·do al·goon
medicamento?   me·dee·ka·men·to

Are you pregnant?
¿Está embarazada?   es·ta em·ba·ra·sa·da

How long are you travelling for?
¿Por cuánto tiempo   por kwan·to tyem·po
va a viajar?   va a vya·khar

Do you ...?   *¿Usted ...?*   oos·ted ...
  drink   *bebe*   be·be
  smoke   *fuma*   foo·ma
  take drugs   *consume drogas*   kon·soo·me dro·gas

You need to be admitted to hospital.
Necesita ingresar al   ne·se·see·ta een·gre·sar al
hospital.   os·pee·tal

You should have it checked when you go home.
Debe revisarse   de·be re·vee·sar·se
cuando vuelva a casa.   kwan·do vwel·va a ka·sa

You should return home for treatment.
Debe regresar a casa   de·be re·gre·sar a ka·sa
para que lo/la atiendan. m/f   pa·ra ke lo/la a·tyen·dan

I feel ...	*Me siento ...*	me *syen*·to ...
anxious	*ansioso/a* m/f	an·*syo*·so/a
better	*mejor*	me·*khor*
depressed	*deprimido/a* m/f	de·pree·*mee*·do/a
dizzy	*mareado/a* m/f	ma·re·*a*·do/a
nauseous	*con náuseas*	kon *now*·se·as
shivery	*destemplado/a* m/f	des·tem·*pla*·do/a
strange	*raro/a* m/f	*ra*·ro/a
weak	*débil*	*de*·veel
worse	*peor*	pe·*or*

I've (recently) had ...
(Hace poco) Tuve ...　　　　　(*a*·se *po*·ko) *too*·ve ...

He's/She's (recently) had ...
(Hace poco) Tuvo ...　　　　　(*a*·se *po*·ko) *too*·vo ...

I'm on medication for ...
Estoy bajo tratamiento　　　　es·*toy ba*·kho tra·ta·*myen*·to
médico contra ...　　　　　　me·*dee*·ko *kon*·tra ...

He's/She's on medication for ...
Está bajo tratamiento　　　　es·*ta ba*·kho tra·ta·*myen*·to
médico contra ...　　　　　　me·*dee*·ko *kon*·tra ...

I'm asthmatic.
Soy asmático/a. m/f　　　　　soy as·*ma*·tee·ko/a

I'm diabetic.
Soy diabético/a. m/f　　　　　soy dya·*be*·tee·ko/a

I'm epileptic.
Soy epiléptico/a. m/f　　　　　soy e·pee·*lep*·tee·ko/a

asthma	*asma* f	*as*·ma
cold	*resfriado* m	res·free·*a*·do
cough	*tos* f	tos
diarrhoea	*diarrea* f	dya·*re*·a
fever	*fiebre* f	*fye*·bre
headache	*dolor* m *de cabeza*	do·*lor* de ka·*be*·sa
infection	*infección* f	een·fek·*syon*
sprain	*torcedura* f	tor·se·*doo*·ra

For more symptoms and conditions, see the **dictionary**.

women's health

salud femenina

I think I'm pregnant.
Creo que estoy embarazada.   kre·o ke es·*toy* em·ba·ra·*sa*·da

I'm pregnant.
Estoy embarazada.   es·*toy* em·ba·ra·*sa*·da

I'm on the Pill.
Tomo pastillas   *to*·mo pas·*tee*·yas
anticonceptivas.   an·tee·kon·sep·*tee*·vas

I haven't had my period for (three) days/weeks.
Hace (tres) días/semanas   *a*·se (tres) *dee*·as/se·*ma*·nas
que no tengo mi periodo.   ke no *ten*·go mee pe·*ryo*·do

I've noticed a lump here.
He notado que tengo una   e no·*ta*·do ke *ten*·go *oo*·na
bola aquí.   *bo*·la a·*kee*

the doctor may say ...

Are you using contraception?
¿Usa anticonceptivos?   *oo*·sa an·tee·kon·sep·*tee*·vos

Are you menstruating?
¿Está menstruando?   es·*ta* men·*strwan*·do

Are you pregnant?
¿Está embarazada?   es·*ta* em·ba·ra·*sa*·da

When did you last have your period?
¿Cuándo tuvo su   *kwan*·do *too*·vo soo
último periodo?   *ool*·tee·mo pe·*ryo*·do

You're pregnant.
Está embarazada.   es·*ta* em·ba·ra·*sa*·da

179

I need ...	*Necesito ...*	ne·se·*see*·to ...
contraception	*algún método*	al·*goon* me·to·do
	anticonceptivo	an·tee·kon·sep·*tee*·vo
the morning-after pill	*tomar la pastilla*	to·*mar* la pas·*tee*·ya
	del día	del *dee*·a
	siguiente	see·*gyen*·te
a pregnancy test	*una prueba del*	*oo*·na *prwe*·ba de
	embarazo	em·ba·*ra*·so

allergies

I have a skin allergy.
  Tengo alergia en la piel.   *ten*·go a·*ler*·gya en la pyel

I'm allergic to ...	*Soy alérgico/a ...* **m/f**	soy a·*ler*·khee·ko/a ...
He's/She's	*Es alérgico/a ...* **m/f**	es a·*ler*·khee·ko/a ...
allergic to ...		
antibiotics	*a los*	a los
	antibióticos	an·tee·*byo*·tee·kos
anti-	*a los anti-*	a los an·tee·
inflammatories	*inflamatorios*	een·fla·ma·*to*·ryos
aspirin	*a la aspirina*	a la as·pee·*ree*·na
antihistamines	*a los anti-*	a los an·tee·
	histamínicos	ees·ta·*mee*·nee·kos
bees	*a las abejas*	a las a·*be*·khas
codeine	*a la codeína*	a la ko·de·*ee*·na
inhalers	*a los inhaladores*	a los ee·na·la·*do*·res
injections	*a las*	a las
	inyecciones	een·yek·*syo*·nes
penicillin	*a la*	a la
	penicilina	pe·nee·see·*lee*·na
pollen	*al polen*	al *po*·len

For food-related allergies, see **vegetarian & special meals**, page 156.

parts of the body

My (stomach) hurts.
 Me duele mi (estómago).   me *dwe*·le mee (es·*to*·ma·go)

I can't move my (ankle).
 No puedo mover mi   no pwe·do mo·*ver* mee
 (tobillo).   (to·*bee*·yo)

I have a cramp in my (foot).
 Tengo calambres en mi (pie).   *ten*·go ka·*lam*·bres en mee (pye)

My (throat) is swollen.
 Mi (garganta) está   mee (gar·*gan*·ta) es·*ta*
 hinchada.   een·*cha*·da

➤For more parts of the body, see the **dictionary**.

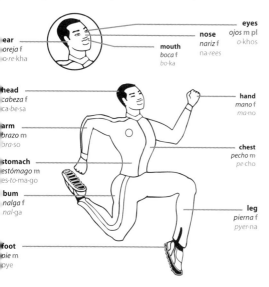

ear
oreja f
o·re·kha

nose
nariz f
na·*rees*

mouth
boca f
bo·ka

eyes
ojos m pl
o·khos

head
cabeza f
ca·*be*·sa

arm
brazo m
bra·so

stomach
estómago m
es·*to*·ma·go

bum
nalga f
nal·ga

foot
pie m
pye

hand
mano f
ma·no

chest
pecho m
pe·cho

leg
pierna f
pyer·na

chemist

I need something for (fever).
Necesito algo para   ne·se·*see*·to *al*·go *pa*·ra
(la fiebre).   (la *fye*·bre)

Do I need a prescription for (antihistamines)?
¿Necesito una receta para   ne·se·*see*·to oo·na re·*se*·ta *pa*·ra
(antihistamínicos)?   (an·tee·ees·ta·*mee*·nee·kos)

How many times a day?
¿Cuántas veces al día?   *kwan*·tas *ve*·ses al *dee*·a

Will it make me drowsy?
¿Me dará sueño?   me da·*ra swe*·nyo

For more chemist items, see the **dictionary**.

listen for ...

a to·*ma*·do *es*·to *an*·tes
¿Ha tomado ésto antes?   **Have you taken this before?**

de·be ter·mee·*nar* el tra·ta·*myen*·to
Debe terminar el   **You must complete**
tratamiento.   **the course.**

dos *ve*·ses al *dee*·a (kon la ko·*mee*·da)
Dos veces al día (con la   **Twice a day (with food).**
comida).

es·ta·*ra lees*·to en (*vayn*·te mee·*noo*·tos)
Estará listo en (veinte   **It'll be ready to pick**
minutos).   **up in (20 minutes).**

dentist

I have a ...	Tengo ...	ten·go ...
broken tooth	un diente roto	oon dyen·te ro·to
cavity	una caries	oo·na ka·ryes
toothache	dolor de muelas	do·lor de mwe·las

I need a/an ...	Necesito una ...	ne·se·see·to oo·na ...
anaesthetic	anestesia	a·nes·te·sya
crown	corona	ko·ro·na
filling	amalgama	a·mal·ga·ma

listen for ...

a·bra gran·de
Abra grande.   Open wide.

en·khwa·ge·se
Enjuáguese.   Rinse.

es·to no le do·le·ra
Esto no le dolerá.   This won't hurt a bit.

es·to le pwe·de do·ler oon po·ko
Esto le puede doler un poco.   This might hurt a little.

mwer·da es·to
Muerda ésto.   Bite down on this.

no se mwe·va
No se mueva.   Don't move.

re·gre·se por ke no e ter·mee·na·do
Regrese, porque no   Come back, I haven't
he terminado.   finished.

I've lost a filling.
Se me cayó una amalgama.   se me ka·*yo oo*·na a·mal·*ga*·ma

My dentures are broken.
Se me rompió la   se me rom·*pyo* la
dentadura postiza.   den·ta·*doo*·ra pos·*tee*·sa

My gums hurt.
Me duelen las encías.   me *dwe*·len las en·*see*·as

I don't want it extracted.
No quiero que me lo saque.   no *kye*·ro ke me lo *sa*·ke

Ouch!
¡Ay!   ai

Nouns in the dictionary have their gender indicated by ⑩ or ⑪. If it's a plural noun, you'll also see pl. Where a word that could be either a noun or a verb has no gender indicated, it's the verb. For all words relating to local food, see the **culinary reader**, page 157.

A

(to be) able *poder* po·der
aboard *a bordo* a bor·do
abortion *aborto* ⑩ a·bor·to
about *sobre* so·bre
above *arriba* a·ree·ba
abroad *en el extranjero* en el ek·stran·khe·ro
accept *aceptar* a·sep·tar
accident *accidente* ⑩ ak·see·den·te
accommodation *alojamiento* ⑩ a·lo·kha·myen·to
across *a través* a tra·ves
activist *activista* ⑩&⑪ ak·tee·vees·ta
acupuncture *acupuntura* ⑪ a·koo·poon·too·ra
adaptor *adaptador* ⑩ a·dap·ta·dor
address *dirección* ⑪ dee·rek·syon
administration *administración* ⑪ ad·mee·nees·tra·syon
admission price *precio* ⑩ *de entrada* pre·syo de en·tra·da
admit (acknowledge) *reconocer* re·ko·no·ser
admit (allow to enter) *dejar entrar* de·khar en·trar
admit (accept) *admitir* ad·mee·teer
adult *adulto/a* ⑩/⑪ a·dool·to/a
advertisement *anuncio* ⑩ a·noon·syo
advice *consejo* ⑩ kon·se·kho
advise *aconsejar* a·kon·se·khar
aerobics *aeróbics* ⑩ a·e·ro·beeks
Africa *África* a·free·ka
after *después de* des·pwes de
aftershave *loción* ⑪ *para después del afeitado* lo·syon pa·ra des·pwes del a·fay·ta·do

again *otra vez* o·tra ves
age *edad* ⑪ e·dad
aggressive *agresivo/a* ⑩/⑪ a·gre·see·vo/a
agree *estar de acuerdo* es·tar de a·kwer·do
agriculture *agricultura* ⑪ a·gree·kool·too·ra
AIDS *SIDA* ⑩ see·da
air *aire* ⑩ ai·re
airmail *correo* ⑩ *aéreo* ko·re·o a·e·re·o
(by) airmail *por vía* ⑪ *aérea* por vee·a a·e·re·a
air-conditioning *aire* ⑩ *acondicionado* ai·re a·kon·dee·syo·na·do
airline *aerolínea* ⑪ a·e·ro·lee·ne·a
airport *aeropuerto* ⑩ a·e·ro·pwer·to
airport tax *tasa* ⑪ *de aeropuerto* ta·sa de a·e·ro·pwer·to
alarm clock *despertador* ⑩ des·per·ta·dor
alcohol *alcohol* ⑩ al·kol
all *todo* to·do
allergy *alergia* ⑪ a·ler·khya
allow *permitir* per·mee·teer
almond *almendra* ⑪ al·men·dra
almost *casi* ka·see
alone *solo/a* ⑩/⑪ so·lo/a
already *ya* ya
also *también* tam·byen
altar *altar* ⑩ al·tar
altitude *altura* ⑪ al·too·ra
always *siempre* syem·pre
amateur *amateur* ⑩&⑪ a·ma·ter
ambassador *embajador/embajadora* ⑩/⑪ em·ba·kha·dor/em·ba·kha·do·ra
among *entre* en·tre
anarchist *anarquista* ⑩&⑪ a·nar·kees·ta

ancient *antiguo/a* ⓜ/ⓕ an·tee·gwo/a
and *y* ee
angry *enojado/a* ⓜ/ⓕ e·no·kha·do/a
animal *animal* ⓜ a·nee·mal
ankle *tobillo* ⓜ to·bee·yo
answer *respuesta* ⓕ res·pwes·ta
answering machine *contestadora* ⓕ
    kon·tes·ta·do·ra
ant *hormiga* ⓕ or·mee·ga
anthology *antología* ⓕ an·to·lo·khee·a
antibiotics *antibióticos* ⓜ pl
    an·tee·byo·tee·kos
antimalarial tablets *pastillas* ⓕ pl
    antipalúdicas pas·tee·yas
    an·tee·pa·loo·dee·kas
antinuclear *antinuclear*
    an·tee·noo·kle·ar
antique *antigüedad* ⓕ
    an·tee·gwe·dad
antiseptic *antiséptico* ⓜ
    an·tee·sep·tee·ko
any (singular) *alguno/a* ⓜ/ⓕ
    al·goo·no/a
any (plural) *algunos/as* ⓜ/ⓕ
    al·goo·nos/as
appendix *apéndice* ⓕ a·pen·dee·se
apple *manzana* ⓕ man·sa·na
appointment *cita* ⓕ see·ta
apricot *chabacano* ⓜ cha·ba·ka·no
archaeological *arqueológico/a* ⓜ/ⓕ
    ar·ke·o·lo·khee·ko/a
archaeologist *arqueólogo/a* ⓜ/ⓕ
    ar·ke·o·lo·go/a
architect *arquitecto/a* ⓜ/ⓕ
    ar·kee·tek·to/a
architecture *arquitectura* ⓕ
    ar·kee·tek·too·ra
argue *discutir* dees·koo·teer
arm *brazo* ⓜ bra·so
army *ejército* ⓜ e·kher·see·to
arrest *arrestar* a·res·tar
arrivals *llegadas* ⓕ pl ye·ga·das
arrive *llegar* ye·gar
art *arte* ⓜ ar·te
art gallery *galería* ⓕ de arte
    ga·le·ree·a de ar·te
artichoke *alcachofa* ⓕ al·ka·cho·fa

artist *artista* ⓜ&ⓕ ar·tees·ta
ashtray *cenicero* ⓜ se·nee·se·ro
Asia *Asia* ⓕ a·sya
ask (a question) *preguntar* pre·goon·t
ask (for something) *pedir* pe·deer
aspirin *aspirina* ⓕ as·pee·ree·na
assault *agresión* ⓕ a·gre·syon
asthma *asma* ⓕ as·ma
at the back (behind) *detrás de* de·tras d
athletics *atletismo* ⓜ at·le·tees·mo
atmosphere *atmósfera* ⓕ at·mos·fe·ra
aubergine *berenjena* ⓕ be·ren·khe·na
aunt *tía* ⓕ tee·a
Australia *Australia* ⓕ ow·stra·lya
Australian Rules football *fútbol* ⓜ
    australiano foot·bol ows·tra·lya·no
automatic teller machine *cajero* ⓜ
    automático ka·khe·ro ow·to·ma·tee·k
autumn *otoño* ⓜ o·to·nyo
avenue *avenida* ⓕ a·ve·nee·da
avocado *aguacate* ⓜ a·gwa·ka·te
Aztec *azteca* ⓜ&ⓕ as·te·ka

B

B&W (film) *blanco y negro*
    blan·ko ee ne·gro
baby *bebé* ⓜ be·be
baby food *alimento* ⓜ *para bebé*
    a·lee·men·to pa·ra be·be
baby powder *talco* ⓜ *para bebé*
    tal·ko pa·ra be·be
babysitter *niñera* ⓕ nee·nye·ra
back (of body) *espalda* ⓕ es·pal·da
back (of chair) *respaldo* ⓜ res·pal·do
backpack *mochila* ⓕ mo·chee·la
bacon *tocino* ⓜ to·see·no
bad *malo/a* ⓜ/ⓕ ma·lo/a
bag *bolsa* ⓕ bol·sa
baggage *equipaje* ⓜ e·kee·pa·khe
baggage allowance *límite* ⓜ *de*
    equipaje lee·mee·te de e·kee·pa·khe
baggage claim *entrega* ⓕ *de equipaje*
    en·tre·ga de e·kee·pa·khe
bakery *panadería* ⓕ pa·na·de·ree·a
balance (account) *saldo* ⓜ sal·do
balcony *balcón* ⓜ bal·kon

ball *pelota* ① pe·lo·ta
ballet *ballet* ⓜ ba·le
banana *plátano* ⓜ pla·ta·no
band *grupo* ⓜ groo·po
bandage *vendaje* ⓜ ven·da·khe
Band-Aids *curitas* ① pl koo·ree·tas
bank *banco* ⓜ ban·ko
bank account *cuenta* ① *bancaria*
  kwen·ta ban·ka·rya
banknotes *billetes* ⓜ pl bee·ye·tes
baptism *bautizo* ⓜ bow·tee·so
bar *bar* ⓜ bar
bar (with live music) *bar* ⓜ *con*
  variedad bar kon va·rye·dad
barber *peluquero* ⓜ pe·loo·ke·ro
baseball *béisbol* ⓜ bays·bol
basket *canasta* ① ka·nas·ta
basketball *baloncesto* ⓜ ba·lon·ses·to
bathtub *tina* ① tee·na
bathing suit *traje* ⓜ *de baño*
  tra·khe de ba·nyo
bathroom *baño* ⓜ ba·nyo
battery (car) *batería* ① ba·te·ree·a
battery (small) *pila* ① pee·la
be (ongoing) *ser* ser
be (temporary) *estar* es·tar
beach *playa* ① pla·ya
beans *frijoles* ⓜ pl free·kho·les
beautiful *hermoso/a* ⓜ/① er·mo·so/a
beauty salon *salón* ⓜ *de belleza*
  sa·lon de be·ye·sa
because *porque* por·ke
bed *cama* ① ka·ma
bedding *ropa* ① *de cama*
  ro·pa de ka·ma
bedroom *habitación* ① a·bee·ta·syon
bee *abeja* ① a·be·kha
beef *carne* ① *de res* kar·ne de res
beer *cerveza* ① ser·ve·sa
beetroot *betabel* ⓜ be·ta·bel
before *antes* an·tes
beggar *limosnero/a* ⓜ/①
  lee·mos·ne·ro/a
begin *comenzar* ko·men·sar
behind *detrás de* de·tras de
below *abajo* a·ba·kho
best *mejor* me·khor

bet *apuesta* ① a·pwes·ta
better *mejor* me·khor
between *entre* en·tre
Bible *Biblia* ① bee·blya
bicycle *bicicleta* ① bee·see·kle·ta
big *grande* gran·de
bike *bici* ① bee·see
bike chain *cadena* ① *de bici*
  ka·de·na de bee·see
bike path *carril* ⓜ *para bici*
  ka·reel pa·ra bee·see
bill (account) *cuenta* ① kwen·ta
biodegradable *biodegradable*
  bee·o·de·gra·da·ble
biography *biografía* ① bee·o·gra·fee·a
bird *pájaro* ⓜ pa·kha·ro
birth certificate *acta* ① *de nacimiento*
  ak·ta de na·see·myen·to
birthday *cumpleaños* ⓜ
  koom·ple·a·nyos
birthday cake *pastel* ⓜ *de cumplea-*
  ños pas·tel de koom·ple·a·nyos
biscuit *galleta* ① ga·ye·ta
bite (dog) *mordedura* ①
  mor·de·doo·ra
bite (food) *bocado* ⓜ bo·ka·do
bite (insect) *picadura* ① pee·ka·doo·ra
black *negro/a* ⓜ/① ne·gro/a
blanket *cobija* ① ko·bee·kha
bleed *sangrar* san·grar
blind *ciego/a* ⓜ/① sye·go/a
blister *ampolla* ① am·po·ya
blocked *bloqueado/a* ⓜ/①
  blo·ke·a·do/a
blood *sangre* ① san·gre
blood group *grupo* ⓜ *sanguíneo*
  groo·po san·gee·ne·o
blood pressure *presión* ① *arterial*
  pre·syon ar·te·ryal
blood test *análisis* ⓜ *de sangre*
  a·na·lee·sees de san·gre
blue *azul* a·sool
board (ship, etc) *embarcar* em·bar·kar
boarding house *pensión* ① pen·syon
boarding pass *pase* ⓜ *de abordar*
  pa·se de a·bor·dar
boat *bote* ⓜ bo·te
body *cuerpo* ⓜ kwer·po

bomb *bomba* ① bom·ba
bone *hueso* ⑩ we·so
book *libro* ⑩ lee·bro
book (reserve) *reservar* re·ser·*var*
booked out *lleno/a* ⑩/① ye·no/a
bookshop *librería* ① lee·bre·ree·a
boots *botas* ① bo·tas
border *frontera* ① fron·te·ra
boring *aburrido/a* ⑩/① a·boo·rree·do/a
borrow *pedir prestado* pe·*deer*
  pres·*ta*·do
botanic garden *jardín* ⑩ *botánico*
  khar·*deen* bo·ta·nee·ko
both *ambos/as* ⑩/① pl am·bos/as
bottle *botella* ① bo·te·ya
bottle opener *destapador* ⑩
  des·ta·pa·*dor*
bowl *refractario* ⑩ re·frak·*ta*·ryo
box *caja* ① ka·kha
boxer shorts *boxers* ⑩ pl bok·sers
boxing *boxeo* ⑩ bok·se·o
boy *niño* ⑩ nee·nyo
boyfriend *novio* ⑩ no·vyo
bra *brassiere* ⑩ bra·*syer*
Braille *Braille* ⑩ brai·le
brakes *frenos* ⑩ pl fre·nos
branch office *sucursal* ① soo·koor·*sal*
brandy *brandy* ⑩ bran·dee
brave *valiente* va·lyen·te
bread *pan* ⑩ pan
  bread roll *bolillo* ⑩ bo·lee·yo
  brown bread *pan* ⑩ *integral*
  pan een·te·*gral*
  rye bread *pan* ⑩ *de centeno*
  pan de sen·te·no
  sourdough bread *pan* ⑩
  de levadura fermentada
  pan de le·va·doo·ra fer·men·*ta*·da
  white bread *pan* ⑩ *blanco* pan
  blan·ko
break *romper* rom·*per*
break down *descomponerse*
  des·kom·po·ner·se
breakfast *desayuno* ⑩ de·sa·*yoo*·no
breast (poultry) *pechuga* ①
  pe·*choo*·ga

breasts *senos* ⑩ pl se·nos
breasts (colloquial) *chichis* ① pl
  chee·chees
breathe *respirar* res·pee·*rar*
bribe *soborno* ⑩ so·bor·no
bribe *sobornar* so·bor·*nar*
bridge *puente* ⑩ pwen·te
briefcase *portafolios* ⑩ por·ta·fo·lyos
brilliant *brillante* bree·yan·te
bring *traer* tra·*er*
brochure *folleto* ⑩ fo·ye·to
broken *roto/a* ⑩/① ro·to/a
bronchitis *bronquitis* ① bron·*kee*·tees
brother *hermano* ⑩ er·ma·no
brown *café* ka·fe
bruise *moretón* ⑩ mo·re·ton
bucket *cubeta* ① koo·be·ta
Buddhist *budista* ⑩&① boo·dees·ta
budget *presupuesto* ⑩
  pre·soo·pwes·to
buffet *buffet* ⑩ boo·fe
bug *bicho* ⑩ bee·cho
build *construir* kon·stroo·*eer*
building *edificio* ⑩ e·dee·fee·syo
bull *toro* ⑩ to·ro
bullfight *corrida* ① *(de toros)*
  ko·*rree*·da (de to·ros)
bullring *plaza* ① *de toros*
  pla·sa de to·ros
bum (ass) *culo* ⑩ koo·lo
burn *quemadura* ① ke·ma·*doo*·ra
burn (something) *quemar* ke·*mar*
bus (city) *camión* ⑩ ka·*myon*
bus (intercity) *autobús* ⑩ ow·to·boos
bus station *estación* ① *de autobuses*
  es·ta·syon de ow·to·boo·ses
bus stop *parada* ① *de camiones*
  pa·*ra*·da de ka·*myo*·nes
business *negocios* ⑩ pl ne·go·syos
business class *clase* ① *ejecutiva*
  kla·se e·khe·koo·tee·va
business person *comerciante* ⑩&①
  ko·mer·syan·te
busker *artista callejero/a* ⑩/①
  ar·*tees*·ta ka·ye·*khe*·ro/a
busy *ocupado/a* ⑩/① o·koo·pa·do/a
but *pero* pe·ro

butcher's shop *carnicería* ⓕ
kar·nee·se·*ree*·a

butter *mantequilla* ⓕ man·te·*kee*·ya

butterfly *mariposa* ⓕ ma·ree·*po*·sa

buttons *botones* ⓜ pl bo·*to*·nes

buy *comprar* kom·*prar*

C

cabbage *col* ⓕ kol

cable *cable* ⓜ *ka*·ble

cable car *teleférico* ⓜ te·le·*fe*·ree·ko

cactus *cactus* ⓜ *kak*·toos

cactus worms *gusanos* ⓜ pl *de maguey* goo·*sa*·nos de ma·*gay*

cafe *café* ⓜ ka·*fe*

cake *pastel* ⓜ pas·*tel*

cake shop *pastelería* ⓕ pas·te·le·*ree*·a

calculator *calculadora* ⓕ
kal·koo·la·*do*·ra

calendar *calendario* ⓜ ka·len·*da*·ryo

calf *becerro* ⓜ be·*se*·ro

camera *cámara* ⓕ *fotográfica*
ka·ma·ra fo·to·*gra*·fee·ka

camera shop *tienda* ⓕ *de fotografía*
tyen·da de fo·to·gra·*fee*·a

camp *acampar* a·kam·*par*

camping store *tienda* ⓕ *de campismo*
tyen·da de kam·*pees*·mo

campsite *área* ⓕ *para acampar*
a·re·a *pa*·ra a·kam·*par*

can (tin) *lata* ⓕ *la*·ta

can (be able) *poder* po·*der*

can opener *abrelatas* ⓜ a·bre·*la*·tas

Canada *Canadá* ka·na·*da*

cancel *cancelar* kan·se·*lar*

cancer *cáncer* ⓜ *kan*·ser

candle *vela* ⓕ *ve*·la

candy *dulces* ⓜ pl *dool*·ses

cantaloupe *melón* ⓜ *cantaloupe*
me·*lon* kan·ta·*loop*

capsicum *pimiento* ⓜ pee·*myen*·to

car *coche* ⓜ *ko*·che

car hire *renta* ⓕ *de coches*
ren·ta de *ko*·ches

car owner's title *factura* ⓕ *del coche*
fak·*too*·ra del *ko*·che

car park *estacionamiento* ⓜ
es·ta·syo·na·*myen*·to

car registration *matrícula* ⓕ
ma·*tree*·koo·la

caravan *caravana* ⓕ ka·ra·*va*·na

cards *cartas* ⓕ pl *kar*·tas

care (about something) *preocuparse por* pre·o·koo·*par*·se por

care (for someone) *cuidar de*
kwee·*dar* de

caring *bondadoso/a* ⓜ/ⓕ
bon·da·*do*·so/a

carpenter *carpintero* ⓜ kar·peen·*te*·ro

carrot *zanahoria* ⓕ sa·na·o·rya

carry *llevar* ye·*var*

carton *cartón* ⓜ kar·*ton*

cash *dinero* ⓜ *en efectivo*
dee·*ne*·ro en e·fek·*tee*·vo

cash (a cheque) *cambiar (un cheque)*
kam·*byar* (oon *che*·ke)

cash register *caja* ⓕ *registradora*
ka·kha re·khees·tra·*do*·ra

cashew nut *nuez* ⓕ *de la India*
nwes de la *een*·dya

cashier *cajero/a* ⓜ/ⓕ ka·*khe*·ro/a

casino *casino* ⓜ ka·*see*·no

cassette *cassette* ⓜ ka·*set*

castle *castillo* ⓜ kas·*tee*·yo

casual work *trabajo* ⓜ *eventual*
tra·*ba*·kho e·ven·*twal*

cat *gato/a* ⓜ/ⓕ *ga*·to/a

cathedral *catedral* ⓕ ka·te·*dral*

Catholic *católico/a* ⓜ/ⓕ ka·*to*·lee·ko/a

cauliflower *coliflor* ⓕ ko·lee·*flor*

caves *cuevas* ⓕ pl *kwe*·vas

CD *cómpact* ⓜ kom·pakt

celebrate (an event) *celebrar*
se·le·*brar*

celebration *celebración* ⓕ
se·le·bra·*syon*

cell phone *teléfono* ⓜ *celular*
te·*le*·fo·no se·loo·*lar*

cemetery *cementerio* ⓜ se·men·*te*·ryo

cent *centavo* ⓜ sen·*ta*·vo

centimetre *centímetro* ⓜ
sen·*tee*·me·tro

Central America *Centroamérica* ⓕ
sen·tro·a·*me*·ree·ka

central heating *calefacción* ① *central*
ka·le·fak·*syon* sen·*tral*
centre *centro* ⓜ sen·tro
ceramic *cerámica* ① se·ra·mee·ka
cereal *cereal* ⓜ se·re·*al*
certificate *certificado* ⓜ
ser·tee·fee·*ka*·do
chair *silla* ① *see*·ya
champagne *champán* ⓜ cham·*pan*
chance *oportunidad* ①
o·por·too·nee·*dad*
change (money) *cambio* ⓜ *kam*·byo
change *cambiar* kam·*byar*
changing rooms *probadores* ⓜ pl
pro·ba·*do*·res
charming *encantador/encantadora*
ⓜ/① en·kan·ta·*dor*/en·kan·ta·*do*·ra
chat up *ligar* lee·*gar*
cheap *barato/a* ⓜ/① ba·*ra*·to/a
cheat *tramposo/a* ⓜ/① tram·po·so/a
check *revisar* re·vee·*sar*
check (bank) *cheque* ⓜ *che*·ke
check (bill) *cuenta* ① *kwen*·ta
check-in (flight) *documentación* ①
do·koo·men·ta·*syon*
check-in (hotel) *registro* ⓜ
re·*khees*·tro
checkpoint *control* ⓜ kon·*trol*
cheese *queso* ⓜ *ke*·so
chef *chef* ⓜ&① chef
chemist (person) *farmacéutico/a* ⓜ/①
far·ma·*sew*·tee·ko/a
chemist (shop) *farmacia* ① far·*ma*·sya
cheque *cheque* ⓜ *che*·ke
chess *ajedrez* ⓜ a·khe·*dres*
chest *pecho* ⓜ *pe*·cho
chewing gum *chicle* ⓜ *chee*·kle
chicken *pollo* ⓜ *po*·yo
chicken breast *pechuga* ① *de pollo*
pe·*choo*·ga de *po*·yo
chickpeas *garbanzos* ⓜ pl gar·*ban*·sos
child *niño/a* ⓜ/① *nee*·nyo/a
child's car seat *asiento* ⓜ *de*
seguridad para bebés a·*syen*·to de
se·goo·ree·*dad* pa·ra be·*bes*
childminding service *guardería* ①
gwar·de·*ree*·a
children *niños* ⓜ&① pl *nee*·nyos

chilli *chile* ⓜ *chee*·le
chilli sauce *salsa* ① *picante*
sal·sa pee·*kan*·te
chocolate *chocolate* ⓜ cho·ko·*la*·te
choose *elegir* e·le·*kheer*
Christian *cristiano/a* ⓜ/①
krees·*tya*·no/a
Christmas Day *Navidad* ① na·vee·*dad*
Christmas Eve *Nochebuena* ①
no·che·*bwe*·na
church *iglesia* ① ee·*gle*·sya
cider *sidra* ① *see*·dra
cigar *puro* ⓜ *poo*·ro
cigarette *cigarro* ⓜ see·*ga*·ro
cigarette lighter *encendedor* ⓜ
en·sen·de·*dor*
cigarette machine *máquina* ① *de*
tabaco *ma*·kee·na de ta·*ba*·ko
cigarette papers *papel* ⓜ *para cigar-*
ros pa·*pel* pa·ra see·*ga*·ros
cinema *cine* ⓜ *see*·ne
cinnamon *canela* ① ka·*ne*·la
circus *circo* ⓜ *seer*·ko
citizenship *ciudadanía* ①
syoo·da·da·*nee*·a
city *ciudad* ① syoo·*dad*
city centre *centro* ⓜ *de la ciudad*
sen·tro de la syoo·*dad*
city walls *murallas* ① pl moo·*ra*·yas
civil rights *derechos* ⓜ pl *civiles*
de·*re*·chos see·*vee*·les
classical *clásico/a* ⓜ/① *kla*·see·ko/a
clean *limpio/a* ⓜ/① *leem*·pyo/a
cleaning *trabajo* ⓜ *de limpieza*
tra·*ba*·kho de leem·*pye*·sa
client *cliente/a* ⓜ/① klee·*en*·te/a
cliff *acantilado* ⓜ a·kan·tee·*la*·do
climb *escalar* es·ka·*lar*
cloak *capa* ⓜ *ka*·pa
cloakroom *guardarropa* ⓜ
gwar·da·*ro*·pa
clock *reloj* ⓜ re·*lokh*
close (nearby) *cerca* *ser*·ka
close (shut) *cerrar* se·*rar*
closed *cerrado/a* ⓜ/① se·*ra*·do/a
clothes line *tendedero* ⓜ ten·de·*de*·ro
clothing *ropa* ① *ro*·pa

clothing store *tienda* ① *de ropa*
tyen·da de *ro*·pa

cloud *nube* ① *noo*·be

cloudy *nublado* noo·*bla*·do

clove (of garlic) *diente (de ajo)*
dyen·te (de *a*·kho)

cloves *clavos* ⓜ pl *de olor*
kla·vos de o·*lor*

clutch *embrague* ⓜ em·*bra*·ge

coach *entrenador/entrenadora* ⓜ/①
en·tre·na·*dor*/en·tre·na·*do*·ra

coast *costa* ① *kos*·ta

cocaine *cocaína* ① ko·ka·*ee*·na

cockroach *cucaracha* ① koo·ka·*ra*·cha

cocoa *cacao* ⓜ ka·*kow*

coconut *coco* ⓜ *ko*·ko

codeine *codeína* ① ko·de·*ee*·na

coffee *café* ⓜ ka·*fe*

coins *monedas* ① pl mo·*ne*·das

cold *frío/a* ⓜ/① *free*·o/a

cold (illness) *resfriado* ⓜ res·free·*a*·do

colleague *colega* ⓜ&① ko·*le*·ga

collect call *llamada* ① *por cobrar*
ya·*ma*·da por ko·*brar*

college *universidad* ①
oo·nee·ver·see·*dad*

colour *color* ⓜ ko·*lor*

colour film *película* ① *en color*
pe·*lee*·koo·la en ko·*lor*

comb *peine* ⓜ *pay*·ne

comb *peinar* pay·*nar*

come *venir* ve·*neer*

come (arrive) *llegar* ye·*gar*

comedy *comedia* ① ko·*me*·dya

comfortable *cómodo/a* ⓜ/①
ko·mo·do/a

communion *comunión* ①
ko·moo·*nyon*

communist *comunista* ⓜ&①
ko·moo·*nees*·ta

companion *compañero/a* ⓜ/①
kom·pa·*nye*·ro/a

company *compañía* ① kom·pa·*nyee*·a

compass *brújula* ① *broo*·khoo·la

complain *quejarse* ke·*khar*·se

computer *computadora* ①
kom·poo·ta·*do*·ra

computer game *juego* ⓜ
de computadora khwe·go de
kom·poo·ta·*do*·ra

concert *concierto* ⓜ kon·*syer*·to

conditioner *acondicionador* ⓜ
a·kon·dee·syo·na·*dor*

condoms *condones* ⓜ pl kon·*do*·nes

confession *confesión* ① kon·fe·*syon*

confirm *confirmar* kon·feer·*mar*

connection *conexión* ① ko·nek·*syon*

conservative *conservador/*
conservadora ⓜ/① kon·ser·va·*dor*/
kon·ser·va·*do*·ra

constipation *estreñimiento* ⓜ
es·tre·nyee·*myen*·to

consulate *consulado* ⓜ kon·soo·*la*·do

contact lenses *lentes* ⓜ pl *de con-*
tacto *len*·tes de kon·*tak*·to

contraceptives *anticonceptivos* ⓜ pl
an·tee·kon·sep·*tee*·vos

contract *contrato* ⓜ kon·*tra*·to

convenience store *tienda* ① *tyen*·da

convent *convento* ⓜ kon·*ven*·to

cook *cocinero* ⓜ ko·see·*ne*·ro

cook *cocinar* ko·see·*nar*

cookie *galleta* ① ga·*ye*·ta

corn *maíz* ⓜ ma·*ees*

corn flakes *hojuelas* ① pl *de maíz*
o·*khwe*·las de ma·*ees*

corner *esquina* ① es·*kee*·na

corrupt *corrupto/a* ⓜ/① ko·*roop*·to/a

cost *costo* ⓜ *kos*·to

cost *costar* kos·*tar*

cottage cheese *queso* ⓜ *cottage*
ke·so ko·*tash*

cotton *algodón* ⓜ al·go·*don*

cotton balls *bolas* ① pl *de algodón*
bo·las de al·go·*don*

cough *tos* ① tos

cough medicine *jarabe* ⓜ *para la tos*
kha·*ra*·be *pa*·ra la tos

count *contar* kon·*tar*

counter (in shop) *mostrador* ⓜ
mos·tra·*dor*

country *país* ⓜ pa·*ees*
countryside *campo* ⓜ *kam*·po
coupon *cupón* ⓜ koo·*pon*
courgette *calabacita* ⓕ ka·la·ba·*see*·ta
court (tennis) *cancha* ⓕ *de tenis*
  kan·cha de te·*nees*
cous cous *cus cus* ⓜ koos koos
cover charge *cover* ⓜ *ko*·ver
cow *vaca* ⓕ *va*·ka
crab *cangrejo* ⓜ kan·*gre*·kho
crackers *galletas* ⓕ pl *saladas*
  ga·*ye*·tas sa·*la*·das
craft *artesanía* ⓕ pl ar·te·sa·*nee*·a
crash *choque* ⓜ *cho*·ke
crazy *loco/a* ⓜ/ⓕ *lo*·ko/a
cream *crema* ⓕ *kre*·ma
cream cheese *queso* ⓜ *crema*
  ke·so *kre*·ma
creche *guardería* ⓕ gwar·de·*ree*·a
credit card *tarjeta* ⓕ *de crédito*
  tar·*khe*·ta de *kre*·dee·to
cricket (sport) *críquet* ⓜ *kree*·ket
crop *cosecha* ⓕ ko·*se*·cha
crowded *lleno/a* ⓜ/ⓕ *ye*·no/a
cucumber *pepino* ⓜ pe·*pee*·no
cuddle *abrazo* ⓜ a·*bra*·so
cuddle *abrazar* a·bra·*sar*
cup *taza* ⓕ *ta*·sa
cupboard *alacena* ⓕ a·la·*se*·na
currency exchange *cambio* ⓜ
  (de moneda) *kam*·byo (de mo·*ne*·da)
current (electricity) *corriente* ⓕ
  ko·*ryen*·te
current affairs *informativo* ⓜ
  een·for·ma·*tee*·vo
curry *curry* ⓜ *koo*·ree
curry powder *curry* ⓜ *en polvo*
  koo·ree en *pol*·vo
custard *flan* ⓜ flan
customs *aduana* ⓕ a·*dwa*·na
cut *cortar* kor·*tar*
cutlery *cubiertos* ⓜ pl koo·*byer*·tos
CV *currículum* ⓜ koo·*ree*·koo·loom
cycle *andar en bicicleta*
  an·*dar* en bee·see·*kle*·ta
cycling *ciclismo* ⓜ see·*klees*·mo
cyclist *ciclista* ⓜ&ⓕ see·*klees*·ta
cystitis *cistitis* ⓕ sees·*tee*·tees

D

dad *papá* ⓜ pa·*pa*
daily *diariamente* dya·rya·*men*·te
dance *bailar* bai·*lar*
dancing *baile* ⓜ *bai*·le
dangerous *peligroso/a* ⓜ/ⓕ
  pe·lee·*gro*·so/a
dark *oscuro/a* ⓜ/ⓕ os·*koo*·ro/a
data projector *cañon* ⓜ *proyector*
  ka·*nyon* pro·yek·*tor*
date (appointment) *cita* ⓕ *see*·ta
date (day) *fecha* ⓕ *fe*·cha
date (a person) *salir con* sa·*leer* kon
date of birth *fecha* ⓕ *de nacimiento*
  fe·cha de na·see·*myen*·to
daughter *hija* ⓕ *ee*·kha
dawn *amanecer* ⓜ a·ma·ne·*ser*
day *día* ⓜ *dee*·a
day after tomorrow *pasado mañana*
  pa·*sa*·do ma·*nya*·na
day before yesterday *antier* an·*tyer*
dead *muerto/a* ⓜ/ⓕ *mwer*·to/a
deaf *sordo/a* ⓜ/ⓕ *sor*·do/a
deal (cards) *repartir* re·par·*teer*
decide *decidir* de·see·*deer*
deep *profundo/a* ⓜ/ⓕ pro·*foon*·do/a
deforestation *deforestación* ⓕ
  de·fo·res·ta·*syon*
degree *título* ⓜ *tee*·too·lo
delay *demora* ⓕ de·*mo*·ra
delirious *delirante* de·lee·*ran*·te
deliver *entregar* en·tre·*gar*
democracy *democracia* ⓕ
  de·mo·*kra*·sya
demonstration (protest) *manifestación* ⓕ ma·nee·fes·ta·*syon*
dental floss *hilo* ⓜ *dental* *ee*·lo den·*tal*
dentist *dentista* ⓜ den·*tees*·ta
deny *negar* ne·*gar*
deodorant *desodorante* ⓜ
  de·so·do·*ran*·te
depart *salir de* sa·*leer* de
department store *tiendas* ⓕ pl
  departamentales *tyen*·das
  de·par·ta·men·*ta*·les
departure *salida* ⓕ sa·*lee*·da

deposit (bank) *depósito* Ⓜ de·*po*·see·to

descendant *descendiente* Ⓜ de·sen·*dyen*·te

desert *desierto* Ⓜ de·*syer*·to

design *diseño* Ⓜ dee·se·nyo

destination *destino* Ⓜ des·*tee*·no

destroy *destruir* des·troo·*eer*

detail *detalle* Ⓜ de·*ta*·ye

diabetes *diabetes* Ⓕ dee·a·*be*·tes

dial tone *línea* Ⓕ *lee*·ne·a

diaper *pañal* Ⓜ pa·*nyal*

diaphragm *diafragma* Ⓜ dee·a·*frag*·ma

diarrhoea *diarrea* Ⓕ dee·a·*re*·a

diary *agenda* Ⓕ a·*khen*·da

dice *dados* Ⓜ pl *da*·dos

dictionary *diccionario* Ⓜ deek·syo·*na*·ryo

die *morir* mo·*reer*

diet *dieta* Ⓕ *dye*·ta

different *diferente* dee·fe·*ren*·te

difficult *difícil* dee·*fee*·seel

dining car *vagón* Ⓜ *restaurante* va·*gon* res·tow·*ran*·te

dinner *cena* Ⓕ *se*·na

direct *directo/a* Ⓜ/Ⓕ dee·*rek*·to/a

direct-dial *marcación* Ⓕ *directa* mar·ka·syon dee·*rek*·ta

director *director/directora* Ⓜ/Ⓕ dee·rek·tor/dee·rek·*to*·ra

dirty *sucio/a* Ⓜ/Ⓕ *soo*·syo/a

disabled *discapacitado/a* Ⓜ/Ⓕ dees·ka·pa·see·*ta*·do/a

disco *discoteca* Ⓕ dees·ko·*te*·ka

discount *descuento* Ⓜ des·*kwen*·to

discover *descubrir* des·koo·*breer*

discrimination *discriminación* Ⓕ dees·kree·mee·na·*syon*

disease *enfermedad* Ⓕ en·fer·me·*dad*

disk *disco* Ⓜ *dees*·ko

disposable *desechable* de·se·*cha*·ble

diving *submarinismo* Ⓜ soob·ma·ree·*nees*·mo

diving equipment *equipo* Ⓜ *para buceo* e·*kee*·po *pa*·ra boo·*se*·o

divorced *divorciado/a* Ⓜ/Ⓕ dee·vor·*sya*·do/a

dizzy *mareado/a* Ⓜ/Ⓕ ma·re·*a*·do/a

do *hacer* a·*ser*

doctor *doctor/doctora* Ⓜ/Ⓕ dok·tor/dok·*to*·ra

documentary *documental* Ⓜ do·koo·men·*tal*

dog *perro/a* Ⓜ/Ⓕ *pe*·ro/a

dole *paro* Ⓜ *pa*·ro

doll *muñeca* Ⓕ moo·*nye*·ka

dollar *dólar* Ⓜ *do*·lar

domestic flight *vuelo* Ⓜ *nacional* *vwe*·lo na·syo·*nal*

donkey *burro* Ⓜ *boo*·ro

door *puerta* Ⓕ *pwer*·ta

dope *droga* Ⓕ *dro*·ga

double *doble* *do*·ble

double bed *cama* Ⓕ *matrimonial* *ka*·ma ma·tree·mo·*nyal*

double room *habitación* Ⓕ *doble* a·bee·ta·syon *do*·ble

down *hacia abajo* a·sya a·*ba*·kho

downhill *cuesta abajo* kwes·ta a·*ba*·kho

dozen *docena* Ⓕ do·*se*·na

drama *drama* Ⓜ *dra*·ma

draw *dibujar* dee·boo·*khar*

dream *soñar* so·*nyar*

dress *vestido* Ⓜ ves·*tee*·do

dried fruit *fruta* Ⓕ *seca* froo·ta se·*ka*

drink *bebida* Ⓕ be·*bee*·da

drink *tomar* to·*mar*

drive *conducir* kon·doo·*seer*

drivers licence *licencia* Ⓕ *de manejo* lee·*sen*·sya de ma·*ne*·kho

drug (medicinal) *medicina* Ⓕ me·dee·*see*·na

drug addiction *drogadicción* Ⓕ dro·ga·deek·*syon*

drug dealer *traficante* Ⓜ&Ⓕ *de drogas* tra·fee·*kan*·te de *dro*·gas

drugs (illegal) *drogas* Ⓕ pl *dro*·gas

drums *batería* Ⓕ ba·te·*ree*·a

drumstick *muslo* Ⓜ *de pollo* *moos*·lo de *po*·yo

drunk *borracho/a* Ⓜ/Ⓕ bo·*ra*·cho/a

dry *seco/a* Ⓜ/Ⓕ *se*·ko/a

dry *secar* se·*kar*

duck *pato* Ⓜ *pa*·to

dummy (pacifier) *chupón* Ⓜ choo·*pon*

during *durante* doo·*ran*·te

DVD *DVD* de ve de

E

each *cada* ka·da

ear *oreja* ① o·re·kha

early *temprano* tem·pra·no

earn *ganar* ga·nar

earplugs *tapones* ⓜ pl *para los oídos* ta·po·nes pa·ra los o·ee·dos

earrings *aretes* ⓜ pl a·re·tes

Earth *Tierra* ① tye·ra

earthquake *terremoto* ⓜ te·re·mo·to

east *este* es·te

Easter *Pascua* ① pas·kwa

easy *fácil* fa·seel

eat *comer* ko·mer

economy class *clase* ① *turista* kla·se too·rees·ta

eczema *eczema* ① ek·se·ma

editor *editor/editora* ⓜ/① e·dee·tor/e·dee·to·ra

education *educación* ① e·doo·ka·syon

eggplant *berenjena* ① be·ren·khe·na

egg *huevo* ⓜ we·vo

elections *elecciones* ① pl e·lek·syo·nes

electrical store *ferretería* ① fe·re·te·ree·a

electricity *electricidad* ① e·lek·tree·see·dad

elevator *elevador* ⓜ e·le·va·dor

embarrassed *apenado/a* ⓜ/① a·pe·na·do/a

embassy *embajada* ① em·ba·kha·da

emergency *emergencia* ① e·mer·khen·sya

emotional *emocional* e·mo·syo·nal

employee *empleado/a* ⓜ/① em·ple·a·do/a

employer *jefe/jefa* ⓜ/① khe·fe/khe·fa

empty *vacío/a* ⓜ/① va·see·o/a

end *fin* ⓜ feen

end *terminar* ter·mee·nar

endangered species *especies* ① pl *en peligro de extinción* es·pe·syes en pe·lee·gro de ek·steen·syon

engine *motor* ⓜ mo·tor

engineer *ingeniero/a* ⓜ/① een·khe·nye·ro/a

engineering *ingeniería* ① een·khe·nye·ree·a

England *Inglaterra* ① een·gla·te·ra

English (language) *inglés* ⓜ een·gles

enjoy (oneself) *divertirse* dee·ver·teer·se

enough *suficiente* soo·fee·syen·te

enter *entrar* en·trar

entertainment guide *guía* ① *del ocio* gee·a del o·syo

envelope *sobre* ⓜ so·bre

environment *medio* ⓜ *ambiente* me·dyo am·byen·te

epilepsy *epilepsia* ① e·pee·lep·sya

equal opportunity *igualdad* ① *de oportunidades* ee·gwal·dad de o·por·too·nee·da·des

equality *igualdad* ① ee·gwal·dad

equipment *equipo* ⓜ e·kee·po

escalator *escaleras* ① pl *eléctricas* es·ka·le·ras e·lek·tree·kas

Euro *euro* ⓜ e·oo·ro

Europe *Europa* ① e·oo·ro·pa

euthanasia *eutanasia* ① e·oo·ta·na·sya

evening *noche* ① no·che

everything *todo* to·do

example *ejemplo* ⓜ e·khem·plo

excellent *excelente* ek·se·len·te

excess baggage *exceso* ⓜ *de equipage* ek·se·so de e·kee·pa·khe

exchange *cambio* ⓜ kam·byo

exchange (money) *cambiar* kam·byar

exchange rate *tipo* ⓜ *de cambio* tee·po de kam·byo

excluded *excluido/a* ⓜ/① ek·skloo·ee·do/a

exhaust *agotar* a·go·tar

exhaust (car) *escape* ⓜ es·ka·pe

exhibit *exponer* ek·spo·ner

exhibition *exposición* ① ek·spo·see·syon

exit *salida* ① sa·lee·da

expensive *caro/a* ⓜ/① ka·ro/a

experience *experiencia* ① ek·spe·ryen·sya

express *expreso* ⓜ ek·spre·so

express mail *correo* ⓜ *expresso*
ko·re·o ek·spre·so
extension (visa) *prórroga* ⓕ pro·ro·ga
eye *ojo* ⓜ o·kho
eyebrows *cejas* ⓕ pl se·khas
eye drops *gotas* ⓕ pl *para los ojos*
go·tas pa·ra los o·khos

F

fabric *tela* ⓕ te·la
face *cara* ⓕ ka·ra
face cloth *toallita* ⓕ *facial*
to·a·yee·ta fa·syal
factory *fábrica* ⓕ fa·bree·ka
factory worker *obrero/a* ⓜ/ⓕ
o·bre·ro/a
fall *caída* ⓕ ka·ee·da
fall (season) *otoño* ⓜ o·to·nyo
family *familia* ⓕ fa·mee·lya
family name *apellido* ⓜ a·pe·yee·do
famous *famoso/a* ⓜ/ⓕ fa·mo·so/a
fan (supporter) *aficionado*
a·fee·syo·na·do
fan (machine) *ventilador* ⓜ
ven·tee·la·dor
far *lejos* le·khos
farewell *despedida* ⓕ des·pe·dee·da
farm *granja* ⓕ gran·kha
farmer *granjero/a* ⓜ/ⓕ gran·khe·ro/a
fart *pedo* ⓜ pe·do
fart *echarse un pedo* e·char·se oon pe·do
fast *rápido/a* ⓜ/ⓕ ra·pee·do/a
fat *gordo/a* ⓜ/ⓕ gor·do/a
fat (grease) *grasa* ⓕ gra·sa
father *padre* ⓜ pa·dre
father-in-law *suegro* ⓜ swe·gro
faucet *llave* ⓕ *(del agua)*
ya·ve (del a·gwa)
fault *falta* ⓕ fal·ta
faulty *defectuoso/a* ⓜ/ⓕ
de·fek·two·so/a
feed *alimentar* a·lee·men·tar
feel *sentir* sen·teer
feelings *sentimientos* ⓜ pl
sen·tee·myen·tos
fence *cerca* ⓕ ser·ka
fencing (sport) *esgrima* ⓕ es·gree·ma

festival *festival* ⓜ fes·tee·val
fever *fiebre* ⓕ fye·bre
few *pocos/as* ⓜ pl po·kos/as
fiance(e) *prometido/a* ⓜ/ⓕ
pro·me·tee·do/a
fiction *ficción* ⓕ feek·syon
field *campo* ⓜ kam·po
fig *higo* ⓜ ee·go
fight *pelea* ⓕ pe·le·a
fight *luchar* loo·char
fill *llenar* ye·nar
film *película* ⓕ pe·lee·koo·la
film speed *sensibilidad* ⓕ
sen·see·bee·lee·dad
filtered *con* ⓕ *filtro* kon feel·tro
find *encontrar* en·kon·trar
fine *multa* ⓕ mool·ta
finger *dedo* ⓜ de·do
finish *terminar* ter·mee·nar
fire (general) *fuego* ⓜ fwe·go
fire (building) *incendio* ⓜ een·sen·dyo
fireplace *chimenea* ⓕ chee·me·ne·a
firewood *leña* ⓕ le·nya
first *primero/a* ⓜ/ⓕ pree·me·ro/a
first class *primera clase* ⓕ
pree·me·ra kla·se
first name *nombre* ⓜ *de pila*
nom·bre de pee·la
first-aid kit *botiquín* ⓜ bo·tee·keen
fish *pez* ⓜ pes
fish (as food) *pescado* ⓜ pes·ka·do
fish shop *pescadería* ⓕ pes·ka·de·ree·a
fishing *pesca* ⓕ pes·ka
fizzy *con gas* kon gas
flag *bandera* ⓕ ban·de·ra
flannel *franela* ⓕ fra·ne·la
flashlight *linterna* ⓕ leen·ter·na
flat *plano/a* ⓜ/ⓕ pla·no/a
flea *pulga* ⓕ pool·ga
flippers *aletas* ⓕ pl a·le·tas
flooding *inundación* ⓕ
ee·noon·da·syon
floor (ground) *suelo* ⓜ swe·lo
floor (storey) *piso* ⓜ pee·so
florist *florista* ⓜ&ⓕ flo·rees·ta
flour *harina* ⓕ a·ree·na
flower *flor* ⓕ flor

flower seller
  vendedor/vendedora de flores ⓜ/ⓕ
  ven·de·*dor*/ven·de·*do*·ra de *flo*·res
flu *gripe* ⓕ *gree*·pe
fly *volar* vo·*lar*
foggy *neblinoso/a* ⓜ/ⓕ ne·blee·*no*·so/a
folk *folklórico/a* ⓜ/ⓕ fol·*klo*·ree·ko/a
follow *seguir* se·*geer*
food *comida* ⓕ ko·*mee*·da
food supplies *víveres* ⓜ pl *vee*·ve·res
fool *imbécil* ⓜ&ⓕ eem·*be*·seel
foot *pie* ⓜ pye
football (soccer) *fútbol* ⓜ *foot*·bol
footpath *banqueta* ⓕ ban·*ke*·ta
for *para* pa·ra
foreign *extranjero/a* ⓜ/ⓕ
  ek·stran·*khe*·ro/a
foreign exchange office *casa* ⓕ *de
  cambio* ka·sa de *kam*·byo
forest *bosque* ⓜ *bos*·ke
forever *para siempre* pa·ra *syem*·pre
forget *olvidar* ol·vee·*dar*
forgive *perdonar* per·do·*nar*
fork *tenedor* ⓜ te·ne·*dor*
fortnight *quincena* ⓕ keen·*se*·na
foul *asqueroso/a* ⓜ/ⓕ as·ke·*ro*·so/a
foyer *vestíbulo* ⓜ ves·*tee*·boo·lo
fragile *frágil* fra·kheel
France *Francia* ⓕ *fran*·sya
free (not bound) *libre* lee·bre
free (of charge) *gratis* *gra*·tees
freeze *congelar* kon·khe·*lar*
friend *amigo/a* ⓜ/ⓕ a·*mee*·go/a
frost *escarcha* ⓕ es·*kar*·cha
frozen foods *productos* ⓜ pl *congelados*
  pro·*dook*·tos kon·khe·*la*·dos
fruit *fruta* ⓕ *froo*·ta
fruit picking *recolección* ⓕ *de fruta*
  re·ko·lek·syon de *froo*·ta
fry *freír* fre·*eer*
frying pan *sartén* ⓜ sar·*ten*
fuck *coger* ko·*kher*
fuel *combustible* ⓜ kom·boos·*tee*·ble
full *lleno/a* ⓜ/ⓕ ye·no/a
full-time *tiempo* ⓜ *completo*
  tyem·po kom·*ple*·to

fun *diversión* ⓕ dee·ver·*syon*
funeral *funeral* ⓜ foo·ne·*ral*
funny *divertido/a* ⓜ/ⓕ
  dee·ver·*tee*·do/a
furniture *muebles* ⓜ pl *mwe*·bles
future *futuro* ⓜ foo·*too*·ro

G

garlic *ajo* ⓜ *a*·kho
gas (for cooking) *gas* ⓜ gas
gas (petrol) *gasolina* ⓕ ga·so·lee·na
gay *gay* gay
gelatin *gelatina* ⓕ khe·la·*tee*·na
general *general* khe·ne·*ral*
Germany *Alemania* ⓕ a·le·*ma*·nya
gift *regalo* ⓜ re·*ga*·lo
gin *ginebra* ⓕ khee·*ne*·bra
ginger *jengibre* ⓜ khen·*khee*·bre
girl *chica* ⓕ *chee*·ka
girl (child) *niña* ⓕ *nee*·nya
girlfriend *novia* ⓕ *no*·vya
give *dar* dar
give (a gift) *regalar* re·ga·*lar*
glandular fever *enfermedad* ⓕ *del
  beso* en·fer·me·*dad* del *be*·so
glass (drinking) *vaso* ⓜ *va*·so
glass (material) *vidrio* ⓜ *vee*·dryo
glass (of wine) *copa* ⓕ *(de vino)*
  ko·pa de *vee*·no
glasses *lentes* ⓜ pl *len*·tes
gloves *guantes* ⓜ pl *gwan*·tes
go *ir* eer
go out with *salir con* sa·*leer* kon
go shopping *ir de compras*
  eer de *kom*·pras
goal *gol* ⓜ gol
goalkeeper *portero/a* ⓜ/ⓕ por·*te*·ro/a
goat *cabra* ⓕ *ka*·bra
god *dios* ⓜ dyos
goddess *diosa* ⓕ *dyo*·sa
goggles *goggles* ⓜ pl *go*·gles
golf *golf* ⓜ golf
golf ball *pelota* ⓕ *de golf*
  pe·*lo*·ta de golf

golf course campo m de golf
kam·po de golf
good bueno/a m/f bwe·no/a
goodbye adiós a·dyos
gorgeous guapo/a m/f gwa·po/a
government gobierno m go·byer·no
gram gramo m gra·mo
grandchild nieto/a m/f nye·to/a
grandfather abuelo m a·bwe·lo
grandmother abuela f a·bwe·la
grapefruit toronja f to·ron·kha
grapes uvas f pl oo·vas
grass pasto m pas·to
grasshoppers chapulines m pl
cha·poo·lee·nes
grave tumba f toom·ba
gray gris grees
grease grasa f gra·sa
great padrísimo/a m/f
pa·dree·see·mo/a
green verde ver·de
greengrocery verdulería f
ver·doo·le·ree·a
grey gris grees
grocery tienda f de abarrotes
tyen·da de a·ba·ro·tes
groundnut cacahuate m ka·ka·wa·te
grow crecer kre·ser
g-string tanga f tan·ga
guess adivinar a·dee·vee·nar
guide (audio) audioguía f
ow·dyo·gee·a
guide (person) guía m&f gee·a
guide dog perro m guía pe·ro gee·a
guidebook guía f turística
gee·a too·rees·tee·ka
guided tour recorrido m guiado
re·ko·ree·do gee·a·do
guilty culpable kool·pa·ble
guitar guitarra f gee·ta·ra
gum goma f go·ma
gymnastics gimnasia f
kheem·na·sya
gynaecologist ginecólogo/a m/f
khee·ne·ko·lo·go/a

H

hair pelo m pe·lo
hairbrush cepillo m se·pee·yo
haircut corte m de pelo kor·te de pe·lo
hairdresser peluquero/a m/f
pe·loo·ke·ro/a
halal halal kha·lal
half medio/a m/f me·dyo/a
half a litre medio litro m me·dyo
lee·tro
hallucinate alucinar a·loo·see·nar
ham jamón m kha·mon
hammer martillo m mar·tee·yo
hammock hamaca f a·ma·ka
hand mano f ma·no
handbag bolsa f bol·sa
handicrafts artesanías f pl
ar·te·sa·nee·as
handkerchief pañuelo m pa·nywe·lo
handlebar manubrio m ma·noo·bryo
handmade hecho/a m/f a mano
e·cho/a a ma·no
handsome guapo/a m/f gwa·po/a
happy feliz fe·lees
harassment acoso m a·ko·so
harbour puerto m pwer·to
hard duro/a m/f doo·ro/a
hardware store tlapalería f
tla·pa·le·ree·a
hash hachís m kha·shees
hat sombrero m som·bre·ro
have tener te·ner
have a cold tener gripa te·ner gree·pa
have fun divertirse dee·ver·teer·se
hay fever alergia f al polen
a·ler·khya al po·len
he él el
head cabeza f ka·be·sa
headache dolor m de cabeza
do·lor de ka·be·sa
headlights faros m pl fa·ros
health salud f sa·lood
hear oír o·eer
hearing aid audífono m ow·dee·fo·no
heart corazón m ko·ra·son

heart condition *cardiopatía* ①
kar·dyo·pa·*tee*·a
heat *calor* ⓜ ka·*lor*
heater *calentador* ⓜ ka·len·ta·*dor*
heating *calefacción* ① ka·le·fak·*syon*
heavy *pesado/a* ⓜ/① pe·*sa*·do/a
helmet *casco* ⓜ *kas*·ko
help *ayudar* a·yoo·*dar*
hepatitis *hepatitis* ① e·pa·*tee*·tees
her *su* soo
herbalist *yerbero/a* ⓜ/① yer·*be*·ro/a
herbs *hierbas* ① pl *yer*·bas
here *aquí* a·*kee*
heroin *heroína* ① e·ro·*ee*·na
herring *arenque* ⓜ a·*ren*·ke
high *alto/a* ⓜ/① *al*·to/a
high school *la preparatoria* ①
la pre·pa·ra·*to*·rya
hike *ir de excursión* eer de
ek·skoor·*syon*
hiking *excursionismo* ⓜ
ek·skoor·syo·*nees*·mo
hiking boots *botas* ① pl *de montaña*
bo·tas de mon·*ta*·nya
hiking routes *caminos* ⓜ pl *rurales*
ka·*mee*·nos roo·*ra*·les
hill *colina* ① ko·*lee*·na
Hindu *hindú* ⓜ&① een·*doo*
hire *rentar* ren·*tar*
his *su* soo
historical *histórico/a* ⓜ/①
ees·*to*·ree·ko/a
hitchhike *pedir aventón*
pe·*deer* a·ven·*ton*
HIV positive *seropositivo/a* ⓜ/①
se·ro·po·see·*tee*·vo/a
hockey *hockey* ⓜ *kho*·kee
holiday *día* ⓜ *festivo* *dee*·a fes·*tee*·vo
holidays *vacaciones* ① pl
va·ka·*syo*·nes
Holy Week *Semana* ① *Santa*
se·*ma*·na *san*·ta
home *casa* ① *ka*·sa
homeless *sin hogar* seen o·*gar*
homemaker *ama* ① *de casa*
a·ma de *ka*·sa

homosexual *homosexual* ⓜ&①
o·mo·sek·*swal*
honey *miel* ① myel
honeymoon *luna* ① *de miel*
loo·na de myel
horoscope *horóscopo* ⓜ o·*ros*·ko·po
horse *caballo* ⓜ ka·*ba*·yo
horse riding *equitación* ①
e·kee·ta·*syon*
hospital *hospital* ⓜ os·pee·*tal*
hospitality *hotelería* ① o·te·le·*ree*·a
hot *caliente* ka·*lyen*·te
hot water *agua* ⓜ *caliente*
a·gwa ka·*lyen*·te
hotel *hotel* ⓜ o·*tel*
house *casa* ① *ka*·sa
housework *trabajo* ⓜ *de casa*
tra·*ba*·kho de *ka*·sa
how *cómo* *ko*·mo
how much *cuánto* *kwan*·to
hug *abrazo* ⓜ a·*bra*·so
huge *enorme* e·*nor*·me
human rights *derechos* ⓜ pl *humanos*
de·*re*·chos oo·*ma*·nos
humanities *humanidades* ① pl
oo·ma·nee·*da*·des
(be) hungry *tener hambre* te·*ner* am·bre
hunting *caza* ① *ka*·sa
(be in a) hurry *tener prisa* te·*ner* *pree*·sa
hurt *lastimar* las·tee·*mar*
husband *esposo* ⓜ es·*po*·so

I

I *yo* yo
ice *hielo* ⓜ *ye*·lo
ice axe *piolet* ⓜ pyo·*let*
ice cream *helado* ⓜ e·*la*·do
ice-cream parlour *heladería* ①
e·la·de·*ree*·a
ice hockey *hockey* ⓜ *sobre hielo*
kho·kee so·bre *ye*·lo
identification *identificación* ①
ee·den·tee·fee·ka·*syon*
idiot *idiota* ⓜ&① ee·*dyo*·ta
if *si* see
ill *enfermo/a* ⓜ/① en·*fer*·mo/a

immigration *inmigración* ①
een·mee·gra·syon
important *importante* eem·por·*tan*·te
in a hurry *de prisa* pree·sa
in front of *enfrente de* en·*fren*·te de
included *incluído/a* ⓜ/①
een·kloo·ee·do/a
income tax *impuesto* ⓜ *sobre la renta*
eem·*pwes*·to so·bre la *ren*·ta
India *India* ① een·dya
indicator *indicador* ⓜ een·dee·ka·*dor*
indigestion *indigestión* ①
een·dee·khes·*tyon*
industry *industria* ① een·*doos*·trya
infection *infección* ① een·fek·*syon*
inflammation *inflamación* ①
een·fla·ma·*syon*
influenza *gripe* ① *gree*·pe
ingredient *ingrediente* ⓜ
een·gre·*dyen*·te
inject *inyectar* een·yek·*tar*
injection *inyección* ① een·yek·*syon*
injury *herida* ① e·*ree*·da
innocent *inocente* ee·no·*sen*·te
inside *adentro* a·*den*·tro
instructor *instructor/instructora* ⓜ/①
een·strook·*tor*/eens·trook·*to*·ra
insurance *seguro* ⓜ se·*goo*·ro
interesting *interesante*
een·te·re·*san*·te
intermission *descanso* ⓜ des·*kan*·so
international *internacional*
een·ter·na·syo·*nal*
Internet *Internet* ① een·ter·*net*
Internet cafe *café Internet* ⓜ
ka·*fe* een·ter·*net*
interpreter *intérprete* ⓜ&①
een·*ter*·pre·te
intersection *intersección* ①
een·ter·sek·*syon*
interview *entrevista* ① en·tre·*vees*·ta
invite *invitar* een·vee·*tar*
Ireland *Irlanda* ① eer·*lan*·da
iron (for clothes) *plancha* ① *plan*·cha
island *isla* ① *ees*·la
IT *informática* ① een·for·*ma*·tee·ka
itch *comezón* ⓜ ko·me·*son*

itemised *detallado/a* ⓜ/①
de·ta·*ya*·do/a
itinerary *itinerario* ⓜ ee·tee·ne·*ra*·ryo
IUD *DIU* ⓜ dee·*oo*

jacket *chamarra* ① cha·*ma*·ra
jail *cárcel* ① *kar*·sel
jam *mermelada* ① mer·me·*la*·da
Japan *Japón* ⓜ kha·*pon*
jar *jarra* ① *kha*·ra
jaw *mandíbula* ① man·*dee*·boo·la
jealous *celoso/a* ⓜ/① se·*lo*·so/a
jeans *jeans* ⓜ pl yeens
jeep *jeep* ⓜ yeep
Jehova's witness *testigo* ⓜ *de Jehová*
tes·*tee*·go de khe·o·*va*
jet lag *jet lag* ⓜ yet lag
jewellery *joyería* ① kho·ye·*ree*·a
Jewish *judío/a* ⓜ/① khoo·*dee*·o/a
job *trabajo* ⓜ tra·*ba*·kho
jockey *jockey* ⓜ *yo*·kee
jogging *correr* ko·*rer*
joke *broma* ① *bro*·ma
joke *bromear* bro·me·*ar*
journalist *periodista* ⓜ&①
pe·ryo·*dees*·ta
judge *juez* ⓜ&① khwes
juice *jugo* ⓜ *khoo*·go
jump *saltar* sal·*tar*
jumper (sweater) *sweater* ⓜ *swe*·ter
jumper leads *cables* ⓜ pl *pasacorrientes*
ka·bles pa·sa·ko·*ryen*·tes

ketchup *cátsup* ⓜ *kat*·soop
key *llave* ① *ya*·ve
keyboard *teclado* ⓜ te·*kla*·do
kick *patear* pa·te·*ar*
kick (a goal) *meter (un gol)*
me·*ter* (oon gol)
kill *matar* ma·*tar*
kilogram *kilo* ⓜ *kee*·lo
kilometre *kilómetro* ⓜ kee·*lo*·me·tro
kind *amable* a·*ma*·ble

kindergarten *jardín* ⓜ *de niños*
khar·*deen* de *nee*·nyos
king *rey* ⓜ ray
kiss *beso* ⓜ *be*·so
kiss *besar* be·*sar*
kitchen *cocina* ① ko·*see*·na
kitten *gatito/a* ⓜ/① ga·*tee*·to/a
kiwifruit *kiwi* ⓜ *kee*·wee
knapsack *mochila* ① mo·*chee*·la
knee *rodilla* ① ro·*dee*·ya
knife *cuchillo* ⓜ koo·*chee*·yo
know (someone) *conocer* ko·no·*ser*
know (something) *saber* sa·*ber*
kosher *kosher* ko·*sher*

L

labourer *obrero/a* ⓜ/① o·*bre*·ro/a
lace *encaje* ⓜ en·*ka*·khe
lager *cerveza* ① *clara* ser·*ve*·sa *kla*·ra
lake *lago* ⓜ *la*·go
lamb *borrego* ⓜ bo·*re*·go
land *tierra* ① *tye*·ra
landlady *propietaria* ① pro·pye·*ta*·rya
landlord *propietario* ① pro·pye·*ta*·ryo
languages *idiomas* ⓜ pl ee·*dyo*·mas
laptop *computadora* ① *portátil*
kom·poo·ta·*do*·ra por·*ta*·teel
lard *manteca* ① man·*te*·ka
large *grande* *gran*·de
laser pointer *señalador* ⓜ *láser*
se·nya·la·*dor* *la*·ser
late *tarde* *tar*·de
laugh *reír* re·*eer*
laundrette *lavandería* ①
la·van·de·*ree*·a
laundry *lavandería* ① la·van·de·*ree*·a
law *ley* ① lay
law (field of study) *derecho* ⓜ
de·*re*·cho
lawyer *abogado/a* ⓜ/① a·bo·*ga*·do/a
leader *líder* ⓜ&① *lee*·der
leaf *hoja* ① *o*·kha
learn *aprender* a·pren·*der*
leather *cuero* ⓜ *kwe*·ro
lecturer *profesor/profesora* ⓜ/①
pro·fe·*sor*/pro·fe·*so*·ra

ledge *saliente* ⓜ sa·*lyen*·te
leek *poro* ⓜ *po*·ro
left *izquierda* ① ees·*kyer*·da
left luggage *consigna* ① kon·*seeg*·na
left-wing *de izquierda* de ees·*kyer*·da
leg *pierna* ① *pyer*·na
legal *legal* le·*gal*
legislation *legislación* ①
le·khees·la·*syon*
lemon *limón* ⓜ lee·*mon*
lemonade *limonada* ① lee·mo·na·da
lens *objetivo* ⓜ ob·khe·*tee*·vo
Lent *Cuaresma* ① kwa·*res*·ma
lentils *lentejas* ① pl len·*te*·khas
lesbian *lesbiana* ① les·bee·*a*·na
less *menos* *me*·nos
letter *carta* ① *kar*·ta
lettuce *lechuga* ① le·*choo*·ga
liar *mentiroso/a* ⓜ/① men·tee·ro·so/a
library *biblioteca* ① bee·blyo·*te*·ka
lice *piojos* ⓜ pl *pyo*·khos
license plate number *número* ⓜ *de*
placa *noo*·me·ro de *pla*·ka
lie (not stand) *recostarse* re·kos·*tar*·se
life *vida* ① *vee*·da
life jacket *chaleco* ⓜ *salvavidas*
cha·*le*·ko sal·va·*vee*·das
lift *elevador* ⓜ e·le·va·*dor*
light (of weight) *ligero/a* ⓜ/①
lee·*khe*·ro/a
light *luz* ① loos
light bulb *foco* ⓜ *fo*·ko
light meter *fotómetro* ⓜ fo·*to*·me·tro
lighter *encendedor* ⓜ en·sen·de·*dor*
lights *luces* ① pl *loo*·ses
like *gustar* goos·*tar*
lime *lima* ① *lee*·ma
line *línea* ① *lee*·ne·a
lip balm *bálsamo* ⓜ *para labios*
bal·sa·mo *pa*·ra *la*·byos
lips *labios* ⓜ pl *la*·byos
lipstick *lápiz* ⓜ *labial* *la*·pees *la*·byal
liquor store *vinatería* ①
vee·na·te·*ree*·a
listen *escuchar* es·koo·*char*
live *vivir* vee·*veer*
liver *hígado* ⓜ *ee*·ga·do

lizard *lagartija* ① la·gar·*tee*·kha
local *local* lo·*kal*
lock *cerradura* ① se·ra·*doo*·ra
lock *cerrar* se·*rar*
locked *cerrado/a con llave* ⑩/① se·ra·do/a kon *ya*·ve
lollies *dulces* ⑩ pl *dool*·ses
long *largo/a* ⑩/① *lar*·go/a
long-distance *larga distancia* ① *lar*·ga dees·*tan*·sya
look *mirar* mee·*rar*
look after *cuidar* kwee·*dar*
look for *buscar* boos·*kar*
lookout *mirador* ⑩ mee·ra·*dor*
loose *suelto/a* ⑩/① *swel*·to/a
loose change *cambio* ⑩ *en monedas* *kam*·byo en mo·*ne*·das
lose *perder* per·*der*
lost *perdido/a* ⑩/① per·*dee*·do/a
lost property office *oficina* ① *de objetos perdidos* o·fee·*see*·na de ob·*khe*·tos per·*dee*·dos
loud *ruidoso/a* ⑩/① rwee·*do*·so/a
love *amar* a·*mar*
lover *amante* ⑩&① a·*man*·te
low *bajo/a* ⑩/① *ba*·kho/a
lubricant *lubricante* ⑩ loo·bree·*kan*·te
luck *suerte* ① *swer*·te
lucky *afortunado/a* ⑩/① a·for·too·*na*·do/a
luggage *equipaje* ⑩ e·kee·*pa*·khe
luggage lockers *casilleros* ⑩ pl ka·see·*ye*·ros
luggage tag *etiqueta* ① *para equipaje* e·tee·*ke*·ta *pa*·ra e·kee·*pa*·khe
lump *bulto* ⑩ *bool*·to
lunch *almuerzo* ⑩ al·*mwer*·so
lungs *pulmones* ⑩ pl pool·*mo*·nes
luxury *lujo* ⑩ *loo*·kho

M

machine *máquina* ① *ma*·kee·na
made of (cotton) *hecho/a* ⑩/① *de (algodón)* e·cho/a de (al·go·*don*)
magazine *revista* ① re·*vees*·ta
magician *mago/a* ⑩/① *ma*·go/a

mail *correo* ⑩ ko·*re*·o
mailbox *buzón* ⑩ boo·*son*
main *principal* preen·see·*pal*
make *hacer* a·*ser*
make fun of *burlarse de* boor·*lar*·se de
make-up *maquillaje* ⑩ ma·kee·*ya*·khe
mammogram *mamograma* ⑩ ma·mo·*gra*·ma
man *hombre* ⑩ *om*·bre
manager *director/directora* ⑩/① dee·rek·*tor*/deerek·*to*·ra
mandarin *mandarina* ① man·da·*ree*·na
mango *mango* ⑩ *man*·go
manual worker *obrero/a* ⑩/① o·*bre*·ro/a
many *muchos/as* ⑩/① pl *moo*·chos/as
map *mapa* ⑩ *ma*·pa
margarine *margarina* ① mar·ga·*ree*·na
marijuana *marihuana* ① ma·ree·*wa*·na
marital status *estado* ⑩ *civil* es·*ta*·do see·*veel*
market *mercado* ⑩ mer·*ka*·do
marmalade *mermelada* ① mer·me·*la*·da
marriage *matrimonio* ⑩ ma·tree·*mo*·nyo
married *casado/a* ⑩/① ka·*sa*·do/a
marry *casarse* ka·*sar*·se
martial arts *artes* ⑩ pl *marciales* *ar*·tes mar·*sya*·les
mass *misa* ① *mee*·sa
massage *masaje* ⑩ ma·*sa*·khe
masseur/masseuse *masajista* ⑩&① ma·sa·*khees*·ta
mat *petate* ⑩ pe·*ta*·te
match (game) *partido* ⑩ par·*tee*·do
matches *cerillos* ⑩ pl se·*ree*·yos
mattress *colchón* ⑩ kol·*chon*
maybe *tal vez* tal ves
mayonnaise *mayonesa* ① ma·yo·*ne*·sa
mayor *alcalde* ⑩&① al·*kal*·de
measles *sarampión* ⑩ sa·ram·*pyon*
meat *carne* ① *kar*·ne

mechanic *mecánico/a* ⓜ/ⓕ
me·*ka*·nee·ko/a
media *medios* ⓜ pl *de comunicación*
me·dyos de ko·moo·nee·ka·*syon*
medicine *medicina* ⓕ me·dee·*see*·na
meet *encontrar* en·kon·*trar*
melon *melón* ⓜ me·*lon*
member *miembro* ⓜ *myem*·bro
menstruation *menstruación* ⓕ
men·strwa·*syon*
menu *menú* ⓜ me·*noo*
message *mensaje* ⓜ men·*sa*·khe
metal *metal* ⓜ me·*tal*
metre *metro* ⓜ *me*·tro
metro station *estación* ⓕ *del metro*
es·ta·*syon* del *me*·tro
microwave *horno* ⓜ *de microondas*
or·no de mee·kro·*on*·das
midnight *medianoche* ⓕ
me·dya·*no*·che
migraine *migraña* ⓕ mee·*gra*·nya
military *militar* mee·lee·*tar*
military service *servicio* ⓜ *militar*
ser·*vee*·syo mee·lee·*tar*
milk *leche* ⓕ *le*·che
millimetre *milímetro* ⓜ mee·*lee*·me·tro
million *millón* ⓜ mee·*yon*
mince meat *carne* ⓕ *molida*
kar·ne mo·*lee*·da
mind *cuidar* kwee·*dar*
mineral water *agua* ⓕ *mineral*
a·gwa mee·ne·*ral*
mints *pastillas* ⓕ pl *de menta*
pas·*tee*·yas de *men*·ta
minute *minuto* ⓜ mee·*noo*·to
mirror *espejo* ⓜ es·*pe*·kho
miscarriage *aborto* ⓜ *natural*
a·*bor*·to na·too·*ral*
miss (feel absence of) *extrañar*
ek·stra·*nyar*
mistake *error* ⓜ e·*ror*
mix *mezclar* mes·*klar*
mobile phone *teléfono* ⓜ *celular*
te·*le*·fo·no se·loo·*lar*
modem *módem* ⓜ *mo*·dem
moisturiser *crema* ⓕ *hidratante*
kre·ma ee·dra·*tan*·te
monastery *monasterio* ⓜ
mo·nas·*te*·ryo

money *dinero* ⓜ dee·*ne*·ro
month *mes* ⓜ mes
monument *monumento* ⓜ
mo·noo·*men*·to
moon *luna* ⓕ *loo*·na
morning *mañana* ⓕ ma·*nya*·na
morning sickness *náuseas* ⓕ pl *del*
embarazo now·se·as del em·ba·*ra*·so
mosque *mezquita* ⓕ mes·*kee*·ta
mosquito *mosquito* ⓜ mos·*kee*·to
mosquito coil *repelente* ⓜ *contra*
mosquitos re·pe·*len*·te *kon*·tra
mos·*kee*·tos
mosquito net *mosquitero* ⓜ
mos·kee·*te*·ro
mother *madre* ⓕ *ma*·dre
mother-in-law *suegra* ⓕ *swe*·gra
motorboat *lancha* ⓕ *de motor*
lan·cha de mo·*tor*
motorcycle *motocicleta* ⓕ
mo·to·see·*kle*·ta
motorway *carretera* ⓕ ka·re·*te*·ra
mountain *montaña* ⓕ mon·*ta*·nya
mountain bike *bicicleta* ⓕ *de mon-*
taña bee·see·*kle*·ta de mon·*ta*·nya
mountain path *brecha* ⓕ *bre*·cha
mountain range *cordillera* ⓕ
kor·dee·*ye*·ra
mountaineering *alpinismo* ⓜ
al·pee·*nees*·mo
mouse *ratón* ⓜ ra·*ton*
mouse (computer) *mouse* ⓜ mows
mouth *boca* ⓕ *bo*·ka
movie *película* ⓕ pe·*lee*·koo·la
MP3 player *reproductor* ⓜ *de MP3*
re·pro·dook·*tor* de e·me pe tres
mud *lodo* ⓜ *lo*·do
muesli *granola* ⓕ gra·*no*·la
mum *mamá* ⓕ ma·*ma*
muscle *músculo* ⓜ *moos*·koo·lo
museum *museo* ⓜ moo·*se*·o
mushroom *champiñón* ⓜ
cham·pee·*nyon*
music *música* ⓕ *moo*·see·ka
musician *músico/a* ⓜ/ⓕ moo·*see*·ko/a
Muslim *musulmán/musulmana* ⓜ/ⓕ
moo·sool·*man*/moo·sool·*ma*·na

mussels *mejillones* ⓜ pl
me·khee·yo·nes
mustard *mostaza* ⓕ mos·ta·sa
mute *mudo/a* ⓜ/ⓕ moo·do/a
my *mi* mee

N

nail clippers *cortauñas* ⓜ
kor·ta·oo·nyas
name *nombre* ⓜ nom·bre
napkin *servilleta* ⓕ ser·vee·ye·ta
nappy *pañal* ⓜ pa·nyal
nappy rash *rosadura* ⓕ ro·sa·doo·ra
national park *parque* ⓜ *nacional*
par·ke na·syo·nal
nationality *nacionalidad* ⓕ
na·syo·na·lee·dad
nature *naturaleza* ⓕ na·too·ra·le·sa
naturopathy *naturopatía* ⓕ
na·too·ro·pa·tee·a
nausea *náusea* ⓕ now·se·a
near *cerca* ser·ka
nearby *cerca* ser·ka
nearest *más cercano/a* ⓜ/ⓕ
mas ser·ka·no/a
necessary *necesario/a* ⓜ/ⓕ
ne·se·sa·ryo/a
neck *cuello* ⓜ kwe·yo
necklace *collar* ⓜ ko·yar
need *necesitar* ne·se·see·tar
needle (sewing) *aguja* ⓕ a·goo·kha
needle (syringe) *jeringa* ⓕ
khe·reen·ga
negatives *negativos* ⓜ pl
ne·ga·tee·vos
neither *tampoco* tam·po·ko
net *red* ⓕ red
network *red* ⓕ red
Netherlands *Holanda* ⓕ o·lan·da
never *nunca* noon·ka
new *nuevo/a* ⓜ/ⓕ nwe·vo/a
New Year *Año Nuevo* ⓜ a·nyo nwe·vo
New Year's Day *día* ⓜ *de Año Nuevo*
dee·a de a·nyo nwe·vo
New Year's Eve *fin* ⓜ *de año*
feen de a·nyo

New Zealand *Nueva* ⓕ *Zelandia*
nwe·va se·lan·dya
news *noticias* ⓕ pl no·tee·syas
news stand *puesto* ⓜ *de periódicos*
pwes·to de pe·ryo·dee·kos
newsagency *agencia* ⓕ *de noticias*
a·khen·sya de no·tee·syas
newspaper *periódico* ⓜ pe·ryo·dee·ko
next *próximo/a* ⓜ/ⓕ prok·see·mo/a
next (month) *(el mes) que viene*
(el mes) ke vye·ne
next to *al lado de* al la·do de
nice *simpático/a* ⓜ/ⓕ
seem·pa·tee·ko/a
nickname *apodo* ⓜ a·po·do
night *noche* ⓕ no·che
no *no* no
noisy *ruidoso/a* ⓜ/ⓕ rwee·do·so/a
none *nada* na·da
non-smoking *no fumar* no foo·mar
noodles *fideos* ⓜ pl fee·de·os
noon *mediodía* ⓜ me·dyo·dee·a
north *norte* ⓜ nor·te
nose *nariz* ⓕ na·rees
notebook *cuaderno* ⓜ kwa·der·no
nothing *nada* na·da
now *ahora* a·o·ra
nuclear energy *energía* ⓕ *nuclear*
e·ner·khee·a noo·kle·ar
nuclear testing *pruebas* ⓕ pl
nucleares prwe·bas noo·kle·a·res
nuclear waste *desperdicios* ⓜ pl
nucleares des·per·dee·syos
noo·kle·a·res
number *número* ⓜ noo·me·ro
nun *monja* ⓕ mon·kha
nurse *enfermero/a* ⓜ/ⓕ en·fer·me·ro/a
nuts *nueces* ⓕ pl nwe·ses

O

oats *avena* ⓕ a·ve·na
ocean *océano* ⓜ o·se·a·no
off (spoiled) *hechado/a* ⓜ/ⓕ *a perder*
e·cha·do/a a per·der
office *oficina* ⓕ o·fee·see·na

office worker *empleado/a* ⓜ/ⓕ
  em·ple·*a*·do/a
offside *fuera de lugar* fwe·ra de loo·*gar*
often *seguido* se·*gee*·do
oil *aceite* ⓜ a·*say*·te
old *viejo/a* ⓜ/ⓕ vye·kho/a
olive oil *aceite de oliva*
  a·*say*·te de o·*lee*·va
Olympic Games *juegos* ⓜ pl *olímpicos*
  khwe·gos o·*leem*·pee·kos
on *en* en
once *una vez* oona ves
one-way ticket *boleto* ⓜ *sencillo*
  bo·*le*·to sen·*see*·yo
onion *cebolla* ⓕ se·*bo*·ya
only *sólo* so·lo
open *abierto/a* ⓜ/ⓕ a·byer·to/a
open *abrir* a·*breer*
opening hours *horario* ⓜ *de servicio*
  o·*ra*·ryo de ser·*vee*·syo
opera *ópera* ⓕ o·pe·ra
operation *operación* ⓕ o·pe·ra·*syon*
operator *operador/operadora* ⓜ/ⓕ
  o·pe·ra·*dor*/o·pe·ra·*do*·ra
opinion *opinión* ⓕ o·pee·*nyon*
opposite *frente a* fren·te a
or *o* o
orange *naranja* ⓕ na·*ran*·kha
orange (colour) *naranja* na·*ran*·kha
orange juice *jugo* ⓜ *de naranja*
  khoo·go de na·*ran*·kha
orchestra *orquesta* ⓕ or·kes·ta
order (command) *orden* ⓕ or·den
order (placement) *orden* ⓜ or·den
order *ordenar* or·de·*nar*
ordinary *corriente* ko·ryen·te
orgasm *orgasmo* ⓜ or·gas·mo
original *original* o·ree·khee·*nal*
other *otro/a* ⓜ/ⓕ o·tro/a
our *nuestro/a* ⓜ/ⓕ nwes·tro/a
outside *exterior* ⓜ ek·ste·*ryor*
ovarian cyst *quiste* ⓜ *ovárico*
  kees·te o·va·ree·ko
oven *horno* ⓜ or·no
overcoat *abrigo* ⓜ a·*bree*·go
overdose *sobredosis* ⓕ so·bre·*do*·sees

overhead projector *proyector* ⓜ *de acetatos* pro·yek·tor de a·se·*ta*·tos
owe *deber* de·*ber*
owner *dueño/a* ⓜ/ⓕ dwe·nyo/a
oxygen *oxígeno* ⓜ ok·*see*·khe·no
oyster *ostión* ⓜ os·tyon
ozone layer *capa* ⓕ *de ozono*
  ka·pa de o·so·no

P

pacemaker *marcapasos* ⓜ
  mar·ka·*pa*·sos
pacifier *chupón* ⓜ choo·*pon*
package *paquete* ⓜ pa·ke·te
packet *paquete* ⓜ pa·ke·te
padlock *candado* ⓜ kan·*da*·do
page *página* ⓕ *pa*·khee·na
pain *dolor* ⓜ do·lor
painful *doloroso/a* ⓜ/ⓕ do·lo·ro·so/a
painkillers *analgésicos* ⓜ pl
  a·nal·*khe*·see·kos
paint *pintar* peen·*tar*
painter *pintor/pintora* ⓜ/ⓕ
  peen·*tor*/peen·*to*·ra
painting *pintura* ⓕ peen·*too*·ra
pair (couple) *pareja* ⓕ pa·re·kha
palace *palacio* ⓜ pa·*la*·syo
palm pilot *palm* ⓜ palm
pan *sartén* ⓜ sar·ten
pants *pantalones* ⓜ pl pan·ta·*lo*·nes
panty liners *pantiprotectores* ⓜ pl
  pan·tee·pro·tek·*to*·res
pantyhose *pantimedias* ⓕ pl
  pan·tee·me·dyas
pap smear *papanicolaou* ⓜ
  pa·pa·nee·ko·low
paper *papel* ⓜ pa·pel
paperwork *trámites* ⓜ *tra*·mee·tes
paraplegic *parapléjico/a* ⓜ/ⓕ
  pa·ra·*ple*·khee·ko/a
parcel *paquete* ⓜ pa·ke·te
parents *padres* ⓜ pl *pa*·dres
park *parque* ⓜ par·ke
park (car) *estacionar* es·ta·syo·*nar*
parliament *parlamento* ⓜ
  par·la·*men*·to

parsley *perejil* ⓜ pe·re·*kheel*
part *parte* ⓕ *par*·te
partner (intimate) *pareja* ⓕ pa·*re*·kha
part-time *medio tiempo*
  me·dyo *tyem*·po
party *fiesta* ⓕ *fyes*·ta
party (political) *partido* ⓜ par·*tee*·do
pass *pase* ⓜ *pa*·se
passenger *pasajero/a* ⓜ/ⓕ
  pa·sa·*khe*·ro/a
passport *pasaporte* ⓜ pa·sa·*por*·te
passport number *número* ⓜ *de*
  pasaporte *noo*·me·ro de pa·sa·*por*·te
past *pasado* ⓜ pa·*sa*·do
pasta *pasta* ⓕ *pas*·ta
pate (food) *paté* ⓜ pa·*te*
path *sendero* ⓜ sen·*de*·ro
pay *pagar* pa·*gar*
payment *pago* ⓜ *pa*·go
peace *paz* ⓕ pas
peach *durazno* ⓜ doo·*ras*·no
peak *cumbre* ⓕ *koom*·bre
peanuts *cacahuates* ⓜ ka·ka·*wa*·tes
pear *pera* ⓕ *pe*·ra
peas *chícharos* ⓜ pl *chee*·cha·ros
pedal *pedal* ⓜ pe·*dal*
pedestrian *peatón* ⓜ pe·a·*ton*
pedestrian crossing *cruce* ⓜ *peatonal*
  kroo·se pe·a·to·*nal*
pen *pluma* ⓕ *ploo*·ma
pencil *lápiz* ⓜ *la*·pees
penis *pene* ⓜ *pe*·ne
penknife *navaja* ⓕ na·*va*·kha
pensioner *jubilado/a* ⓜ/ⓕ
  khoo·bee·*la*·do/a
people *gente* ⓕ *khen*·te
pepper (bell) *pimiento* ⓜ
  pee·*myen*·to
pepper (spice) *pimienta* ⓕ
  pee·*myen*·ta
per (day) *por (día)* por (*dee*·a)
percent *por ciento* por *syen*·to
performance *desempeño* ⓜ
  des·em·*pe*·nyo
perfume *perfume* ⓜ per·*foo*·me
period pain *cólico* ⓜ *menstrual*
  ko·lee·ko men·*strwal*
permission *permiso* ⓜ per·*mee*·so

permit *permiso* ⓜ per·*mee*·so
permit *permitir* per·mee·*teer*
person *persona* ⓕ per·*so*·na
perspire *sudar* soo·*dar*
petition *petición* ⓕ pe·tee·*syon*
petrol *gasolina* ⓕ ga·so·*lee*·na
pharmacy *farmacia* ⓕ far·*ma*·sya
phone book *directorio* ⓜ *telefónico*
  dee·rek·*to*·ryo te·le·*fo*·nee·ko
phone box *teléfono* ⓜ *público*
  te·*le*·fo·no *poo*·blee·ko
phone card *tarjeta* ⓕ *de teléfono*
  tar·*khe*·ta de te·*le*·fo·no
photo *fotografía* ⓕ fo·to·gra·*fee*·a
photocopier *fotocopiadora* ⓕ
  fo·to·ko·pya·*do*·ra
photographer *fotógrafo/a* ⓜ/ⓕ
  fo·*to*·gra·fo/a
photography *fotografía* ⓕ
  fo·to·gra·*fee*·a
phrasebook *libro* ⓜ *de frases*
  lee·bro de *fra*·ses
pick-up (truck) *pickup* pee·*kop*
pick up (lift) *levantar* le·van·*tar*
pick up (seduce) *ligar* lee·*gar*
pickaxe *pico* ⓜ *pee*·ko
picnic *día* ⓜ *de campo*
  dee·a de *kam*·po
pie *pay* ⓜ pay
piece *pedazo* ⓜ pe·*da*·so
pig *cerdo* ⓜ *ser*·do
pill *pastilla* ⓕ pas·*tee*·ya
the Pill *la píldora* ⓕ la *peel*·do·ra
pillow *almohada* ⓕ al·*mwa*·da
pillowcase *funda* ⓕ *de almohada*
  foon·da de al·*mwa*·da
pineapple *piña* ⓕ *pee*·nya
pink *rosa* *ro*·sa
pistachio *pistache* ⓜ pees·*ta*·che
place *lugar* ⓜ loo·*gar*
place of birth *lugar* ⓜ *de nacimiento*
  loo·*gar* de na·see·*myen*·to
plane *avión* ⓜ a·*vyon*
planet *planeta* ⓜ pla·*ne*·ta
plant *planta* ⓕ *plan*·ta
plant *sembrar* sem·*brar*
plastic *plástico* ⓜ *plas*·tee·ko
plate *plato* ⓜ *pla*·to

plateau *meseta* ① me·se·ta
platform *plataforma* ① pla·ta·for·ma
play *obra* ① o·bra
play (an instrument) *tocar* to·kar
play (game/sport) *jugar* khoo·gar
plug (bath) *tapón* ① ta·pon
plug (electrical) *chavija* ① cha·vee·kha
plum *ciruela* ① seer·we·la
pocket *bolsillo* ⓜ bol·see·yo
poetry *poesía* ① po·e·see·a
point *apuntar* a·poon·tar
point (tip) *punto* ⓜ poon·to
poisonous *venenoso/a* ⓜ/①
    ve·ne·no·so/a
poker *póquer* ⓜ po·ker
police *policía* ① po·lee·see·a
police officer *oficial de policía*
    o·fee·syal de po·lee·see·a
police station *estación* ① *de policía*
    es·ta·syon de po·lee·see·a
policy *política* ① po·lee·tee·ka
policy (insurance) *póliza* ① po·lee·sa
politician *político* ⓜ po·lee·tee·ko
politics *política* ① po·lee·tee·ka
pollen *polen* ⓜ po·len
polls *encuestas* ① pl en·kwes·tas
pollution *contaminación* ①
    kon·ta·mee·na·syon
pony *pony* ⓜ po·nee
pool (game) *billar* ⓜ bee·yar
pool (swimming) *alberca* ① al·ber·ka
poor *pobre* po·bre
pope *Papa* ⓜ pa·pa
popular *popular* po·poo·lar
pork *cerdo* ⓜ ser·do
pork sausage *chorizo* ⓜ cho·ree·so
port *puerto* ⓜ pwer·to
port (wine) *oporto* ⓜ o·por·to
portable CD player *reproductor* ⓜ *de*
    compacts portátil re·pro·dook·tor de
    kom·pakts por·ta·teel
possible *posible* po·see·ble
post code *código* ⓜ *postal*
    ko·dee·go pos·tal
post office *oficina* ① *de correos*
    o·fee·see·na de ko·re·os
postage *timbre* ⓜ teem·bre

postcard *postal* ① pos·tal
poste restante *lista* ① *de correos*
    lees·ta de ko·re·os
poster *póster* ⓜ pos·ter
pot (kitchen) *cazuela* ① kas·we·la
pot (for plant) *maceta* ① ma·se·ta
pot (marijuana) *mota* ① mo·ta
potato *papa* ① pa·pa
pottery *alfarería* ① al·fa·re·ree·a
pound (money) *libra* ① lee·bra
poverty *pobreza* ① po·bre·sa
power *poder* ⓜ po·der
prawn *camarón* ① ka·ma·ron
prayer *oración* ① o·ra·syon
prayer book *libro* ⓜ *de oraciones*
    lee·bro de o·ra·syo·nes
prefer *preferir* pre·fe·reer
pregnancy test kit *prueba* ① *de*
    embarazo prwe·ba de em·ba·ra·so
pregnant *embarazada* em·ba·ra·sa·da
premenstrual tension *síndrome* ⓜ
    premenstrual seen·dro·me
    pre·men·strwal
prepare *preparar* pre·pa·rar
president *presidente/a* ⓜ/①
    pre·see·den·te/a
pressure *presión* ① pre·syon
pretty *bonito/a* ⓜ/① bo·nee·to/a
prevent *prevenir* pre·ve·neer
price *precio* ⓜ pre·syo
priest *sacerdote* ⓜ sa·ser·do·te
primary school *la primaria* ⓜ
    la pree·ma·rya
prime minister (man) *primer ministro*
    ⓜ pree·mer mee·nees·tro
prime minister (woman) *primera*
    ministra ① pree·me·ra mee·nees·tra
printer *impresora* ① eem·pre·so·ra
prison *cárcel* ① kar·sel
prisoner *prisionero/a* ⓜ/①
    pree·syo·ne·ro/a
private *privado/a* ⓜ/① pre·va·do/a
private hospital *hospital* ⓜ *privado*
    os·pee·tal pree·va·do
produce *producir* pro·doo·seer
profit *ganancia* ⓜ ga·nan·sya

programme *programa* ⓜ pro-*gra*-ma
projector *proyector* ⓜ pro-yek-*tor*
promise *promesa* ① pro-*me*-sa
protect *proteger* pro-te-*kher*
protected *protegido/a* ⓜ/①
  pro-te-*khee*-do/a
protest *protesta* ① pro-*tes*-ta
protest *protestar* pro-tes-*tar*
provisions *provisiones* ① pl
  pro-vee-*syo*-nes
prune *ciruela* ① pasa seer-*we*-la *pa*-sa
pub *bar* ⓜ bar
public telephone *teléfono* ⓜ *público*
  te-*le*-fo-no *poo*-blee-ko
public toilets *baños* ⓜ pl *públicos*
  ba-nyos *poo*-blee-kos
pull *jalar* kha-*lar*
pump *bomba* ① *bom*-ba
pumpkin *calabaza* ① ka-la-*ba*-sa
puncture *ponchar* pon-*char*
punish *castigar* kas-tee-*gar*
puppy *cachorro* ⓜ ka-*cho*-ro
pure *puro/a* ⓜ/① *poo*-ro/a
purple *morado/a* ⓜ/① mo-*ra*-do/a
push *empujar* em-poo-*khar*
put *poner* po-*ner*

Q

qualifications *aptitudes* ① pl
  ap-tee-*too*-des
quality *calidad* ① ka-lee-*dad*
quarantine *cuarentena* ①
  kwa-ren-*te*-na
quarrel *pelea* ① pe-*le*-a
quarter *cuarto* ⓜ *kwar*-to
queen *reina* ① *ray*-na
question *pregunta* ① pre-*goon*-ta
question *preguntar* pre-goon-*tar*
queue *cola* ① *ko*-la
quick *rápido/a* ⓜ/① *ra*-pee-do/a
quiet *tranquilo/a* ⓜ/① tran-*kee*-lo/a
quiet *tranquilidad* ① tran-kee-lee-*dad*
quit *renunciar* re-noon-*syar*

R

rabbit *conejo* ⓜ ko-*ne*-kho
race (sport) *carrera* ① ka-*re*-ra
racetrack *pista* ① *pees*-ta
racing bike *bicicleta* ① *de carreras*
  bee-see-*kle*-ta de ka-*re*-ras
racquet *raqueta* ① ra-*ke*-ta
radiator *radiador* ⓜ ra-dya-*dor*
railway station *estación* ① *de tren*
  es-ta-*syon* de tren
rain *lluvia* ① *yoo*-vya
raincoat *impermeable* ⓜ
  eem-per-me-*a*-ble
rainbow *arcoiris* ⓜ ar-ko-ee-*rees*
raisin *uva* ① *pasa* *oo*-va *pa*-sa
rally *rally* ⓜ *ra*-lee
rape *violar* vyo-*lar*
rare *raro/a* ⓜ/① *ra*-ro/a
rash *irritación* ① ee-ree-ta-*syon*
raspberry *frambuesa* ① fram-*bwe*-sa
rat *rata* ① *ra*-ta
rate of pay *salario* ⓜ sa-*la*-ryo
raw *crudo/a* ⓜ/① *kroo*-do/a
razor *rastrillo* ⓜ ras-*tree*-yo
razor blades *navajas* ① pl *de razurar*
  na-*va*-khas de ra-soo-*rar*
read *leer* le-*er*
ready *listo/a* ⓜ/① *lees*-to/a
real estate agent *agente* ⓜ *inmobili-*
  ario a-*khen*-te een-mo-bee-*lya*-ryo
realise *darse cuenta de*
  dar-se kwen-ta de
realistic *realista* re-a-*lees*-ta
reason *razón* ① ra-*son*
receipt *recibo* ⓜ re-*see*-bo
receive *recibir* re-see-*beer*
recently *recientemente*
  re-syen-te-*men*-te
recognise *reconocer* re-ko-no-*ser*
recommend *recomendar*
  re-ko-men-*dar*
recording *grabación* ① gra-ba-*syon*
recyclable *reciclable* re-see-*kla*-ble
recycle *reciclar* re-see-*klar*
red *rojo/a* ⓜ/① *ro*-kho/a
referee *árbitro* ⓜ *ar*-bee-tro

reference *referencia* ① re·fe·*ren*·sya
refrigerator *refrigerador* ⑩ re·free·khe·ra·dor
refugee *refugiado/a* ⑩/① re·foo·*khya*·do/a
refund *reembolso* ⑩ re·em·*bol*·so
refund *reembolsar* re·em·bol·*sar*
refuse *negar(se)* ne·*gar*·(se)
registered mail *correo* ⑩ *certificado* ko·*re*·o ser·tee·fee·*ka*·do
regret *lamentar* la·men·*tar*
relationship *relación* ① re·la·*syon*
relax *relajarse* re·la·*khar*·se
relic *reliquia* ① re·*lee*·kya
religion *religión* ① re·lee·*khyon*
religious *religioso/a* ⑩/① re·lee·*khyo*·so/a
remember *recordar* re·kor·*dar*
remote *remoto/a* ⑩/① re·*mo*·to/a
remote control *control* ⑩ *remoto* kon·*trol* re·*mo*·to
rent *renta* ① *ren*·ta
rent *rentar* ren·*tar*
repair *reparar* re·pa·*rar*
repeat *repetir* re·pe·*teer*
republic *república* ① re·*poo*·blee·ka
reservation *reservación* ① re·ser·va·*syon*
reserve *reservar* re·ser·*var*
rest *descansar* des·kan·*sar*
restaurant *restaurante* ⑩ res·tow·*ran*·te
resumé *currículum* ⑩ koo·*ree*·koo·loom
retired *jubilado/a* ⑩/① khoo·bee·*la*·do/a
return *volver* vol·*ver*
return ticket *boleto* ⑩ *de viaje redondo* bo·*le*·to de *vya*·khe re·*don*·do
review *crítica* ① *kree*·tee·ka
rhythm *ritmo* ⑩ *reet*·mo
rice *arroz* ⑩ a·*ros*
rich *rico/a* ⑩/① *ree*·ko/a
ride *paseo* ⑩ pa·*se*·o
ride *montar* mon·*tar*
right (correct) *correcto/a* ⑩/① ko·*rek*·to/a
right (not left) *derecha* de·*re*·cha
right-wing *de derecha* de de·*re*·cha
ring *anillo* ① a·*nee*·yo

ring *llamar por teléfono* ya·*mar* por te·*le*·fo·no
rip-off *estafa* ① es·*ta*·fa
risk *riesgo* ⑩ *ryes*·go
river *río* ⑩ *ree*·o
road *camino* ⑩ ka·*mee*·no
rob *robar* ro·*bar*
rock *roca* ① *ro*·ka
rock (music) *rock* ⑩ rok
rock climbing *escalada* ① *en roca* es·ka·*la*·da en *ro*·ka
rock group *grupo* ⑩ *de rock* *groo*·po de rok
rollerblading *patinar* pa·*tee*·nar
romantic *romántico/a* ⑩/① ro·*man*·tee·ko/a
room *habitación* ① a·bee·ta·*syon*
room number *número* ⑩ *de habitación* *noo*·me·ro de a·bee·ta·*syon*
rope *cuerda* ① *kwer*·da
round *redondo/a* ⑩/① re·*don*·do/a
roundabout *glorieta* ① glo·*rye*·ta
route *ruta* ① *roo*·ta
rowing *remo* ⑩ *re*·mo
rubbish *basura* ① ba·*soo*·ra
rug *alfombra* ① al·*fom*·bra
rugby *rugby* ⑩ *roog*·bee
ruins *ruinas* ① pl *rwee*·nas
rules *reglas* ① pl *re*·glas
rum *ron* ⑩ ron
run *correr* ko·*rer*
run out of *quedarse sin* ke·*dar*·se seen

S

Sabbath *Sabbath* ⑩ sa·*bat*
sad *triste* *trees*·te
saddle *silla* ① *de montar* *see*·ya de mon·*tar*
safe *caja* ① *fuerte* ka·kha *fwer*·te
safe *seguro/a* ⑩/① se·*goo*·ro/a
safe sex *sexo* ⑩ *seguro* sek·so se·*goo*·ro
saint *santo/a* ⑩/① *san*·to/a
salad *ensalada* ① en·sa·*la*·da
salami *salami* ⑩ sa·*la*·mee
salary *salario* ⑩ sa·*la*·ryo
sales tax *IVA* ⑩ *ee*·va

salmon *salmón* ⓜ sal·*mon*

salt *sal* ⓕ sal

same *igual* ee·*gwal*

sand *arena* ⓕ a·*re*·na

sandals *sandalias* ⓕ pl san·*da*·lyas

sanitary napkins *toallas* ⓕ pl *femeninas* to·*a*·yas fe·me·*nee*·nas

sauna *sauna* ⓕ *sow*·na

sausage *salchicha* ⓕ sal·*chee*·cha

save *salvar* sal·*var*

save (money) *ahorrar* a·o·*rar*

say *decir* de·*seer*

scale (climb) *escalar* es·ka·*lar*

scarf *bufanda* ⓕ boo·*fan*·da

school *escuela* ⓕ es·*kwe*·la

science *ciencias* ⓕ pl *syen*·syas

scientist *científico/a* ⓜ/ⓕ syen·*tee*·fee·ko/a

scissors *tijeras* ⓕ pl tee·*khe*·ras

score *anotar* a·no·*tar*

scoreboard *marcador* ⓜ mar·ka·*dor*

Scotland *Escocia* ⓕ es·*ko*·sya

screen *pantalla* ⓕ pan·*ta*·ya

script *guión* ⓜ gee·*on*

sculpture *escultura* ⓕ es·kool·*too*·ra

sea *mar* ⓜ mar

seasick *mareado/a* ⓜ/ⓕ ma·re·*a*·do/a

seaside *costa* ⓕ *kos*·ta

season *estación* ⓕ es·ta·*syon*

season (in sport) *temporada* ⓕ tem·po·*ra*·da

seat *asiento* ⓜ a·*syen*·to

seatbelt *cinturón* ⓜ *de seguridad* seen·too·*ron* de se·goo·ree·*dad*

second *segundo* ⓜ se·*goon*·do

second *segundo/a* ⓜ/ⓕ se·*goon*·do/a

secondary school *la secundaria* ⓕ la se·goon·*da*·rya

second-hand *de segunda mano* de se·*goon*·da *ma*·no

secretary *secretario/a* ⓜ/ⓕ se·kre·*ta*·ryo/a

see *ver* ver

selfish *egoísta* e·go·*ees*·ta

self-service *autoservicio* ⓜ ow·to·ser·*vee*·syo

sell *vender* ven·*der*

send *enviar* en·*vyar*

sensible *sensible* sen·*see*·ble

sensual *sensual* sen·*swal*

separate *separado/a* ⓜ/ⓕ se·pa·*ra*·do/a

separate *separar* se·pa·*rar*

series *serie* ⓕ *se*·rye

serious *serio/a* ⓜ/ⓕ *se*·ryo/a

service station *gasolinera* ⓕ ga·so·lee·*ne*·ra

service-charge *cubierto* ⓜ koo·*byer*·to

several *varios/as* ⓜ/ⓕ *va*·ryos/as

sew *coser* ko·*ser*

sex *sexo* ⓜ *sek*·so

sexism *sexismo* ⓜ sek·*sees*·mo

sexy *sexy* *sek*·see

shadow *sombra* ⓕ *som*·bra

shampoo *shampoo* ⓜ sham·*poo*

shape *forma* ⓕ *for*·ma

share (with) *compartir* kom·par·*teer*

shave *rasurar* ra·soo·*rar*

shaving cream *espuma* ⓕ *de rasurar* es·*poo*·ma de ra·soo·*rar*

she *ella* e·ya

sheep *oveja* ⓕ o·*ve*·kha

sheet (bed) *sábana* ⓕ *sa*·ba·na

sheet (of paper) *hoja* ⓕ o·kha

shelf *repisa* ⓕ re·*pee*·sa

ship *barco* ⓜ *bar*·ko

ship *enviar* en·vee·*ar*

shirt *camisa* ⓕ ka·*mee*·sa

shoe shop *zapatería* ⓕ sa·pa·te·*ree*·a

shoes *zapatos* ⓜ pl sa·*pa*·tos

shoot *disparar* dees·pa·*rar*

shop *tienda* ⓕ *tyen*·da

shopping centre *centro* ⓜ *comercial* *sen*·tro ko·mer·*syal*

short (height) *bajo/a* ⓜ/ⓕ *ba*·kho/a

short (length) *corto/a* ⓜ/ⓕ *kor*·to/a

shortage *escasez* ⓕ es·ka·*ses*

shorts *shorts* ⓜ pl shorts

shoulder *hombro* ⓜ *om*·bro

shout *gritar* gree·*tar*

show *espectáculo* ⓜ es·pek·*ta*·koo·lo

show *mostrar* mos·*trar*

shower *regadera* ⓕ re·ga·*de*·ra

shrine *capilla* ① ka·*pee*·ya
shut *cerrado/a* ⓜ/① se·*ra*·do/a
shut *cerrar* se·*rar*
shy *tímido/a* ⓜ/① *tee*·mee·do/a
sick *enfermo/a* ⓜ/① en·*fer*·mo/a
side *lado* ⓜ *la*·do
sign *señal* ① se·*nyal*
sign *firmar* feer·*mar*
signature *firma* ① *feer*·ma
silk *seda* ① *se*·da
silver *plateado/a* ⓜ/① pla·te·*a*·do/a
silver *plata* ① *pla*·ta
SIM card *tarjeta* ① SIM
 tar·*khe*·ta seem
similar *similar* see·mee·*lar*
simple *sencillo/a* ⓜ/① sen·*see*·yo/a
since (time) *desde* *des*·de
sing *cantar* kan·*tar*
singer *cantante* ⓜ&① kan·*tan*·te
single *soltero/a* ⓜ/① sol·*te*·ro/a
single room *habitación* ① *individual*
 a·bee·ta·*syon* een·dee·vee·*dwal*
singlet *camiseta* ① ka·mee·*se*·ta
sister *hermana* ① er·*ma*·na
sit *sentarse* sen·*tar*·se
size (clothes) *talla* ① *ta*·ya
size (general) *tamaño* ① ta·*ma*·nyo
skateboarding *andar en patineta*
 an·*dar* en pa·tee·*ne*·ta
skateboard *patineta* ① pa·tee·*ne*·ta
ski *esquiar* es·kee·*ar*
skiing *esquí* ⓜ es·*kee*
skimmed milk *leche* ① *descremada*
 le·che des·kre·*ma*·da
skin *piel* ① pyel
skirt *falda* ① *fal*·da
sky *cielo* ⓜ *sye*·lo
sleep *dormir* dor·*meer*
sleeping bag *bolsa* ① *de dormir*
 bol·sa de dor·*meer*
sleeping car *coche* ⓜ *cama*
 ko·che *ka*·ma
sleeping pills *pastillas* ① pl *para*
 dormir pas·*tee*·yas *pa*·ra dor·*meer*
(be) sleepy *tener sueño* te·*ner* *swe*·nyo
slide *transparencia* ① trans·pa·*ren*·sya
slow *lento/a* ⓜ/① *len*·to/a

slowly *despacio* des·*pa*·syo
small *pequeño/a* ⓜ/① pe·*ke*·nyo/a
smell *olor* ⓜ o·*lor*
smell *oler* o·*ler*
smile *sonreír* son·re·*eer*
smoke *fumar* foo·*mar*
SMS capability *capacidad* ① *de SMS*
 ka·pa·see·*dad* de *e*·se *e*·me *e*·se
snack *botana* ① bo·*ta*·na
snail *caracol* ⓜ ka·ra·*kol*
snake *serpiente* ① ser·*pyen*·te
snorkelling *esnorkelear* es·nor·ke·le·*ar*
snow *nieve* ① *nye*·ve
snowboarding *snowboarding*
 es·now·bor·*deen*
soap *jabón* ⓜ kha·*bon*
soap opera *telenovela* ① te·le·no·*ve*·la
soccer *fútbol* ⓜ *foot*·bol
social welfare *seguridad* ① *social*
 se·goo·ree·*dad* so·*syal*
socialist *socialista* ⓜ&① so·sya·*lees*·ta
socks *calcetines* ⓜ pl kal·se·*tee*·nes
soft drink *refresco* ⓜ re·*fres*·ko
soldier *militar* ⓜ mee·lee·*tar*
some *algún* al·*goon*
someone *alguien* al·gyen
something *algo* al·go
sometimes *de vez en cuando*
 de ves en *kwan*·do
son *hijo* ⓜ *ee*·kho
song *canción* ① kan·*syon*
soon *pronto* *pron*·to
sore *adolorido/a* ⓜ/① a·do·lo·*ree*·do/a
soup *sopa* ① *so*·pa
sour cream *crema* ① *agria*
 kre·ma *a*·grya
south *sur* ⓜ soor
souvenir *suvenir* ⓜ soo·ve·*neer*
souvenir shop *tienda* ① *de suvenirs*
 tyen·da de soo·ve·*neers*
soy milk *leche* ① *de soya*
 le·che de so·*ya*
soy sauce *salsa* ① *de soya*
 sal·sa de so·*ya*
space *espacio* ⓜ es·*pa*·syo
Spain *España* ① es·*pa*·nya

sparkling *espumoso/a* ⓜ/ⓕ
es·poo·mo·so/a

speak *hablar* a·blar

special *especial* es·pe·syal

specialist *especialista* ⓜ&ⓕ
es·pe·sya·lees·ta

speed *velocidad* ⓕ ve·lo·see·dad

speedometer *velocímetro* ⓜ
ve·lo·see·me·tro

spermicide *espermecida* ⓕ
es·per·me·see·da

spider *araña* ⓕ a·ra·nya

spinach *espinaca* ⓕ es·pee·na·ka

spoon *cuchara* ⓕ koo·cha·ra

sport *deportes* ⓜ pl de·por·tes

sports store *tienda* ⓕ *de deportes*
tyen·da de de·por·tes

sportsperson *deportista* ⓜ&ⓕ
de·por·tees·ta

sprain *torcedura* ⓕ tor·se·doo·ra

spring (wire) *resorte* ⓜ re·sor·te

spring (season) *primavera* ⓕ
pree·ma·ve·ra

square *cuadrado* ⓜ kwa·dra·do

square (town) *zócalo* ⓜ so·ka·lo

stadium *estadio* ⓜ es·ta·dyo

stage *escenario* ⓜ e·se·na·ryo

stairway *escalera* ⓕ es·ka·le·ra

stamp *sello* ⓜ se·yo

stand-by ticket *boleto* ⓜ *en lista de
espera* bo·le·to en lees·ta de es·pe·ra

stars *estrellas* ⓕ pl es·tre·yas

start *comenzar* ko·men·sar

station *estación* ⓕ es·ta·syon

statue *estatua* ⓕ es·ta·twa

stay (at a hotel) *alojarse* a·lo·khar·se

stay (remain) *permanecer*
per·ma·ne·ser

stay (somewhere) *quedarse* ke·dar·se

steak (beef) *bistec* ⓜ bees·tek

steal *robar* ro·bar

steep *empinado/a* ⓜ/ⓕ
em·pee·na·do/a

step *paso* ⓜ pa·so

stereo *equipo* ⓜ *estereofónico*
e·kee·po es·te·re·o·fo·nee·ko

stingy *tacaño/a* ⓜ/ⓕ ta·ka·nyo/a

stock (broth) *caldo* ⓜ kal·do

stockings *calcetas* ⓕ pl kal·se·tas

stomach *estómago* ⓜ es·to·ma·go

stomachache *dolor* ⓜ *de estómago*
do·lor de es·to·ma·go

stone *piedra* ⓕ pye·dra

stoned *ciego/a* ⓜ/ⓕ sye·go/a

stop *parada* ⓕ pa·ra·da

stop *parar* pa·rar

store *tienda* ⓕ tyen·da

storm *tormenta* ⓕ tor·men·ta

story *cuento* ⓜ kwen·to

stove *estufa* ⓕ es·too·fa

straight *derecho/a* ⓜ/ⓕ de·re·cho/a

strange *extraño/a* ⓜ/ⓕ ek·stra·nyo/a

stranger *desconocido/a* ⓜ/ⓕ
des·ko·no·see·do/a

strawberry *fresa* ⓕ fre·sa

stream *arroyo* ⓜ a·ro·yo

street *calle* ⓕ ka·ye

string *cuerda* ⓕ kwer·da

strong *fuerte* fwer·te

stubborn *terco/a* ⓜ/ⓕ ter·ko/a

student *estudiante* ⓜ&ⓕ
es·too·dyan·te

studio *estudio* ⓜ es·too·dyo

stupid *estúpido/a* ⓜ/ⓕ es·too·pee·do/a

style *estilo* ⓜ es·tee·lo

subtitles *subtítulos* ⓜ pl
soob·tee·too·los

suburb *colonia* ⓜ ko·lo·nya

subway *metro* ⓜ me·tro

suffer *sufrir* soo·freer

sugar *azúcar* ⓜ&ⓕ a·soo·kar

suitcase *maleta* ⓕ ma·le·ta

summer *verano* ⓜ ve·ra·no

sun *sol* ⓜ sol

sunblock *bloqueador* ⓜ *solar*
blo·ke·a·dor so·lar

sunburn *quemadura* ⓕ *de sol*
ke·ma·doo·ra de sol

sun-dried tomatoes *tomates* ⓜ pl
deshidratados to·ma·tes
des·ee·dra·ta·dos

sunflower oil *aceite* ⓜ *de girasol*
a·say·te de khee·ra·sol

sunglasses *lentes* ① pl *de sol*
len·tes de sol

sunny *soleado* so·le·a·do

sunrise *amanecer* ⓜ a·ma·ne·ser

sunset *puesta* ① *de sol* pwes·ta de sol

supermarket *supermercado* ⓜ
soo·per·mer·ka·do

superstition *superstición* ①
soo·per·stee·syon

supporters *aficionados* ⓜ&① pl
a·fee·syo·na·dos

surf *surfear* sor·fe·ar

surface mail *correo* ⓜ *terrestre*
ko·re·o te·res·tre

surfboard *tabla* ① *de surf*
ta·bla de sorf

surname *apellido* ⓜ a·pe·yee·do

surprise *sorpresa* ① sor·pre·sa

survive *sobrevivir* so·bre·vee·veer

sweater *sueter* ⓜ swe·ter

sweet *dulce* dool·se

sweets (candy) *dulces* ⓜ pl dool·ses

swim *nadar* na·dar

swimming pool *alberca* ① al·ber·ka

swimsuit *traje* ⓜ *de baño*
tra·khe de ba·nyo

synagogue *sinagoga* ① see·na·go·ga

synthetic *sintético/a* ⓜ/①
seen·te·tee·ko/a

syringe *jeringa* ① khe·reen·ga

T

table *mesa* ① me·sa

table tennis *ping pong* ⓜ peen pon

tablecloth *mantel* ⓜ man·tel

tail *cola* ① ko·la

tailor *sastre* ⓜ sas·tre

take (away) *llevar* lye·var

take (the train) *tomar (el tren)*
to·mar (el tren)

take (photos) *tomar (fotos)*
to·mar fo·tos

talk *hablar* a·blar

tall *alto/a* ⓜ/① al·to/a

tampons *tampones* ⓜ pl tam·po·nes

tanning lotion *bronceador* ⓜ
bron·se·a·dor

tap *grifo* ⓜ gree·fo

tasty *sabroso/a* ⓜ/① sa·bro·so/a

tax *impuesto* ⓜ pl eem·pwes·to

taxi *taxi* ⓜ tak·see

taxi driver *taxista* ⓜ&① tak·sees·ta

taxi stand *sitio* ⓜ *de taxis*
see·tyo de tak·sees

tea *té* ⓜ te

teacher *maestro/maestra* ⓜ/①
ma·es·tro/ma·es·tra

team *equipo* ⓜ e·kee·po

teaspoon *cucharita* ① koo·cha·ree·ta

technique *técnica* ① tek·nee·ka

teeth *dientes* ⓜ pl dyen·tes

telegram *telegrama* ⓜ te·le·gra·ma

telephone *teléfono* ⓜ te·le·fo·no

telephone *llamar (por teléfono)*
ya·mar (por te·le·fo·no)

telephone centre *central* ① *telefónica*
sen·tral te·le·fo·nee·ka

telephoto lens *teleobjetivo* ⓜ
te·le·ob·khe·tee·vo

telescope *telescopio* ⓜ te·les·ko·pyo

television *televisión* ① te·le·vee·syon

tell *decir* de·seer

temperature (fever) *fiebre* ① fye·bre

temperature (weather) *temperatura* ①
tem·pe·ra·too·ra

temple *templo* ⓜ tem·plo

tennis *tenis* ⓜ te·nees

tennis court *cancha* ① *de tenis*
kan·cha de te·nees

tent *tienda* ① *(de campaña)*
tyen·da (de kam·pa·nya)

tent pegs *estacas* ① pl es·ta·kas

terrible *terrible* te·ree·ble

test *prueba* ① prwe·ba

thank *dar gracias* dar gra·syas

theatre *teatro* ⓜ te·a·tro

their *su* soo

they *ellos/ellas* ⓜ/① e·yos/e·yas

thief *ladrón/ladrona* ⓜ/①
la·dron/la·dro·na

thin *delgado/a* ⓜ/① del·ga·do/a

think *pensar* pen·sar

third *tercio* ⓜ *ter*·syo

(be) thirsty *tener sed* te·*ner* sed

this *éste/ésta* ⓜ/ⓕ *es*·te/es·ta

this (month) *este mes* es·te mes

throat *garganta* ⓕ gar·*gan*·ta

thrush *infección* ⓕ *de garganta* een·fek·syon de gar·*gan*·ta

ticket *boleto* ⓜ bo·*le*·to

ticket collector *inspector/inspectora* ⓜ/ⓕ een·spek·*tor*/een·spek·*to*·ra

ticket machine *venta* ⓕ *automática de boletos* ven·ta ow·to·ma·tee·ka de bo·*le*·tos

ticket office *taquilla* ⓕ ta·*kee*·ya

tide *marea* ⓕ ma·*re*·a

tight *apretado/a* ⓜ/ⓕ a·pre·*ta*·do/a

time *tiempo* ⓜ *tyem*·po

time difference *diferencia* ⓕ *de horas* dee·fe·*ren*·sya de o·ras

timetable *horario* ⓜ o·*ra*·ryo

tin *lata* ⓕ *la*·ta

tin opener *abrelatas* ⓜ a·bre·*la*·tas

tiny *pequeño/a* ⓜ/ⓕ pe·ke·*nyo*/a

tip (gratuity) *propina* ⓕ pro·*pee*·na

tired *cansado/a* ⓜ/ⓕ kan·*sa*·do/a

tissues *kleenex* ⓜ pl *klee*·neks

toast *pan tostado* ⓜ pan tos·*ta*·do

toaster *tostador* ⓜ tos·ta·*dor*

tobacco *tabaco* ⓜ ta·*ba*·ko

tobacconist *tabaquería* ⓕ ta·ba·ke·*ree*·a

today *hoy* oy

toe *dedo* ⓜ *del pie* de·do del pye

tofu *tofu* ⓜ to·*foo*

together *juntos/as* ⓜ/ⓕ *khoon*·tos/as

toilet *baño* ⓜ *ba*·nyo

toilet paper *papel* ⓜ *higiénico* pa·pel ee·*khye*·nee·ko

tomato *jitomate* ⓜ khee·to·*ma*·te

tomato sauce *catsup* ⓜ *kat*·soop

tomorrow *mañana* ma·*nya*·na

tomorrow afternoon *mañana en la tarde* ma·*nya*·na en la *tar*·de

tomorrow evening *mañana en la noche* ma·*nya*·na en la *no*·che

tomorrow morning *mañana en la mañana* ma·*nya*·na en la ma·*nya*·na

tonight *esta noche* es·ta *no*·che

too (expensive) *muy (caro/a)* ⓜ/ⓕ mooy (*ka*·ro/a)

too much *demasiado* de·ma·*sya*·do

tooth (back) *muela* ⓕ *mwe*·la

toothache *dolor* ⓜ *de muelas* do·*lor* de *mwe*·las

toothbrush *cepillo* ⓜ *de dientes* se·*pee*·yo de *dyen*·tes

toothpaste *pasta* ⓕ *de dientes* *pas*·ta de *dyen*·tes

toothpick *palillo* ⓜ pa·*lee*·yo

torch *linterna* ⓕ leen·*ter*·na

touch *tocar* to·*kar*

tour *excursión* ⓕ ek·skoor·*syon*

tourist *turista* ⓜ&ⓕ too·*rees*·ta

tourist office *oficina* ⓕ *de turismo* o·fee·*see*·na de too·*rees*·mo

towards *hacia* a·sya

towel *toalla* ⓕ to·a·ya

tower *torre* ⓕ *to*·re

toxic waste *residuos* ⓜ pl *tóxicos* re·*see*·dwos tok·*see*·kos

toyshop *juguetería* ⓕ khoo·ge·te·*ree*·a

track (footprints) *rastro* ⓜ *ras*·tro

track (path) *sendero* ⓜ sen·*de*·ro

track (sport) *pista* ⓕ *pees*·ta

trade *comercio* ⓜ ko·*mer*·syo

traffic *tráfico* ⓜ *tra*·fee·ko

traffic lights *semáforos* ⓜ pl se·*ma*·fo·ros

trail *camino* ⓜ ka·*mee*·no

train *tren* ⓜ tren

train station *estación* ⓕ *de tren* es·ta·*syon* de tren

tram *tranvía* ⓕ tran·*vee*·a

transit lounge *sala* ⓕ *de tránsito* *sa*·la de *tran*·see·to

translate *traducir* tra·doo·*seer*

transport *transporte* ⓜ trans·*por*·te

travel *viajar* vya·*khar*

travel agency *agencia* ⓕ *de viajes* a·*khen*·sya de *vya*·khes

travel books *guías* ⓕ pl *turísticas* *gee*·as too·*rees*·tee·kas

travel sickness *mareo* ⓜ ma·*re*·o

travellers cheques *cheques* ⓜ pl *de viajero* che·kes de vya·khe·ro

tree *árbol* ⓜ ar·bol

trip *viaje* ⓜ vya·khe

trousers *pantalones* ⓜ pl pan·ta·lo·nes

truck *camión* ⓜ ka·myon

trust *confianza* ⓕ kon·fee·an·sa

trust *confiar* kon·fee·ar

try *probar* pro·bar

try (attempt) *intentar* een·ten·tar

T-shirt *camiseta* ⓕ ka·mee·se·ta

tube (tyre) *cámara* ⓕ *de llanta* ka·ma·ra de yan·ta

tuna *atún* ⓜ a·toon

tune *melodía* ⓕ me·lo·dee·a

turkey *pavo* ⓜ pa·vo

turn *dar vuelta* dar vwel·ta

TV *televisión* ⓕ te·le·vee·syon

TV series *serie* ⓕ se·rye

tweezers *pinzas* ⓕ pl peen·sas

twice *dos veces* dos ve·ses

twin beds *dos camas* dos ka·mas

twins *gemelos/as* ⓜ/ⓕ pl khe·me·los/as

type *tipo* ⓜ tee·po

type *escribir a máquina* es·kree·beer a ma·kee·na

typical *típico/a* ⓜ/ⓕ tee·pee·ko/a

tyre *llanta* ⓕ yan·ta

U

ultrasound *ultrasonido* ⓜ ool·tra·so·nee·do

umbrella *paraguas* ⓜ pa·ra·gwas

umpire *árbitro* ⓜ ar·bee·tro

uncomfortable *incómodo/a* ⓜ/ⓕ een·ko·mo·do/a

underpants (men) *truzas* ⓕ pl troo·sas

underpants (women) *pantaletas* ⓕ pl pan·ta·le·tas

understand *comprender* kom·pren·der

underwear *ropa* ⓕ *interior* ro·pa een·te·ryor

unemployed *desempleado/a* ⓜ/ⓕ des·em·ple·a·do/a

unfair *injusto/a* ⓜ/ⓕ een·khoos·to/a

uniform *uniforme* ⓜ oo·nee·for·me

universe *universo* ⓜ oo·nee·ver·so

university *universidad* ⓕ oo·nee·ver·see·dad

unleaded *sin plomo* seen plo·mo

unsafe *inseguro/a* ⓜ/ⓕ een·se·goo·ro/a

until (June) *hasta (junio)* as·ta (khoo·nyo)

unusual *raro/a* ⓜ/ⓕ ra·ro/a

up *arriba* a·ree·ba

uphill *cuesta arriba* kwes·ta a·ree·ba

urgent *urgente* oor·khen·te

USA *Estados* ⓜ pl *Unidos de América* es·ta·dos oo·nee·dos de a·me·ree·ka

useful *útil* oo·teel

V

vacant *vacante* va·kan·te

vacation *vacaciones* ⓕ pl va·ka·syo·nes

vaccination *vacuna* ⓕ va·koo·na

vagina *vagina* ⓕ va·khee·na

validate *validar* va·lee·dar

valley *valle* ⓜ va·ye

valuable *valioso/a* ⓜ/ⓕ va·lyo·so/a

value *valor* ⓜ va·lor

van *camioneta* ⓕ ka·myo·ne·ta

veal *ternera* ⓕ ter·ne·ra

vegan *vegetariano/a estricto/a* ⓜ/ⓕ ve·khe·ta·rya·no/a es·treek·to/a

vegetable *legumbre* ⓕ le·goom·bre

vegetables *verduras* ⓕ ver·doo·ras

vegetarian *vegetariano/a* ⓜ/ⓕ ve·khe·ta·rya·no/a

vein *vena* ⓕ ve·na

venereal disease *enfermedad* ⓕ *venérea* en·fer·me·dad ve·ne·re·a

venue *jurisdicción* ⓕ khoo·rees·deek·syon

very *muy* mooy

video tape *videocassette* ⓕ vee·de·o·ka·set

view *vista* ⓕ vees·ta

village *pueblo* ⓜ pwe·blo

vine *vid* ⓕ veed

vinegar *vinagre* ⓜ vee·na·gre

vineyard *viñedo* ⓜ vee·*nye*·do
virus *virus* ⓜ *vee*·roos
visa *visa* ⓕ *vee*·sa
visit *visitar* vee·see·*tar*
vitamins *vitaminas* ⓕ pl
   vee·ta·*mee*·nas
vodka *vodka* ⓕ *vod*·ka
voice *voz* ⓕ vos
volume *volumen* ⓜ vo·*loo*·men
vote *votar* vo·*tar*

W

wage *sueldo* ⓜ *swel*·do
wait *esperar* es·pe·*rar*
waiter *mesero/a* ⓜ/ⓕ me·*se*·ro/a
waiting room *sala* ⓕ *de espera*
   sa·la de es·*pe*·ra
walk *caminar* ka·mee·*nar*
wall (inside) *pared* ⓕ pa·*red*
wallet *cartera* ⓕ kar·*te*·ra
want *querer* ke·*rer*
WAP enabled *capacidad* ⓕ *de WAP*
   ka·pa·see·*dad* de wap
war *guerra* ⓕ *ge*·ra
wardrobe *closet* ⓜ *klo*·set
warm *templado/a* ⓜ/ⓕ tem·*pla*·do/a
warn *advertir* ad·ver·*teer*
wash (oneself) *lavarse* la·*var*·se
wash (something) *lavar* la·*var*
wash cloth *jerga* ⓕ *kher*·ga
washing machine *lavadora* ⓕ
   la·va·*do*·ra
watch *reloj* ⓜ *de pulsera*
   re·*lokh* de pool·*se*·ra
watch *mirar* mee·*rar*
water *agua* ⓕ *a*·gwa
   boiled water *agua* ⓕ *hervida*
   a·gwa er·*vee*·da
   still water *agua* ⓕ *sin gas*
   a·gwa seen gas
   tap water *agua* ⓕ *de la llave*
   a·gwa de la *ya*·ve
waterfall *cascada* ⓕ kas·*ka*·da
watermelon *sandía* ⓕ san·*dee*·a
waterproof *impermeable*
   eem·per·me·*a*·ble

waterskiing *esquí* ⓜ *acuático*
   es·*kee* a·*kwa*·tee·ko
wave *ola* ⓕ *o*·la
way *camino* ⓜ ka·*mee*·no
we *nosotros/as* ⓜ/ⓕ pl no·*so*·tros/as
weak *débil* *de*·beel
wealthy *rico/a* ⓜ/ⓕ *ree*·ko/a
wear *llevar* ye·*var*
weather *tiempo* ⓜ *tyem*·po
wedding *boda* ⓕ *bo*·da
wedding cake *pastel* ⓜ *de bodas*
   pas·*tel* de *bo*·das
wedding present *regalo* ⓜ *de bodas*
   re·*ga*·lo de *bo*·das
weekend *fin* ⓜ *de semana*
   feen de se·*ma*·na
weigh *pesar* pe·*sar*
weight *peso* ⓜ *pe*·so
weights *pesas* ⓕ pl *pe*·sas
welcome *bienvenida* ⓕ
   byen·ve·*nee*·da
welcome *dar la bienvenida*
   dar la byen·ve·*nee*·da
welfare *bienestar* ⓜ byen·es·*tar*
well *bien* byen
well *pozo* ⓜ *po*·so
west *oeste* ⓜ o·*es*·te
wet *mojado/a* ⓜ/ⓕ mo·*kha*·do/a
wetsuit *wetsuit* ⓜ wet·*soot*
what *qué* ke
wheel *rueda* ⓕ *rwe*·da
wheelchair *silla* ⓕ *de ruedas*
   see·ya de *rwe*·das
when *cuándo* *kwan*·do
where *dónde* *don*·de
white *blanco/a* ⓜ/ⓕ *blan*·ko/a
whiteboard *pizzarón* ⓜ *blanco*
   pee·sa·*ron* *blan*·ko
who *quién* kyen
why *por qué* por ke
wide *ancho/a* ⓜ/ⓕ *an*·cho/a
wife *esposa* ⓕ es·*po*·sa
win *ganar* ga·*nar*
wind *viento* ⓜ *vyen*·to
window *ventana* ⓕ ven·*ta*·na
window-shopping *mirar los aparadores* mee·*rar* los a·pa·ra·*do*·res

windscreen *parabrisas* ⓜ
pa·ra·*bree*·sas
windsurfing *hacer windsurf*
a·*ser weend*·sorf
wine *vino* ⓜ *vee*·no
  red wine *vino* ⓜ *tinto vee*·no *teen*·to
  sparkling wine *vino* ⓜ *espumoso*
  vee·no es·poo·*mo*·so
  white wine *vino* ⓜ *blanco*
  vee·no *blan*·ko
winery *bodega* ⓕ *de vinos*
bo·*de*·ga de *vee*·nos
wings *alas* ⓕ pl *a*·las
winner *ganador/ganadora* ⓜ/ⓕ
ga·na·*dor*/ga·na·*do*·ra
winter *invierno* ⓜ een·*vyer*·no
wire *alambre* ⓜ a·*lam*·bre
wish *desear* de·se·*ar*
with *con* kon
within (an hour) *dentro de (una hora)*
den·tro de (*oo*·na o·ra)
without *sin* seen
woman *mujer* ⓕ moo·*kher*
wonderful *maravilloso/a* ⓜ/ⓕ
ma·ra·vee·*yo*·so/a
wood *madera* ⓕ ma·*de*·ra
wool *lana* ⓕ *la*·na
word *palabra* ⓕ pa·*la*·bra
work *trabajo* ⓜ tra·*ba*·kho
work *trabajar* tra·ba·*khar*
work experience *experiencia* ⓕ
laboral ek·spe·*ryen*·sya la·bo·*ral*
work permit *permiso* ⓜ *de trabajo*
per·*mee*·so de tra·*ba*·kho
workout *entrenamiento* ⓜ
en·tre·na·*myen*·to
workshop *taller* ⓜ ta·*yer*
world *mundo* ⓜ *moon*·do

World Cup *Copa* ⓕ *Mundial*
ko·pa moon·*dyal*
worms *lombrices* ⓕ pl lom·*bree*·ses
worried *preocupado/a* ⓜ/ⓕ
pre·o·koo·*pa*·do/a
worship *rezar* re·*sar*
wrist *muñeca* ⓕ moo·*nye*·ka
write *escribir* es·kree·*beer*
writer *escritor/escritora* ⓜ/ⓕ
es·kree·*tor*/es·kree·*to*·ra
wrong *equivocado/a* ⓜ/ⓕ
e·kee·vo·*ka*·do/a

Y

year *año* ⓜ *an*·yo
yellow *amarillo/a* ⓜ/ⓕ a·ma·*ree*·yo/a
yes *sí* see
(not) yet *todavía (no)* to·da·*vee*·a (no)
yesterday *ayer* a·*yer*
yoga *yoga* ⓜ *yo*·ga
yogurt *yogurt* ⓜ *yo*·goort
you sg inf *tú* too
you sg pol *usted* oos·*ted*
you pl inf&pol *ustedes* oos·*te*·des
young *joven* kho·ven
your inf *tu* too
your pol *su* soo
youth hostel *albergue* ⓜ *juvenil*
al·*ber*·ge khoo·ve·*neel*

Z

zodiac *zodíaco* ⓜ so·*dee*·a·ko
zoo *zoológico* ⓜ so·o·*lo*·khee·ko
zoom lens *telefoto* ⓜ te·le·*fo*·to

Nouns in the dictionary have their gender indicated by ⓜ or ⓕ. If it's a plural noun, you'll also see pl. Where a word that could be either a noun or a verb has no gender indicated, it's the verb. For all words relating to local food, see the **culinary reader**, page 157.

A

a bordo a *bor*·do aboard
abajo a·*ba*·kho below · down
abeja ⓕ a·*be*·kha bee
abierto/a ⓜ/ⓕ a·*byer*·to/a open
abogado/a ⓜ/ⓕ a·bo·*ga*·do/a lawyer
aborto ⓜ a·*bor*·to abortion
— **natural** na·too·*ral* miscarriage
abrazar a·bra·*sar* cuddle · hug
abrazo ⓜ a·*bra*·so hug
abrelatas a·bre·*la*·tas can opener · tin opener
abrigo ⓜ a·*bree*·go overcoat
abrir a·*breer* open
abuela a·*bwe*·la grandmother
abuelo a·*bwe*·lo grandfather
aburrido/a a·boo·*ree*·do/a boring
acabar a·ka·*bar* end
acampar a·kam·*par* camp
acantilado ⓜ a·kan·tee·*la*·do cliff
accidente ⓜ ak·see·*den*·te accident
aceite a·*say*·te oil
— **de girasol** de khee·ra·*sol* sunflower oil
— **de oliva** de o·*lee*·va olive oil
aceptar a·sep·*tar* accept
acondicionador ⓜ a·kon·dee·syo·na·*dor* conditioner
acoso ⓜ a·*ko*·so harassment
acta ⓕ **de nacimiento** *ak*·ta de na·see·*myen*·to birth certificate
activista ⓜ&ⓕ ak·tee·*vees*·ta activist
acupuntura ⓕ a·koo·poon·*too*·ra acupuncture
adaptador ⓜ a·dap·ta·*dor* adaptor
adentro a·*den*·tro inside
adiós a·*dyos* goodbye

adivinar a·dee·vee·*nar* guess
administración ⓕ ad·mee·nees·tra·*syon* administration
admitir ad·mee·*teer* admit · allow
adolorido/a ⓜ/ⓕ ado·lo·*ree*·do/a sore
aduana ⓕ a·*dwa*·na customs
adulto/a ⓜ/ⓕ a·*dool*·to/a adult
advertir ad·ver·*teer* warn
aeróbics ⓜ a·e·ro·beeks aerobics
aerolínea ⓕ a·e·ro·lee·ne·a airline
aeropuerto ⓜ a·e·ro·*pwer*·to airport
aficionados ⓜ&ⓕ pl a·fee·syo·*na*·dos supporters
afortunado/a ⓜ/ⓕ a·for·too·*na*·do/a lucky
África *a*·free·ka Africa
agencia ⓕ **de noticias** a·*khen*·sya de no·*tee*·syas newsagency
agencia ⓕ **de viajes** a·*khen*·sya de *vya*·khes travel agency
agenda ⓕ a·*khen*·da diary
agente ⓜ **inmobiliario** a·*khen*·te een·mo·bee·*lya*·ryo real estate agent
agotar a·go·*tar* exhaust
agresivo/a ⓜ/ⓕ a·gre·*see*·vo/a aggressive
agricultura ⓕ a·gree·kool·*too*·ra agriculture
agua ⓕ *a*·gwa water
— **caliente** ka·*lyen*·te hot water
— **hervida** er·*vee*·da boiled water
— **mineral** mee·ne·*ral* mineral water
aguacate ⓜ a·gwa·*ka*·te avocado

aguja ① a·*goo*·kha *needle (sewing)*

ahora a·*o*·ra *now*

ahorrar a·o·*rar* *save (money)*

aire ⓜ *ai*·re *air*

— **acondicionado**
a·kon·dee·syo·*na*·do *air-conditioning*

ajedrez ⓜ a·khe·*dres* *chess*

ajo ⓜ *a*·kho *garlic*

al lado de al *la*·do de *next to*

alacena ① a·la·se·na *cupboard*

alambre ⓜ a·*lam*·bre *wire*

alas ① pl *a*·las *wings*

alba ① *al*·ba *dawn*

alberca ① al·*ber*·ka *swimming pool*

albergue ⓜ **juvenil** al·*ber*·ge
khoo·ve·*neel* *youth hostel*

alcachofa ① al·ka·cho·fa *artichoke*

alcalde ⓜ&① al·*kal*·de *mayor*

alcohol ⓜ al·*kol* *alcohol*

Alemania ① a·le·*ma*·nya *Germany*

alergia ① a·*ler*·khya *allergy*

— **al polen** al po·len *hay fever*

aletas pl ① a·*le*·tas *flippers*

alfarería ① al·fa·re·*ree*·a *pottery*

alfombra ① al·*fom*·bra *rug*

algo *al*·go *something*

algodón ⓜ al·go·*don* *cotton*

alguien *al*·gyen *someone*

algún al·*goon* *some*

alguno/a ⓜ/① sg al·*goo*·no/a *any*

algunos/as ⓜ/① pl al·*goo*·nos/as
some

alimentar a·lee·men·*tar* *feed*

alimento para bebé a·lee·*men*·to
pa·ra be·*be* *baby food*

almendra ① al·*men*·dra *almond*

almohada ① al·*mwa*·da *pillow*

almuerzo ⓜ al·*mwer*·so *lunch*

alojamiento ⓜ a·lo·kha·*myen*·to
accommodation

alojarse a·lo·*khar*·se *stay (somewhere)*

alpinismo ⓜ al·pee·*nees*·mo
mountaineering

altar ⓜ al·*tar* *altar*

alto/a ⓜ/① *al*·to/a *high • tall*

altura ① al·*too*·ra *altitude*

alucinar a·loo·see·*nar* *hallucinate*

ama de casa *a*·ma de *ka*·sa
homemaker

amable a·*ma*·ble *kind*

amanecer ⓜ a·ma·ne·*ser* *dawn •
sunrise*

amante ⓜ&① a·*man*·te *lover*

amar a·*mar* *love*

amarillo/a ⓜ/① a·ma·*ree*·yo/a *yellow*

amateur ⓜ&① a·ma·*ter* *amateur*

amigo/a ⓜ/① a·*mee*·go/a *friend*

ampolla ① am·*po*·ya *blister*

analgésicos ⓜ pl a·nal·*khe*·see·kos
painkillers

análisis ⓜ **de sangre** a·*na*·lee·sees de
san·gre *blood test*

anarquista ⓜ&① a·nar·*kees*·ta
anarchist

ancho/a ⓜ/① *an*·cho/a *wide*

andar an·*dar* *go • walk*

— **en bicicleta** en bee·see·*kle*·ta
cycle

— **en patineta** en pa·tee·ne·ta
skateboarding

anillo ① a·*nee*·yo *ring*

animal ⓜ a·ne·*mal* *animal*

anotar a·no·*tar* *score*

antier an·*tyer* *day before yesterday*

anteojos ⓜ pl an·te·o·khos *glasses*

antibióticos ⓜ pl an·tee·*byo*·tee·kos
antibiotics

anticonceptivos ⓜ pl
an·tee·kon·sep·*tee*·vos
contraceptives

antigüedad ① an·tee·gwe·*dad*
antique

antiguo/a ⓜ/① an·*tee*·gwo/a *ancient*

antinuclear an·tee·noo·kle·*ar*
antinuclear

antiséptico ⓜ an·tee·*sep*·tee·ko
antiseptic

antología ① an·to·lo·*khee*·a
anthology

anuncio ⓜ a·*noon*·syo *advertisement*

año ⓜ *a*·nyo *year*

apellido ⓜ a·pe·*yee*·do *family name*

apenado/a ⓜ/① a·pe·*na*·do/a
embarrassed

apéndice ⓜ a·*pen*·dee·se *appendix*

apodo ⓜ a·*po*·do *nickname*

aprender a·pren·der *learn*

apretado/a ⓜ/ⓕ a·pre·ta·do/a *tight*

aptitudes ⓕ pl ap·tee·too·des *qualifications*

apuesta ⓕ a·pwes·ta *bet*

apuntar a·poon·tar *point*

aquí a·kee *here*

araña ⓕ a·ra·nya *spider*

árbitro ⓜ ar·bee·tro *umpire • referee*

árbol ⓜ ar·bol *tree*

arcoiris ⓜ ar·co·ee·rees *rainbow*

área ⓕ **para acampar** a·re·a pa·ra a·kam·par *campsite*

arena ⓕ a·re·na *sand*

arenque ⓜ a·ren·ke *herring*

aretes ⓜ pl a·re·tes *earrings*

arqueológico/a ⓜ/ⓕ ar·ke·o·lo·khee·ko/a *archaeological*

archeólogo/a ⓜ/ⓕ ar·ke·o·lo·go/a *archeologist*

arquitecto/a ⓜ/ⓕ ar·kee·tek·to/a *architect*

arquitectura ⓕ ar·kee·tek·too·ra *architecture*

arriba a·ree·ba *above • up*

arroyo ⓜ a·ro·yo *stream*

arroz ⓜ a·ros *rice*

arte ⓜ ar·te *art*

artes ⓕ pl **marciales** ar·tes mar·sya·les *martial arts*

artesanía ⓕ ar·te·sa·nee·a *handicraft*

artista ⓜ&ⓕ ar·tees·ta *artist*
— **callejero/a** ⓜ/ⓕ ka·ye·khe·ro/a *busker*

Asia ⓕ a·sya *Asia*

asiento ⓜ a·syen·to *seat*
— **de seguridad para bebés** de se·goo·ree·dad pa·ra be·bes *child seat*

asma ⓜ as·ma *asthma*

aspirina ⓕ as·pee·ree·na *aspirin*

asqueroso/a ⓜ/ⓕ as·ke·ro·so/a *foul*

atletismo ⓜ at·le·tees·mo *athletics*

atmósfera ⓕ at·mos·fe·ra *atmosphere*

atún ⓜ a·toon *tuna*

audífono ⓜ ow·dee·fo·no *hearing aid*

audioguía ⓕ ow·dyo·gee·a *a guide (audio)*

Australia ⓕ ow·stra·lya *Australia*

autobús ⓜ ow·to·boos *bus (intercity)*

autoservicio ⓜ ow·to·ser·vee·syo *self-service*

avena ⓕ a·ve·na *oats*

avenida ⓕ a·ve·nee·da *avenue*

avión ⓜ a·vyon *plane*

ayer a·yer *yesterday*

ayudar a·yoo·dar *help*

azteca as·te·ka *Aztec*

azúcar a·soo·kar *sugar*

azul a·sool *blue*

B

bailar bai·lar *dance*

baile ⓜ bai·le *dancing*

bajo/a ⓜ/ⓕ ba·kho/a *low • short (height)*

balcón ⓜ bal·kon *balcony*

ballet ⓜ ba·le *ballet*

baloncesto ⓜ ba·lon·ses·to *basketball*

bálsamo ⓜ **para labios** bal·sa·mo pa·ra la·byos *lip balm*

banco ⓜ ban·ko *bank*

bandera ⓕ ban·de·ra *flag*

baño ⓜ ba·nyo *toilet • bathroom*

baños ⓜ pl **públicos** ba·nyos poo·blee·kos *public toilet*

banqueta ⓕ ban·ke·ta *footpath*

bar ⓜ bar *bar • pub*
— **con variedad** kon va·rye·dad *bar (with live music)*

barato/a ⓜ/ⓕ ba·ra·to/a *cheap*

barco ⓜ bar·ko *ship*

barrio ⓜ bar·yo *suburb*

basura ⓕ ba·soo·ra *rubbish*

batería ⓕ ba·te·ree·a *drums • battery (car)*

bautizo ⓜ bow·tee·so *baptism*

bebé ⓜ be·be *baby*

bebida ⓕ be·bee·da *drink*

becerro ⓜ be·se·ro *calf*

béisbol ⓜ bays·bol *baseball*

berenjena ① be·ren·*khe*·na
aubergine • eggplant
besar be·*sar* kiss
beso ⓜ be·so kiss
betabel ⓜ be·ta·*bel* beetroot
Biblia ① *bee*·blya Bible
biblioteca ① bee·blyo·*te*·ka library
bicho ⓜ *bee*·cho bug
bici ① *bee*·see bike
bicicleta ① bee·see·*kle*·ta bicycle
— **de carreras** de ka·*re*·ras
racing bike
— **de montaña** de mon·*ta*·nya
mountain bike
bien byen well
bienestar ⓜ byen·es·*tar* welfare
bienvenida ① byen·ve·*nee*·da
welcome
billetes ⓜ pl bee·*ye*·tes banknotes
biodegradable byo·de·gra·*da*·ble
biodegradable
biografía ① byo·gra·*fee*·a biography
bistec ⓜ bees·*tek* steak (beef)
blanco *blan*·ko white
blanco y negro *blan*·ko ee *ne*·gro
B&W (film)
blanco/a ⓜ/① *blan*·ko/a white
bloqueado/a ⓜ/① blo·ke·*a*·do/a
blocked
bloqueador ⓜ **solar** blo·ke·a·*dor*
so·*lar* sunblock
boca ① *bo*·ka mouth
bocado ⓜ bo·*ka*·do bite (food)
boda ① *bo*·da wedding
bodega ① **de vinos** bo·*de*·ga de
vee·nos winery
bolas ① pl **de algodón** bo·las de
al·go·*don* cotton balls
boleto ⓜ bo·*le*·to ticket
— **de viaje redondo** de *vya*·khe
re·*don*·do return ticket
— **en lista de espera** en *lees*·ta de
es·*pe*·ra standby ticket
— **sencillo** sen·*see*·yo one-way
ticket
bolillo ⓜ bo·*lee*·yo bread roll

bolsa ① *bol*·sa bag • handbag
— **de dormir** de dor·*meer* sleeping
bag
bolsillo ⓜ bol·*see*·yo pocket
bomba ① *bom*·ba pump • bomb
bondadoso/a ⓜ/① bon·da·*do*·so/a
caring
bonito/a ⓜ/① bo·*nee*·to/a pretty
borracho/a ⓜ/① bo·*ra*·cho/a drunk
borrego ⓜ bo·*re*·go lamb
bosque ⓜ *bos*·ke forest
botana ① bo·*ta*·na snack
botas ① pl *bo*·tas boots
— **de montaña** de mon·*ta*·nya
hiking boots
bote ⓜ *bo*·te boat
botella ① bo·*te*·ya bottle
botiquín ⓜ bo·tee·*keen* first-aid kit
botones ⓜ pl bo·*to*·nes buttons
boxeo ⓜ bok·*se*·o boxing
boxers ⓜ pl bok·sers boxer shorts
Braille ⓜ *brai*·le Braille
brandy ⓜ *bran*·dee brandy
brassiere ① bra·*syer* bra
brazo ⓜ *bra*·so arm
brecha ① *bre*·cha mountain path
brillante bree·*yan*·te brilliant
broma ① *bro*·ma joke
bromear bro·me·*ar* joke
bronceador ⓜ bron·se·a·*dor*
tanning lotion
bronquitis ① bron·*kee*·tees
bronchitis
brújula ① *broo*·khoo·la compass
budista boo·*dees*·ta Buddhist
bueno/a ⓜ/① *bwe*·no/a good
bufanda ① boo·*fan*·da scarf
buffet ⓜ boo·*fet* buffet
bulto ⓜ *bool*·to lump
burlarse de boor·*lar*·se de
make fun of
burro ⓜ *boo*·ro donkey
buscar boos·*kar* look for
buzón ⓜ boo·*son* mailbox

C

caballo ⓜ ka·*ba*·yo *horse*
cabeza ⓕ ka·*be*·sa *head*
cable ⓜ *ka*·ble *cable*
cables ⓜ pl **pasacorriente** *ka*·bles pa·sa·ko·ryen·tes *jumper leads*
cabra ⓕ *ka*·bra *goat*
cacahuates ⓜ ka·ka·*wa*·tes *peanuts*
cacao ⓜ ka·*kow cocoa*
cachorro ⓜ ka·*cho*·ro *puppy*
cactus ⓜ kak·*toos cactus*
cada *ka*·da *each*
cadena ⓕ **de bici** ka·*de*·na de *bee*·see *bike chain*
café ⓜ ka·*fe coffee • cafe*
— **Internet** een·ter·net *Internet cafe*
caída ⓕ ka·*ee*·da *fall (tumble)*
caja ⓕ *ka*·kha *box*
— **fuerte** *fwer*·te *safe*
— **registradora** re·khees·tra·*do*·ra *cash register*
cajero/a ⓜ/ⓕ ka·*khe*·ro/a *cashier*
cajero ⓜ **automático** ka·*khe*·ro ow·to·*ma*·tee·ko *automatic teller machine*
calabacita ⓕ ka·la·ba·*see*·ta *courgette*
calabaza ⓕ ka·la·*ba*·sa *pumpkin*
calcetines ⓜ pl kal·se·*tee*·nes *socks*
calculadora ⓕ kal·koo·la·*do*·ra *calculator*
caldo ⓜ *kal*·do *stock*
calefacción ⓕ **central** ka·le·fak·*syon* sen·*tral central heating*
calendario ⓜ ka·len·*da*·ryo *calendar*
calentador ⓜ ka·len·ta·*dor heater*
calidad ⓕ ka·lee·*dad quality*
caliente ka·*lyen*·te *hot*
calor ⓜ ka·*lor heat*
calle ⓕ *ka*·ye *street*
cama ⓕ *ka*·ma *bed*
— **matrimonial** ma·tree·mo·*nyal double bed*
cámara ⓕ **de llanta** *ka*·ma·ra de *yan*·ta *tube (tyre)*

cámara ⓕ **fotográfica** *ka*·ma·ra fo·to·*gra*·fee·ka *camera*
camarón ⓜ ka·ma·*ron prawn*
cambiar kam·*byar change • exchange (money)*
— **un cheque** oon *che*·ke *cash a cheque*
cambio ⓜ *kam*·byo *exchange • change (money)*
— **de moneda** de mo·*ne*·da *currency exchange*
— **en monedas** en mo·*ne*·das *loose change*
caminar ka·mee·*nar walk*
camino ⓜ ka·*mee*·no *road • trail • way*
caminos ⓜ pl **rurales** ka·*mee*·nos roo·*ra*·les *hiking route*
camión ⓜ ka·*myon bus • truck*
camioneta ⓕ ka·myo·*ne*·ta *van*
camisa ⓕ ka·*mee*·sa *shirt*
camiseta ⓕ ka·mee·*se*·ta *singlet • T-shirt*
campo ⓜ *kam*·po *field • countryside*
— **de golf** de golf *golf course*
Canadá ka·na·*da Canada*
canasta ⓕ ka·*nas*·ta *basket*
cancelar kan·se·*lar cancel*
cáncer ⓜ *kan*·ser *cancer*
cancha ⓕ **de tenis** *kan*·cha de *te*·nees *tennis court*
canción ⓕ kan·*syon song*
candado ⓜ kan·*da*·do *padlock*
canela ⓕ ka·*ne*·la *cinnamon*
cangrejo ⓜ kan·*gre*·kho *crab*
cansado/a ⓜ/ⓕ kan·*sa*·do/a *tired*
cantante ⓜ&ⓕ kan·*tan*·te *singer*
cantar kan·*tar sing*
cantimplora ⓕ kan·teem·*plo*·ra *water bottle*
capa ⓕ *ka*·pa *cloak*
— **de ozono** de o·*so*·no *ozone layer*
capilla ⓕ ka·*pee*·ya *shrine*
cara ⓕ *ka*·ra *face*
caracol ⓜ ka·ra·*kol snail*
caravana ⓕ ka·ra·*va*·na *caravan*
cárcel ⓕ *kar*·sel *prison • jail*
cardiopatía ⓕ kar·dyo·pa·*tee*·a *heart condition*

carne ① *kar*·ne *meat*
— **de res** de res *beef*
— **molida** mo·*lee*·da *mince meat*
carnicería ① kar·nee·se·*ree*·a
butcher's shop
caro/a ⓜ/① *ka*·ro/a *expensive*
carpintero ⓜ kar·peen·*te*·ro *carpenter*
carrera ① ka·*re*·ra *race (sport) • university studies*
carretera ① ka·re·*te*·ra *motorway*
carril ⓜ **para bici** ka·*reel* pa·ra
bee·see *bike path*
carta ① *kar*·ta *letter*
cartas ① pl *kar*·tas *playing cards*
cartón ⓜ kar·*ton* *carton*
casa ① *ka*·sa *house*
— **de cambio** *foreign exchange office* *ka*·sa de *kam*·byo
casarse ka·*sar*·se *marry*
cascada ① kas·*ka*·da *waterfall*
casco ⓜ *kas*·ko *helmet*
casi *ka*·see *almost*
casilleros ⓜ pl ka·see·*ye*·ros
luggage lockers
casino ⓜ ka·*see*·no *casino*
cassette ⓜ ka·*set* *cassette*
castigar kas·tee·*gar* *punish*
castillo ⓜ kas·*tee*·yo *castle*
catedral ① ka·te·*dral* *cathedral*
católico/a ⓜ/① ka·to·*lee*·ko/a *Catholic*
cátsup ⓜ *kat*·soop *tomato sauce • ketchup*
caza ① *ka*·sa *hunting*
cazuela ① ka·*swe*·la *pot (kitchen)*
cebolla ① se·*bo*·ya *onion*
cejas ① pl *se*·khas *eyebrows*
celebración ① se·le·bra·*syon*
celebration
celebrar se·le·*brar* *celebrate (an event)*
celoso/a ⓜ/① se·*lo*·so/a *jealous*
cementerio ⓜ se·men·*te*·ryo
cemetery
cena ① *se*·na *dinner*
cenicero ⓜ se·nee·*se*·ro *ashtray*
centavo ⓜ sen·*ta*·vo *cent*
centímetro ⓜ sen·*tee*·me·tro
centimetre

central ① **telefónica** sen·*tral*
te·le·*fo*·nee·ka *telephone centre*
centro ⓜ *sen*·tro *centre*
— **comercial** ko·mer·*syal*
shopping centre
— **de la ciudad** de la syoo·*dad*
city centre
Centroamérica ① sen·tro·a·*me*·ree·ka
Central America
cepillo ⓜ se·*pee*·yo *hairbrush*
— **de dientes** de *dyen*·tes
toothbrush
cerámica ① se·*ra*·mee·ka *ceramic*
cerca ① *ser*·ka *fence*
cerca *ser*·ka *near • nearby*
cerdo ⓜ *ser*·do *pork • pig*
cereal ⓜ se·re·*al* *cereal*
cerillos ⓜ pl se·*ree*·yos *matches*
cerrado/a ⓜ/① se·ra·do/a *closed • shut*
— **con llave** kon *ya*·ve *locked*
cerradura ① se·ra·*doo*·ra *lock*
cerrar se·*rar* *close • lock • shut*
certificado ⓜ ser·tee·fee·*ka*·do
certificate
cerveza ① ser·*ve*·sa *beer*
— **clara** *kla*·ra *lager*
cibercafé ⓜ see·ber·ka·*fe* *Internet cafe*
ciclismo ⓜ see·*klees*·mo *cycling*
ciclista ⓜ&① see·*klees*·ta *cyclist*
ciego/a ⓜ/① *sye*·go/a *blind • stoned*
cielo ⓜ *sye*·lo *sky*
ciencias ① pl *syen*·syas *science*
científico/a ⓜ/① syen·*tee*·fee·ko/a
scientist
cigarro ⓜ see·*ga*·ro *cigarette*
cine ⓜ *see*·ne *cinema*
cinturón ⓜ **de seguridad**
seen·too·*ron* de se·goo·ree·*dad*
seatbelt
circo ⓜ *seer*·ko *circus*
ciruela ① seer·*we*·la *plum*
— **pasa** *pa*·sa *prune*
cistitis ① sees·*tee*·tees *cystitis*
cita ① *see*·ta *appointment • date*
ciudad ① syoo·*dad* *city*

ciudadanía ⓕ syoo·da·da·*nee*·a
citizenship

clase ⓕ ejecutiva kla·se
e·khe·koo·*tee*·va business class

clase ⓕ turística kla·se
too·*rees*·tee·ka economy class

clásico/a ⓜ/ⓕ kla·see·ko/a classical

clavos ⓜ pl de olor kla·vos de o·lor
cloves

cliente/a ⓜ/ⓕ klee·en·te/a client

closet ⓜ klo·set wardrobe

cobija ⓕ ko·*bee*·kha blanket

cocaína ⓕ ko·ka·ee·na cocaine

coche ⓜ ko·che car

— cama ka·ma sleeping car

cocina ⓕ ko·*see*·na kitchen

cocinar ko·see·nar cook

cocinero ⓜ ko·see·*ne*·ro cook

coco ⓜ ko·ko coconut

codeína ⓕ ko·de·ee·na codeine

código ⓜ postal ko·dee·go pos·tal
post code

congelar kon·khe·lar freeze

coger ko·kher fuck

col ⓕ kol cabbage

colchón ⓜ kol·chon mattress

colega ⓜ&ⓕ ko·*le*·ga colleague

cólico ⓜ menstrual ko·lee·ko
men·strwal period pain

coliflor ⓕ ko·lee·flor cauliflower

colina ⓕ ko·*lee*·na hill

collar ⓜ ko·yar necklace

colonia ⓕ ko·lo·nya suburb

color ⓜ ko·lor colour

combustible ⓜ kom·boos·*tee*·ble
fuel

comedia ⓕ ko·*me*·dya comedy

comenzar ko·men·sar begin · start

comer ko·mer eat

comerciante ⓜ&ⓕ ko·mer·*syan*·te
business person

comercio ⓜ ko·*mer*·syo trade

comezón ⓕ ko·me·son itch

comida ⓕ ko·*mee*·da food

cómo ko·mo how

cómodo/a ⓜ/ⓕ ko·mo·do/a
comfortable

cómpact ⓜ kom·pakt CD

compañero/a ⓜ/ⓕ kom·pa·*nye*·ro/a
companion

compañía ⓕ kom·pa·*nyee*·a company

compartir kom·par·teer share (with)

comprar kom·prar buy

comprender kom·pren·der
understand

compromiso ⓜ kom·pro·*mee*·so
commitment

computadora ⓕ kom·poo·ta·*do*·ra
computer

— portátil por·ta·teel laptop

comunión ⓕ ko·moo·nyon
communion

comunista ⓜ&ⓕ ko·moo·*nees*·ta
communist

con kon with

concierto ⓜ kon·syer·to concert

condones ⓜ pl kon·do·nes condoms

conducir kon·doo·seer drive

conectar ko·nek·tar plug

conejo ⓜ ko·*ne*·kho rabbit

conexión ⓕ ko·nek·syon connection

confesión ⓕ kon·fe·syon confession

confianza ⓕ kon·fee·*an*·sa trust

confiar kon·fee·ar trust

confirmar kon·feer·mar confirm

conocer ko·no·ser know (someone)

consejo ⓜ kon·*se*·kho advice

conservador(a) ⓜ/ⓕ kon·ser·va·*dor*/
kon·ser·va·*do*·ra conservative

consigna ⓕ kon·*seeg*·na left luggage

construir kon·stroo·eer build

consulado ⓜ kon·soo·la·do consulate

contaminación ⓕ
kon·ta·mee·na·syon pollution

contar kon·tar count

contestadora ⓕ kon·tes·ta·*do*·ra
answering machine

contrato ⓜ kon·*tra*·to contract

cóntrol ⓜ kon·*trol* checkpoint

— remoto re·mo·to remote control

convento ⓜ kon·ven·to convent

copa (de vino) ⓕ ko·pa (de vee·no)
glass (of wine)

Copa ① **Mundial** *ko·pa moon·dyal* World Cup

corazón ⓜ *ko·ra·son* heart

cordillera ① *kor·dee·ye·ra* mountain range

correcto/a ⓜ/① *ko·rek·to/a* right (correct)

correo ⓜ *ko·re·o* mail
— **aéreo** *a·e·re·o* airmail
— **certificado** *ser·tee·fee·ka·do* registered mail
— **expresso** *ek·spre·so* express mail
— **terrestre** *te·res·tre* surface mail

correr *ko·rer* run

corrida (de toros) ① *ko·ree·da (de to·ros)* bullfight

corriente ① *ko·ryen·te* current (electricity)

corriente *ko·ryen·te* ordinary

corrupto/a ⓜ/① *ko·roop·to/a* corrupt

cortar *kor·tar* cut

cortauñas ⓜ *kor·ta·oo·nyas* nail clippers

corte ⓜ **de pelo** *kor·te de pe·lo* haircut

corto/a ⓜ/① *kor·to/a* short (length)

cosecha ① *ko·se·cha* crop

coser *ko·ser* sew

costa ① *kos·ta* coast · seaside

costar *kos·tar* cost

costo ⓜ *kos·to* cost

cover ⓜ *ko·ver* cover charge

crecer *kre·ser* grow

crema ① *kre·ma* cream
— **agria** *a·grya* sour cream
— **hidratante** *ee·dra·tan·te* moisturiser

críquet ⓜ *kree·ket* cricket

cristiano/a ⓜ/① *krees·tya·no/a* Christian

crítica ① *kree·tee·ka* review

crudo/a ⓜ/① *kroo·do/a* raw

cuaderno ⓜ *kwa·der·no* notebook

cuadrado ⓜ *kwa·dra·do* square (shape)

cuando *kwan·do* when

cuánto *kwan·to* how much

cuarentena ① *kwa·ren·te·na* quarantine

Cuaresma ① *kwa·res·ma* Lent

cuarto ⓜ *kwar·to* quarter

cubeta ① *koo·be·ta* bucket

cubiertos ⓜ pl *koo·byer·tos* cutlery

cucaracha ① *koo·ka·ra·cha* cockroach

cuchara ① *koo·cha·ra* spoon

cucharita ① *koo·cha·ree·ta* teaspoon

cuchillo ⓜ *koo·chee·yo* knife

cuenta ① *kwen·ta* bill (account)
— **bancaria** *ban·ka·rya* bank account

cuento ⓜ *kwen·to* story

cuerda ① *kwer·da* rope · string

cuero ⓜ *kwe·ro* leather

cuerpo ⓜ *kwer·po* body

cuesta abajo *kwes·ta a·ba·kho* downhill

cuesta arriba *kwes·ta a·ree·ba* uphill

cuevas ① pl *kwe·vas* caves

cuidar *kwee·dar* look after · mind

cuidar de *kwee·dar de* care for

culo ⓜ *koo·lo* bum (ass)

culpable *kool·pa·ble* guilty

cumbre ① *koom·bre* peak

cumpleaños ⓜ *koom·ple·a·nyos* birthday

cupón ⓜ *koo·pon* coupon

curitas ① pl *koo·ree·tas* Band-Aids

currículum ⓜ *koo·ree·koo·loom* CV · resumé

curry ⓜ *koo·ree* curry
— **en polvo** *en pol·vo* curry powder

cus cus ⓜ *koos koos* cous cous

CH

chabacano ⓜ *cha·ba·ka·no* apricot

chaleco ⓜ **salvavidas** *cha·le·ko sal·va·vee·das* life jacket

chamarra ① *cha·ma·ra* jacket

champán ⓜ *cham·pan* champagne

champiñón ⓜ *cham·pee·nyon* mushroom

chapulines ⓜ pl cha·poo·*lee*·nes *grasshoppers*

chavija ⓕ cha·*vee*·kha *plug (electrical)*

cheque ⓜ *che*·ke *cheque · check (bank)*

cheques ⓜ pl **de viajero** *che*·kes de vya·*khe*·ro *travellers cheques*

chícharos ⓜ pl *chee*·cha·ros *peas*

chichis ⓕ pl inf *chee*·chees *breasts*

chicle ⓜ *chee*·kle *chewing gum*

chica ⓕ *chee*·ka *girl*

chico ⓜ *chee*·ko *boy*

chico/a ⓜ/ⓕ *chee*·ko/a *small*

chile ⓜ *chee*·le *chilli*

chimenea ⓕ chee·me·*ne*·a *fireplace*

chocolate ⓜ cho·ko·*la*·te *chocolate*

choque ⓜ *cho*·ke *crash*

chorizo ⓜ cho·*ree*·so *pork sausage*

chupón ⓜ choo·*pon* *dummy · pacifier*

D

dados ⓜ pl *da*·dos *dice*

dar dar *give*

— **gracias** *gra*·syas *thank*

— **la bienvenida** la byen·ve·*nee*·da *welcome*

— **vuelta** *vwel*·ta *turn*

darse cuenta de *dar*·se *kwen*·ta de *realise*

de de of · *from*

— **(cuatro) estrellas** (*kwa*·tro) es·*tre*·yas *(four-)star*

— **derecha** de·*re*·cha *right-wing*

— **izquierda** ees·*kyer*·da *left-wing*

— **segunda mano** se·*goon*·da *ma*·no *second-hand*

— **vez en cuando** ves en *kwan*·do *sometimes*

deber de·*ver* *owe*

débil *de*·beel *weak*

decidir de·see·*deer* *decide*

decir de·*seer* say · *tell*

dedo *de*·do *finger*

— **del pie** del pye *toe*

defectuoso/a ⓜ/ⓕ de·fek·*two*·so/a *faulty*

deforestación ⓕ de·fo·res·ta·*syon* *deforestation*

dejar de·*khar* *quit*

delgado/a ⓜ/ⓕ del·*ga*·do/a *thin*

delirante de·lee·*ran*·te *delirious*

demasiado de·ma·*sya*·do too *(much)*

democracia ⓕ de·mo·*kra*·sya *democracy*

demora ⓕ de·*mo*·ra *delay*

dentista ⓜ den·*tees*·ta *dentist*

dentro de (una hora) *den*·tro de (*oo*·na *o*·ra) *within (an hour)*

deportes ⓜ pl de·*por*·tes *sport*

deportista ⓜ&ⓕ de·por·*tees*·ta *sportsperson*

depósito ⓜ de·*po*·see·to *deposit (bank)*

derecha de·*re*·cha *right (not left)*

derecho de·*re*·cho *straight*

derechos ⓜ pl *rights*

— **civiles** see·*vee*·les *civil rights*

— **humanos** oo·*ma*·nos *human rights*

desayuno ⓜ de·sa·*yoo*·no *breakfast*

descansar des·kan·*sar* *rest*

descanso ⓜ des·*kan*·so *intermission*

descendiente ⓜ de·sen·*dyen*·te *descendant*

descomponerse des·kom·po·*ner*·se *break down*

desconocido/a ⓜ/ⓕ des·ko·no·*see*·do/a *stranger*

descubrir des·koo·*breer* *discover*

descuento ⓜ des·*kwen*·to *discount*

desde *des*·de *since (time)*

desear de·se·*ar* *wish*

desechable de·se·*cha*·ble *disposable*

desempeño ⓜ des·em·*pe*·nyo *performance*

desempleado/a ⓜ/ⓕ des·em·*ple*·a·do/a *unemployed*

desierto ⓜ de·*syer*·to *desert*

desodorante ⓜ de·so·do·*ran*·te *deodorant*

despacio des·*pa*·syo *slowly*

despedida ⓕ des·pe·*dee*·da *farewell*

desperdicios ⓜ pl **nucleares** des·per·*dee*·syos noo·kle·*a*·res *nuclear waste*

despertador ⓜ des·per·ta·*dor*
alarm clock
después de des·*pwes* de *after*
destapador ⓜ des·ta·pa·*dor* *bottle
opener*
destino ⓜ des·*tee*·no *destination*
destruir des·troo·*eer destroy*
detallado/a ⓜ/ⓕ de·ta·ya·*do*/a
itemised
detalle ⓜ de·*ta*·ye *detail*
detener de·te·*ner arrest*
detrás de de·*tras* de *behind • at the
back*
día ⓜ *dee*·a *day*
 — **de Año Nuevo** de *a*·nyo nwe·vo
 New Year's Day
 — **de campo** de *kam*·po *picnic*
 — **festivo** fes·*tee*·vo *holiday*
diabetes ⓕ dee·a·*be*·tes *diabetes*
diafragma ⓜ dee·a·*frag*·ma
diaphragm
diariamente dya·rya·*men*·te *daily*
diarrea ⓕ dee·a·*re*·a *diarrhoea*
dibujar dee·boo·*khar draw*
diccionario ⓜ deek·syo·*na*·ryo
dictionary
diente ⓜ **(de ajo)** *dyen*·te (de *a*·kho)
clove (of garlic)
dientes ⓜ pl *dyen*·tes *teeth*
dieta ⓜ *dye*·ta *diet*
diferencia ⓕ **de horas** de·fe·*ren*·sya
de o·ras *time difference*
diferente dee·fe·*ren*·te *different*
difícil dee·*fee*·seel *difficult*
dinero ⓜ dee·*ne*·ro *money*
 — **en efectivo** en e·fek·*tee*·vo *cash*
dios ⓜ dyos *god*
diosa ⓕ *dyo*·sa *goddess*
dirección ⓕ dee·rek·*syon address*
directo/a ⓜ/ⓕ dee·*rek*·to/a *direct*
director(a) ⓜ/ⓕ dee·rek·*tor*/
dee·rek·to·ra *director • manager*
directorio ⓜ **telefónico**
dee·rek·to·ryo te·le·*fo*·nee·ko
phone book
discapacitado/a ⓜ/ⓕ
dees·ka·pa·see·*ta*·do/a *disabled*
disco ⓜ *dees*·ko *disk*

discoteca ⓕ dees·ko·*te*·ka *disco*
discriminación ⓕ
dees·kree·mee·na·*syon*
discrimination
discutir dees·koo·*teer argue*
diseño ⓜ dee·*se*·nyo *design*
disparar dees·pa·*rar shoot*
DIU ⓜ dee·oo *IUD*
diversión ⓕ dee·ver·*syon fun*
divertido/a ⓜ/ⓕ dee·ver·*tee*·do/a
funny
divertirse dee·ver·*teer*·se
enjoy oneself • have fun
divorciado/a ⓜ/ⓕ dee·vor·*sya*·do/a
divorced
doble *do*·ble *double*
docena ⓕ do·*se*·na *dozen*
doctor(a) ⓜ/ⓕ dok·*tor*/dok·*to*·ra
doctor
documentación ⓕ
do·koo·men·ta·*syon check-in •
paperwork*
documental ⓜ do·koo·men·*tal*
documentary
dólar ⓜ *do*·lar *dollar*
dolor ⓜ do·*lor pain*
 — **de cabeza** de ka·*be*·sa *headache*
 — **de estómago** de es·*to*·ma·go
 stomachache
 — **de muelas** de *mwe*·las
 toothache
doloroso/a ⓜ/ⓕ do·lo·ro·*so*/a
painful
donde *don*·de *where*
dormir dor·*meer sleep*
dos camas dos *ka*·mas *twin beds*
dos veces dos *ve*·ses *twice*
drama ⓜ *dra*·ma *drama*
droga ⓕ *dro*·ga *dope*
drogadicción ⓕ dro·ga·deek·*syon*
drug addiction
drogas ⓕ pl *dro*·gas *drugs (illegal)*
dueño/a ⓜ/ⓕ *dwe*·nyo/a *owner*
dulce *dool*·se *sweet*
dulces ⓜ pl *dool*·ses
lollies • sweets • candy
durazno ⓜ doo·*ras*·no *peach*
duro/a ⓜ/ⓕ *doo*·ro/a *hard*

E

echarse un pedo e·*char*·se oon pe·do
fart

eczema ① ek·*se*·ma *eczema*

edad ① e·*dad age*

edificio ⓜ e·dee·*fee*·syo *building*

editor(a) ⓜ/① e·dee·*tor*/e·dee·*to*·ra
editor

educación ① e·doo·ka·*syon*
education

egoísta e·go·*ees*·ta *selfish*

ejemplo ⓜ e·*khem*·plo *example*

él el *he*

elecciones ① pl e·lek·*syo*·nes
elections

electricidad ① e·lek·tree·see·*dad*
electricity

elegir e·le·*kheer choose*

elevador ⓜ e·le·va·*dor lift* • *elevator*

ella e·ya *she*

ellos/ellas ⓜ/① e·yos/e·yas *they*

embajada ① em·ba·*kha*·da *embassy*

embajador(a) ⓜ/① em·ba·kha·*dor*/
em·ba·kha·*do*·ra *ambassador*

embarazada em·ba·ra·*sa*·da *pregnant*

embarcar em·bar·*kar board (ship, etc)*

embrague ⓜ em·*bra*·ge *clutch*

emergencia ① e·mer·*khen*·sya
emergency

emocional e·mo·syo·*nal emotional*

empinado/a ⓜ/① em·pee·*na*·do/a
steep

empleado/a ⓜ&① em·ple·*a*·do/a
office worker • *employee*

empujar em·poo·*khar push*

en en *on*
 — **casa** *ka*·sa *(at) home*
 — **el extranjero** el ek·stran·*khe*·ro
 abroad

encaje ⓜ en·*ka*·khe *lace*

encantador(a) ⓜ/① en·kan·ta·*dor*/
en·kan·ta·*do*·ra *charming*

encendedor ⓜ en·sen·de·*dor*
cigarette lighter

encontrar en·kon·*trar find* • *meet*

encuestas ① pl en·*kwes*·tas *polls*

energía ① **nuclear** e·ner·*khee*·a
noo·kle·*ar nuclear energy*

enfermedad ① en·fer·me·*dad*
disease
 — **del beso** del be·so *glandular*
 fever
 — **venérea** ve·ne·re·a *venereal*
 disease

enfermero/a ⓜ/① en·fer·*me*·ro/a
nurse

enfermo/a ⓜ/① en·*fer*·mo/a *sick* • *ill*

enfrente de en·*fren*·te de *in front of*

enojado/a ⓜ/① e·no·*kha*·do/a *angry*

enorme e·*nor*·me *huge*

ensalada ① en·sa·*la*·da *salad*

enseñar en·se·*nyar teach* • *show*

entrar en·*trar enter*

entre en·tre *between* • *among*

entrega ① **de equipaje** en·*tre*·ga de
e·kee·pa·khe *baggage claim*

entregar en·tre·*gar deliver*

entrenador(a) ⓜ/① en·tre·na·*dor*/
en·tre·na·*do*·ra *coach*

entrenamiento ⓜ en·tre·na·*myen*·to
workout

entrevista ① en·tre·*vees*·ta *interview*

enviar en·*vyar send*

epilepsia ① e·pee·*lep*·sya *epilepsy*

equipaje ⓜ e·kee·*pa*·khe *luggage* •
baggage

equipo ⓜ e·*kee*·po *team* • *equipment*
 — **estereofónico**
 es·te·re·o·fo·nee·ko *stereo*
 — **para buceo** pa·ra boo·se·o
 diving equipment

equitación ① e·kee·ta·*syon*
horse riding

equivocado/a ⓜ/① e·kee·vo·*ka*·do/a
wrong (mistaken)

error ⓜ e·*ror mistake*

escalada ① **en roca** es·ka·*la*·da en
ro·ka *rock climbing*

escalar es·ka·*lar climb*

escalera ① es·ka·*le*·ra *stairway*

escaleras ① pl **eléctricas** es·ka·*le*·ras
e·lek·tree·kas *escalator*

escape ⓜ es·*ka*·pe *exhaust pipe*

escarcha ① es·*kar*·cha *frost*

escasez ① es·ka·*ses shortage*

escenario ⓜ e·se·*na*·ryo *stage*

Escocia ① es·*ko*·sya *Scotland*

escribir es·kree·*beer* *write*
— **a máquina** a *ma*·kee·na *type*

escritor(a) ⓜ/① es·kree·*tor*/
es·kree·*to*·ra *writer*

escuchar es·koo·*char* *listen*

escuela ① es·*kwe*·la *school*

escultura ① es·kool·*too*·ra *sculpture*

esa ① *e*·sa *that*

ese ⓜ *e*·se *that*

esgrima ① es·*gree*·ma *fencing (sport)*

esnorkelear es·nor·ke·le·ar
snorkelling

espacio ⓜ es·*pa*·syo *space*

espalda ① es·*pal*·da *back (body)*

España ① es·*pa*·nya *Spain*

especial es·pe·*syal* *special*

especialista ⓜ&① es·pe·sya·*lees*·ta
specialist

especies ① pl **en peligro de extinción**
es·*pe*·syes en pe·*lee*·gro de
ek·steen·*syon* *endangered species*

espectáculo ⓜ es·pek·*ta*·koo·lo *show*

espejo ⓜ es·*pe*·kho *mirror*

esperar es·pe·*rar* *wait*

espinaca ① es·pee·*na*·ka *spinach*

esposa ① es·*po*·sa *wife*

esposo ⓜ es·*po*·so *husband*

espuma ① **de rasurar** es·*poo*·ma de
ra·soo·*rar* *shaving cream*

espumoso/a ⓜ/① es·poo·*mo*·so/a
sparkling

esquí ⓜ es·*kee* *skiing*
— **acuático** a·*kwa*·tee·ko
waterskiing

esquiar es·kee·*ar* *ski*

esquina ① es·*kee*·na *corner*

estacas ① pl es·*ta*·kas *tent pegs*

estación ① es·ta·*syon* *station •
season*
— **de autobuses** de ow·to·*boo*·ses
bus station
— **del metro** es·ta·*syon* del *me*·tro
metro station
— **de policía** de po·lee·*see*·a
police station
— **de tren** de tren *railway station •
train station*

estacionamiento ⓜ
es·ta·syo·na·*myen*·to *car park*

estacionar es·ta·syo·*nar* *park (car)*

estadio ⓜ es·*ta*·dyo *stadium*

estado ⓜ **civil** es·*ta*·do see·*veel*
marital status

Estados ⓜ pl **Unidos de América**
es·*ta*·dos oo·*nee*·dos de a·*me*·ree·ka
USA

estafa ① es·*ta*·fa *rip-off*

estar es·*tar* *be*
— **de acuerdo** de a·*kwer*·do *agree*

estatua ① es·*ta*·twa *statue*

este es·te *east*

éste/a ⓜ/① *es*·te/a *this*

estilo ⓜ es·*tee*·lo *style*

ésto *es*·to *this one*

estómago ⓜ es·*to*·ma·go *stomach*

estrella ① es·*tre*·ya *star*

estreñimiento ⓜ es·tre·nyee·*myen*·to
constipation

estudiante ⓜ&① es·too·*dyan*·te
student

estudio ⓜ es·*too*·dyo *studio*

estufa ① es·*too*·fa *stove*

estúpido/a ⓜ/① es·*too*·pee·do/a
stupid

etiqueta ① **para equipaje** e·tee·*ke*·ta
pa·ra e·kee·*pa*·khe *luggage tag*

euro ⓜ e·oo·ro *Euro*

Europa ① e·oo·ro·pa *Europe*

eutanasia ① e·oo·ta·*na*·sya
euthanasia

eventual e·ven·*twal* *part-time*

excelente ek·se·*len*·te *excellent*

excluído/a ⓜ/① ek·skloo·*ee*·do/a
excluded

excursión ① ek·skoor·*syon* *tour*

excursionismo ⓜ
ek·skoor·syo·*nees*·mo *hiking*

experiencia ① ek·spe·*ryen*·sya
experience
— **laboral** la·bo·*ral* *work experience*

exponer ek·spo·*ner* *exhibit*

exposición ① ek·spo·see·*syon*
exhibition

expreso ek·*spre*·so *express*

exterior ⓜ ek·ste·*ryor* *outside*

extrañar ek·stra·*nyar* miss
(feel absence)
extranjero/a ⓜ/ⓕ ek·stran·*khe*·ro/a
foreign
extraño/a ⓜ/ⓕ ek·*stra*·nyo/a strange

F

fábrica ⓕ *fa*·bree·ka factory
fácil *fa*·seel easy
factura ⓕ **del coche** fak·*too*·ra del
ko·che car owner's title
falda ⓕ *fal*·da skirt
falta ⓕ *fal*·ta fault
familia ⓕ fa·*mee*·lya family
famoso/a ⓜ/ⓕ fa·*mo*·so/a famous
farmacéutico/a ⓜ/ⓕ
far·ma·*sew*·tee·ko chemist (person)
farmacia ⓕ far·*ma*·sya pharmacy ·
chemist (shop)
faros ⓜ pl *fa*·ros headlights
fecha ⓕ *fe*·cha date (time)
— **de nacimiento** de
na·see·*myen*·to date of birth
feliz fe·*lees* happy
ferretería ⓕ fe·re·te·*ree*·a
electrical store
festival ⓜ fes·tee·*val* festival
ficción ⓕ feek·*syon* fiction
fideos ⓜ pl fee·*de*·os noodles
fiebre ⓕ *fye*·bre fever
fiesta ⓕ *fyes*·ta party
filete ⓜ fee·*le*·te fillet
fin ⓜ feen end
— **de año** de *a*·nyo New Year's Eve
— **de semana** de se·*ma*·na
weekend
firma ⓕ *feer*·ma signature
firmar feer·*mar* sign
flan ⓜ flan custard
flor ⓕ flor flower
florista ⓜ&ⓕ flo·*rees*·ta florist
foco ⓜ *fo*·ko light bulb
folklórico/a ⓜ/ⓕ fol·*klo*·ree·ko/a folk
folleto ⓜ fo·*ye*·to brochure
forma ⓕ *for*·ma shape

fotografía ⓕ fo·to·gra·*fee*·a photo ·
photography
fotógrafo/a ⓜ/ⓕ fo·*to*·gra·fo/a
photographer
fotómetro ⓜ fo·*to*·me·tro light meter
frágil *fra*·kheel fragile
frambuesa ⓕ fram·*bwe*·sa raspberry
France ⓕ *fran*·sya France
franela ⓕ fra·*ne*·la flannel
freír fre·*eer* fry
frenos ⓜ pl *fre*·nos brakes
frente a *fren*·te a opposite
fresa ⓕ *fre*·sa strawberry
frijoles ⓜ pl free·*kho*·les beans
frío/a ⓜ/ⓕ *free*·o/a cold
frontera ⓕ fron·*te*·ra border
fruta ⓕ *froo*·ta fruit
— **seca** se·*ka* dried fruit
fuego ⓜ *fwe*·go fire
fuera de lugar *fwe*·ra de loo·*gar*
offside
fuerte *fwer*·te strong
fumar foo·*mar* smoke
funda ⓕ **de almohada** *foon*·da de
al·*mwa*·da pillowcase
funeral ⓜ foo·ne·*ral* funeral
fútbol ⓜ *foot*·bol football · soccer
— **australiano** ow·stra·*lya*·no
Australian Rules football
futuro ⓜ foo·*too*·ro future

G

galería ⓕ **de arte** ga·le·*ree*·a de *ar*·te
art gallery
galleta ⓕ ga·*ye*·ta biscuit · cookie
galletas ⓕ pl **saladas** ga·*ye*·tas
sa·*la*·das crackers
ganador(a) ⓜ/ⓕ ga·na·*dor*/
ga·na·*do*·ra winner
ganancia ⓕ ga·*nan*·sya profit
ganar ga·*nar* win · earn
garbanzos ⓜ pl gar·*ban*·sos
chickpeas
garganta ⓕ gar·*gan*·ta throat
gasolina ⓕ ga·so·*lee*·na petrol

gasolinera ① ga·so·lee·*ne*·ra *service station*

gatito/a ⓜ/① ga·*tee*·to/a *kitten*

gato/a ⓜ/① *ga*·to/a *cat*

gay gay *gay*

gelatina ① khe·la·*tee*·na *gelatin*

gemelos/as ⓜ/① pl khe·*me*·los/as *twins*

general khe·ne·*ral general*

gente ① *khen*·te *people*

gimnasia ① kheem·*na*·sya *gymnastics*

ginebra ① khee·*ne*·bra *gin*

ginecólogo/a ⓜ/① khee·ne·*ko*·lo·go/a *gynaecologist*

glorieta ① glo·*rye*·ta *roundabout*

gobierno ⓜ go·*byer*·no *government*

goggles ⓜ pl *go*·gles *goggles*

gol ⓜ gol *goal*

goma ① *go*·ma *gum*

gordo/a ⓜ/① *gor*·do/a *fat*

gotas ① pl **para los ojos** *go*·tas *pa*·ra los *o*·khos *eye drops*

grabación ① gra·ba·*syon recording*

gramo ⓜ *gra*·mo *gram*

grande *gran*·de *big* • *large*

granja ① *gran*·kha *farm*

granjero/a ⓜ/① gran·*khe*·ro/a *farmer*

granola ① gra·*no*·la *muesli*

grasa *gra*·sa *fat (meat)* • *grease*

gratis *gra*·tees *free (of charge)*

gripe ① *gree*·pe *influenza*

gris grees *grey*

gritar gree·*tar shout*

grupo ⓜ *groo*·po *band*
  — **de rock** de rok *rock group*
  — **sanguíneo** san·*gee*·ne·o *blood group*

guantes ⓜ pl *gwan*·tes *gloves*

guapo/a ⓜ/① *gwa*·po/a *gorgeous*

guardarropa ⓜ gwar·da·*ro*·pa *cloakroom*

guardería ① gwar·de·*ree*·a *childminding service* • *creche*

guerra ① *ge*·ra *war*

güey ⓜ gway *mate* • *pal*

guía ⓜ&① *gee*·a *guide (person)*

guía ① *gee*·a *guidebook*
  — **del ocio** del *o*·syo *entertainment guide*
  — **turística** too·*rees*·tee·ka *guidebook*

guión ⓜ gee·*on script*

guitarra ① gee·*ta*·ra *guitar*

gusanos ⓜ pl **de maguey** goo·*sa*·nos de ma·*gay cactus worms*

gustar goos·*tar like*

habitación ① a·bee·ta·*syon room* • *bedroom*
  — **doble** *do*·ble *double room*
  — **individual** een·dee·vee·*dwal single room*

hablar a·*blar speak* • *talk*

hacer a·*ser do* • *make*

hachís ⓜ kha·*shees hash*

hacia *a*·sya *towards*

halal kha·*lal halal*

hamaca ① a·*ma*·ka *hammock*

hambre ① *am*·bre *hunger*

harina ① a·*ree*·na *flour*

hasta (junio) *as*·ta (khoo·nyo) *until (June)*

hechado/a ⓜ/① **a perder** e·*cha*·do/a a per·*der off (spoiled)*

hecho/a ⓜ/① *e*·cho/a *made*
  — **a mano** a *ma*·no *handmade*
  — **de (algodón)** de (al·go·*don*) *made of (cotton)*

heladería ① e·la·de·*ree*·a *ice-cream parlour*

helado ⓜ e·*la*·do *ice cream*

hepatitis ① e·pa·*tee*·tees *hepatitis*

herida ① e·*ree*·da *injury*

hermana ① er·*ma*·na *sister*

hermano ⓜ er·*ma*·no *brother*

hermoso/a ⓜ/① er·mo·*so*/a *beautiful*

heroína ① e·ro·*ee*·na *heroin*

hielo m *ye·lo* ice

hierbas f pl *yer·bas* herbs

hígado m *ee·ga·do* liver

higo m *ee·go* fig

hija f *ee·kha* daughter

hijo m *ee·kho* son

hijos m pl *ee·khos* children

hilo — **dental** *ee·lo den·tal* dental floss

hindú een·*doo* Hindu

hipódromo m *ee·po·dro·mo* racetrack (horses)

histórico/a m/f *ees·to·ree·ko/a* historical

hockey m *kho·kee* hockey
— **sobre hielo** *so·bre ye·lo* ice hockey

hoja f *o·kha* leaf · sheet (of paper)

hojuelas f pl **de maíz** *o·khwe·las de ma·ees* corn flakes

Holanda f *o·lan·da* Netherlands

hombre m *om·bre* man

hombro m *om·bro* shoulder

homosexual m&f *o·mo·sek·swal* homosexual

hora f *o·ra* time · hour

horario m *o·ra·ryo* timetable
— **de servicio** de ser·*vee·*syo opening hours

hormiga f *or·mee·ga* ant

horno m *or·no* oven
— **de microondas** de mee·kro·*on·*das microwave oven

horóscopo m *o·ros·ko·po* horoscope

hospital m *os·pee·tal* hospital
— **privado** pree·*va·*do private hospital

hotel m *o·tel* hotel

hotelería f *o·te·le·ree·a* hospitality

hoy oy today

hueso m *we·so* bone

huevo m *we·vo* egg

humanidades f pl *oo·ma·nee·da·des* humanities

I

identificación f *ee·den·tee·fee·ka·syon* identification

idiomas m pl *ee·dyo·*mas languages

idiota m&f *ee·dyo·ta* idiot

iglesia f *ee·gle·sya* church

igual ee·*gwal* same

igualdad f *ee·gwal·dad* equality
— **de oportunidades** de o·por·too·nee·*da·*des equal opportunity

imbécil m&f *eem·be·seel* fool

impermeable m *eem·per·me·a·*ble raincoat

impermeable *eem·per·me·a·*ble waterproof

importante *eem·por·tan·*te important

impuesto m *eem·pwes·*to tax
— **sobre la renta** *so·*bre la *ren·*ta income tax

incendio m *een·sen·*dyo fire

incluído/a m/f *een·kloo·ee·*do/a included

incómodo/a m/f *een·ko·mo·*do/a uncomfortable

India f *een·*dya India

indicador m *een·dee·ka·*dor indicator

indigestión f *een·dee·khes·*tyon indigestion

industria f *een·doos·*trya industry

infección f *een·fek·*syon infection
— **de garganta** de gar·*gan·*ta thrush

inflamación f *een·fla·ma·*syon inflammation

informática f *een·for·ma·*tee·ka IT

informativo m *een·for·ma·*tee·vo current affairs

ingeniería f *een·khe·nye·*ree·a engineering

ingeniero/a m/f *een·khe·nye·*ro/a engineer

Inglaterra f *een·gla·te·*ra England

inglés m *een·*gles English (language)

ingrediente ⓜ een·gre·*dyen*·te
ingredient

injusto/a ⓜ/ⓕ een·*khoos*·to/a *unfair*

inmigración ⓕ een·mee·gra·*syon*
immigration

inocente ee·no·*sen*·te *innocent*

inseguro/a ⓜ/ⓕ een·se·*goo*·ro/a
unsafe

inspector(a) ⓜ/ⓕ een·spek·*tor*/
een·spek·*to*·ra *ticket collector ·
inspector*

instructor(a) ⓜ/ⓕ een·strook·*tor*/
eens·trook·*to*·ra *instructor*

intentar een·ten·*tar* *try (attempt)*

interesante een·te·re·*san*·te
interesting

internacional een·ter·na·syo·*nal*
international

Internet ⓕ *een*·ter·net *Internet*

intérprete ⓜ&ⓕ een·*ter*·pre·te
interpreter

inundación ⓕ ee·noon·da·*syon*
flooding

invierno ⓜ een·*vyer*·no *winter*

invitar een·vee·*tar* *invite*

inyección ⓕ een·yek·*syon* *injection*

inyectar een·yek·*tar* *inject*

ir eer *go*
— **de compras** de *kom*·pras
go shopping
— **de excursión** de ek·skoor·*syon*
hike

Irlanda ⓕ eer·*lan*·da *Ireland*

irritación ⓕ ee·rree·ta·*syon* *rash*

isla ⓕ *ees*·la *island*

itinerario ⓜ ee·tee·ne·*ra*·ryo *itinerary*

IVA ⓜ *ee*·va *sales tax*

izquierda ⓕ ees·*kyer*·da *left*

J

jabón ⓜ kha·*bon* *soap*

jalar kha·*lar* *pull*

jamón ⓜ kha·*mon* *ham*

Japón ⓜ kha·*pon* *Japan*

jarabe (para la tos) ⓜ kha·*ra*·be
(*pa*·ra la tos) *cough medicine*

jardín ⓜ khar·*deen* *garden*
— **botánico** bo·*ta*·nee·ko *botanic
garden*
— **de niños** de *nee*·nyos
kindergarten

jarra ⓕ *kha*·ra *jar*

jeep ⓜ yeep *jeep*

jefe/a ⓜ/ⓕ *khe*·fe/a *employer ·
manager*

jengibre ⓜ khen·*khee*·bre *ginger*

jerga ⓕ *kher*·ga *wash cloth*

jeringa ⓕ khe·*reen*·ga *syringe*

jitomate ⓜ khee·to·*ma*·te *tomato*

joven *kho*·ven *young*

joyería ⓕ kho·ye·*ree*·a *jewellery*

jubilado/a ⓜ/ⓕ khoo·bee·*la*·do/a
retired · pensioner

judío/a ⓜ/ⓕ khoo·*dee*·o/a *Jewish*

juego ⓜ **de computadora** *khwe*·go
de kom·poo·ta·*do*·ra *computer
game*

juegos ⓜ pl **olímpicos** *khwe*·gos
o·*leem*·pee·kos *Olympic Games*

juez ⓜ&ⓕ khwes *judge*

jugar khoo·*gar* *play (sport/games)*
— **a las cartas** a las *kar*·tas
play (cards)

jugo ⓜ *khoo*·go *juice*
— **de naranja** de na·*ran*·kha
orange juice

juguetería ⓕ khoo·ge·te·*ree*·a
toyshop

juntos/as ⓜ/ⓕ *khoon*·tos/as
together

K

kilo ⓜ *kee*·lo *kilogram*

kilómetro ⓜ kee·*lo*·me·tro *kilometre*

kiwi ⓜ *kee*·wee *kiwifruit*

kleenex ⓜ pl *klee*·neks *tissues*

kosher *ko*·sher *kosher*

L

labios ⓜ pl *la*·byos lips
lado ⓜ *la*·do side
ladrón ⓜ la·*dron* thief
lagartija ⓕ la·gar·*tee*·kha small lizard
lago ⓜ *la*·go lake
lamentar la·men·*tar* regret
lana ⓕ *la*·na wool
lancha ⓕ **de motor** *lan*·cha de
mo·*tor* motorboat
lápiz ⓜ *la*·pees pencil
— **labial** *la*·byal lipstick
larga distancia *lar*·ga dees·*tan*·sya
long-distance
largo/a ⓜ/ⓕ *lar*·go/a long
lastimar las·tee·*mar* hurt
lata ⓕ *la*·ta can • tin
lavadora ⓕ la·va·*do*·ra washing
machine
lavandería ⓕ la·van·de·*ree*·a
laundry • laundrette
lavar la·*var* wash (something)
lavarse la·*var*·se wash (oneself)
leche ⓕ *le*·che milk
— **de soya** de *so*·ya soy milk
— **descremada** des·kre·*ma*·da
skimmed milk
lechuga ⓕ le·*choo*·ga lettuce
leer le·*er* read
legal le·*gal* legal
legislación ⓕ le·khees·la·*syon*
legislation
legumbre ⓕ le·*goom*·bre vegetable
lejos *le*·khos far
leña ⓕ *le*·nya firewood
lentejas ⓕ pl len·*te*·khas lentils
lentes ⓜ&ⓕ pl *len*·tes glasses
— **de contacto** de kon·*tak*·to
contact lenses
— **de sol** de sol sunglasses
lento/a ⓜ/ⓕ *len*·to/a slow
lesbiana ⓕ les·bee·*a*·na lesbian
ley ⓕ lay law
libra ⓕ *lee*·bra pound (money)
libre *lee*·bre free (not bound)

librería ⓕ lee·bre·*ree*·a bookshop
libro ⓜ *lee*·bro book
— **de frases** de *fra*·ses phrasebook
— **de oraciones** de o·ra·*syo*·nes
prayer book
licencia ⓕ **de manejo** lee·*sen*·sya de
ma·*ne*·kho drivers licence
licenciatura ⓕ lee·sen·sya·*too*·ra
university
líder ⓜ&ⓕ *lee*·der leader
ligar lee·*gar* chat up • pick up
ligero/a ⓜ/ⓕ lee·*khe*·ro/a
light (of weight)
lima ⓕ *lee*·ma lime
límite ⓜ **de equipaje** *lee*·mee·te de
e·kee·*pa*·khe baggage allowance
limón ⓜ lee·*mon* lemon
limonada ⓕ lee·mo·*na*·da lemonade
limosnero/a ⓜ/ⓕ lee·mos·*ne*·ro/a
beggar
limpio/a ⓜ/ⓕ *leem*·pyo/a clean
línea ⓕ *lee*·ne·a line • dial tone
linterna ⓕ leen·*ter*·na torch •
flashlight
listo/a ⓜ/ⓕ *lees*·to/a ready
local lo·*kal* local
loción ⓕ **para después del afeitado**
lo·*syon* pa·ra des·*pwes* del
a·fay·*ta*·do aftershave
loco/a ⓜ/ⓕ *lo*·ko/a crazy
lodo ⓜ *lo*·do mud
lombrices ⓕ pl lom·*bree*·ses worms
lubricante ⓜ loo·bree·*kan*·te
lubricant
luces ⓕ pl *loo*·ses lights
luchar loo·*char* fight
lugar ⓜ loo·*gar* place
— **de nacimiento** de
na·see·*myen*·to place of birth
lujo ⓜ *loo*·kho luxury
luna ⓕ *loo*·na moon
— **de miel** de myel honeymoon
— **llena** *ye*·na full moon
luz ⓕ loos light

LL

llamada ① **por cobrar** ya·*ma*·da por ko·*brar* *collect call*
llamar ya·*mar* *call*
 — **por teléfono** por te·*le*·fo·no *telephone • ring*
llanta ① yan·ta *tyre*
llave ① *ya*·ve *key*
 — **del agua** del *a*·gwa *faucet*
llegadas ① pl ye·*ga*·das *arrivals*
llegar ye·*gar* *arrive*
llenar ye·*nar* *fill*
lleno/a ⓜ/① *ye*·no/a *booked out • crowded • full*
llevar ye·*var* *carry • take (away) • wear*
lluvia ① *yoo*·vya *rain*

M

maceta ① ma·*se*·ta *pot (for plant)*
machismo ⓜ ma·*chees*·mo *machismo*
madera ① ma·*de*·ra *wood*
madre ① *ma*·dre *mother*
maestro/a ⓜ/① ma·*es*·tro/a *teacher*
mago/a ⓜ/① *ma*·go/a *magician*
maíz ⓜ ma·*ees* *corn*
maleta ① ma·*le*·ta *suitcase*
malo/a ⓜ/① *ma*·lo/a *bad*
mamá ① ma·*ma* *mum*
mamograma ⓜ ma·mo·*gra*·ma *mammogram*
mañana ① ma·*nya*·na *morning*
mañana ma·*nya*·na *tomorrow*
 — **en la mañana** en la ma·*nya*·na *tomorrow morning*
 — **en la noche** en la *no*·che *tomorrow evening*
 — **en la tarde** en la *tar*·de *tomorrow afternoon*
mandarina ① man·da·*ree*·na *mandarin*
mandíbula ① man·*dee*·boo·la *jaw*
mango ⓜ *man*·go *mango*
manifestación ① ma·nee·fes·ta·*syon* *demonstration (protest)*

mano ① *ma*·no *hand*
manteca ① man·*te*·ka *lard*
mantel ⓜ man·*tel* *tablecloth*
mantequilla ① man·te·*kee*·ya *butter*
manubrio ⓜ ma·*noo*·bryo *handlebar*
manzana ① man·*sa*·na *apple*
mapa ⓜ *ma*·pa *map*
maquillaje ⓜ ma·kee·ya·khe *make-up*
máquina ① *ma*·kee·na *machine*
 — **de tabaco** de ta·*ba*·ko *cigarette machine*
mar ⓜ mar *sea*
maravilloso/a ⓜ/① ma·ra·vee·*yo*·so/a *wonderful*
marcación ① **directa** mar·ka·*syon* dee·*rek*·ta *direct-dial*
marcador ⓜ mar·ka·*dor* *scoreboard*
marcapasos ⓜ mar·ka·*pa*·sos *pacemaker*
marea ① ma·*re*·a *tide*
mareado/a ⓜ/① ma·re·*a*·do/a *dizzy • seasick*
mareo ⓜ ma·*re*·o *travel sickness*
margarina ① mar·ga·*ree*·na *margarine*
marihuana ① ma·ree·*wa*·na *marijuana*
mariposa ① ma·ree·*po*·sa *butterfly*
martillo ⓜ mar·*tee*·yo *hammer*
más mas *more*
 — **cercano/a** ⓜ/① mas ser·*ka*·no/a *nearest*
masaje ⓜ ma·*sa*·khe *massage*
masajista ⓜ&① ma·sa·*khees*·ta *masseur/masseuse*
matar ma·*tar* *kill*
matrícula ① ma·*tree*·koo·la *car registration*
matrimonio ⓜ ma·tree·*mo*·nyo *marriage*
mayonesa ① ma·yo·*ne*·sa *mayonnaise*
mecánico/a ⓜ/① me·*ka*·nee·ko/a *mechanic*
medianoche ① me·dya·*no*·che *midnight*
medicina ① me·dee·*see*·na *medicine*

medio ⓜ **ambiente** me·dyo am·*byen*·te *environment*

medio litro ⓜ me·dyo lee·tro *half a litre*

medio/a ⓜ/ⓕ me·dyo/a *half*

mediodía ⓜ me·dyo·*dee*·a *noon*

medios ⓜ pl **de comunicación** me·dyos de ko·moo·nee·ka·*syon* *media*

mejillones ⓜ pl me·khee·yo·nes *mussels*

mejor me·*khor* *better* • *best*

melodía ⓕ me·lo·*dee*·a *a tune*

melón ⓜ me·*lon* *melon*
— cantaloupe kan·ta·*loop* *cantaloupe*

menos me·nos *less*

mensaje ⓜ men·*sa*·khe *message*

menstruación ⓕ men·strwa·*syon* *menstruation*

mentiroso/a ⓜ/ⓕ men·tee·ro·so/a *liar*

menú ⓜ me·*noo* *menu*

mercado ⓜ mer·*ka*·do *market*

mermelada ⓕ mer·me·*la*·da *jam* • *marmalade*

mes ⓜ mes *month*

mesa ⓕ me·sa *table*

mesero/a ⓜ/ⓕ me·se·ro/a *waiter*

meseta ⓕ me·se·ta *plateau*

metal ⓜ me·*tal* *metal*

meter ⓜ me·*ter* *put*
— un gol oon gol *kick a goal*

metro ⓜ me·tro *metre* • *subway*

mezclar mes·*klar* *mix*

mezquita ⓕ mes·*kee*·ta *mosque*

mi mee *my*

miel ⓕ myel *honey*

miembro ⓜ *myem*·bro *member*

migraña ⓕ mee·*gra*·nya *migraine*

milímetro ⓜ mee·*lee*·me·tro *millimetre*

militar ⓜ mee·lee·*tar* *military*

millón ⓜ mee·*yon* *million*

minuto ⓜ mee·*noo*·to *minute*

mirador ⓜ mee·ra·*dor* *lookout*

mirar mee·*rar* *look* • *watch*
— los aparadores los a·pa·ra·do·res *window-shopping*

misa ⓕ *mee*·sa *mass*

mochila ⓕ mo·*chee*·la *backpack* • *knapsack*

módem ⓜ *mo*·dem *modem*

mojado/a ⓜ/ⓕ mo·*kha*·do/a *wet*

monasterio ⓜ mo·nas·*te*·ryo *monastery*

monedas ⓕ pl mo·*ne*·das *coins*

monja ⓕ mon·kha *nun*

montaña ⓕ mon·*ta*·nya *mountain*

montar mon·*tar* *ride*

monumento ⓜ mo·noo·*men*·to *monument*

morado/a ⓜ/ⓕ mo·*ra*·do/a *purple*

mordedura ⓕ mor·de·*doo*·ra *bite (dog)*

moretón ⓜ mo·re·*ton* *bruise*

morir mo·*reer* *die*

mosquitero ⓜ mos·kee·*te*·ro *mosquito net*

mosquito ⓜ mos·*kee*·to *mosquito*

mostaza ⓕ mos·*ta*·sa *mustard*

mostrador ⓜ mos·tra·*dor* *counter*

mostrar mos·*trar* *show*

mota ⓕ *mo*·ta *pot (marijuana)*

motocicleta ⓕ mo·to·see·*kle*·ta *motorcycle*

motor ⓜ mo·*tor* *engine*

muchos/as ⓜ/ⓕ pl moo·chos/as *many*

mudo/a ⓜ/ⓕ moo·do/a *mute*

muebles ⓜ pl mwe·bles *furniture*

muela ⓕ mwe·la *tooth (back)*

muerto/a ⓜ/ⓕ mwer·to/a *dead*

mujer ⓕ moo·*kher* *woman*

multa ⓕ *mool*·ta *fine*

mundo ⓜ moon·do *world*

muñeca ⓕ moo·*nye*·ka *doll* • *wrist*

murallas ⓕ pl moo·*ra*·yas *city walls*

músculo ⓜ *moos*·koo·lo *muscle*

museo ⓜ moo·*se*·o *museum*

música ⓕ *moo*·see·ka *music*

músico ⓜ&ⓕ *moo*·see·ko *musician*

musulmán/musulmana ⓜ/ⓕ moo·sool·*man*/moo·sool·*ma*·na *Muslim*

muy mooy *very*

muy (caro/a) ⓜ/ⓕ mooy (*ka*·ro/a) *too (expensive)*

N

nacionalidad ① na·syo·na·lee·*dad*
nationality
nada *na*·da *none · nothing*
nadar na·*dar* *swim*
naranja ① na·*ran*·kha *orange*
naranja na·*ran*·kha *orange (colour)*
nariz ① na·*rees* *nose*
naturaleza ① na·too·ra·*le*·sa *nature*
naturopatía ① na·too·ro·*pa*·tee·a
naturopathy
náusea ① *now*·se·a *nausea*
náuseas ① pl
now·se·as del em·ba·*ra*·so *morning
sickness*
navaja ① na·*va*·kha *penknife*
navajas ① pl **de razurar** na·*va*·khas
de ra·soo·*rar* *razor blades*
Navidad ① na·vee·*dad*
Christmas Day
neblinoso ne·blee·*no*·so *foggy*
necesario/a ⓜ/① ne·se·*sa*·ryo/a
necessary
necesitar ne·se·see·*tar* *need*
negar ne·*gar* *deny*
negar(se) ne·*gar*·(se) *refuse*
negativos ⓜ pl ne·ga·*tee*·vos
negatives (film)
negocios ⓜ pl ne·*go*·syos *business*
negro/a ⓜ/① *ne*·gro/a *black*
nieto/a ⓜ/① *nye*·to/a *grandchild*
nieve ① *nye*·ve *snow*
niñera ① nee·*nye*·ra *babysitter*
niño/a ⓜ/① *nee*·nyo/a *child*
niños ⓜ&① pl *nee*·nyos *children*
no no *no*
no fumar no foo·*mar* *non-smoking*
noche ① *no*·che *evening*
Nochebuena ① no·che·*bwe*·na
Christmas Eve
nombre ⓜ *nom*·bre *name*
— de pila de *pee*·la *first name*
norte ⓜ *nor*·te *north*
nosotros/as ⓜ/① pl no·*so*·tros/as *we*
noticias ① pl no·*tee*·syas *news*

novia ① *no*·vya *girlfriend*
novio ⓜ *no*·vyo *boyfriend*
nube ① *noo*·be *cloud*
nublado noo·*bla*·do *cloudy*
nueces ① pl *nwe*·ses *nuts*
— crudas *kroo*·das *raw nuts*
— tostadas tos·*ta*·das *roasted nuts*
nuestro/a ⓜ/① *nwes*·tro/a *our*
Nueva ① **Zelandia** *nwe*·va se·*lan*·dya
New Zealand
nuevo/a ⓜ/① *nwe*·vo/a *new*
nuez ① **de la India** nwes de la
een·dya *cashew nut*
número ⓜ *noo*·me·ro *number*
— de habitación de a·bee·ta·*syon*
room number
— de pasaporte de pa·sa·*por*·te
passport number
— de placa de *pla*·ka
license plate number
nunca *noon*·ka *never*

O

o o *or*
objetivo ⓜ ob·khe·*tee*·vo *lens*
obra ① *o*·bra *play*
obrero/a ⓜ/① o·*bre*·ro/a
labourer · manual worker
océano ⓜ o·*se*·a·no *ocean*
ocupado/a ⓜ/① o·koo·*pa*·do/a *busy*
oeste ⓜ o·*es*·te *west*
oficina ① o·fee·*see*·na *office*
— de correos de ko·*re*·os *post
office*
— de turismo de too·*rees*·mo
tourist office
— de objetos perdidos de
ob·*khe*·tos per·*dee*·dos *lost property
office*
oír o·*eer* *hear*
ojo ⓜ *o*·kho *eye*
ola ① *o*·la *wave*
oler o·*ler* *smell*
olor ⓜ o·*lor* *smell*

olvidar ol·vee·*dar* forget
ópera ① *o*·pe·ra opera
operación ① o·pe·ra·*syon* operation
operador(a) ⑩/① o·pe·ra·*dor*/
o·pe·ra·*do*·ra operator
opinión ① o·pee·*nyon* opinion
oporto ⑩ o·*por*·to port (wine)
oportunidad ① o·por·too·nee·*dad*
chance
oración ① o·ra·*syon* prayer
orden ⑩ *or*·den order (placement)
orden ① *or*·den order (command)
ordenar or·de·*nar* order
oreja ① o·*re*·kha ear
orgasmo ⑩ or·*gas*·mo orgasm
original o·ree·khee·*nal* original
orquesta ① or·*kes*·ta orchestra
oscuro/a ⑩/① os·*koo*·ro/a dark
ostión ⑩ os·*tyon* oyster
otoño ⑩ o·*to*·nyo autumn
otra vez *o*·tra ves again
otro/a ⑩/① *o*·tro/a other
oveja ① o·*ve*·kha sheep
oxígeno ⑩ ok·*see*·khe·no oxygen

P

pacheco/a ⑩/① pa·*che*·ko/a stoned ·
high
padre ⑩ *pa*·dre father
padres ⑩ pl *pa*·dres parents
padrísimo/a ⑩/① pa·*dree*·see·mo/a
great
pagar pa·*gar* pay
página ① *pa*·khee·na page
pago ⑩ *pa*·go payment
país ⑩ pa·*ees* country
pájaro ⑩ *pa*·kha·ro bird
palabra ① pa·*la*·bra word
palacio ⑩ pa·*la*·syo palace
palillo ⑩ pa·*lee*·yo toothpick
pan ⑩ pan bread
— **de levadura fermentada**
de le·va·*doo*·ra fer·men·*ta*·da
sourdough
— **integral** een·te·*gral* brown bread
— **tostado** tos·*ta*·do toast

panadería ① pa·na·de·*ree*·a bakery
pantaletas ① pl pan·ta·*le*·tas
underpants (women)
pantalla ① pan·*ta*·ya screen
pantalones ⑩ pl pan·ta·*lo*·nes
pants · trousers
— **de mezclilla** de mes·*klee*·ya
jeans
pantimedias ① pl pan·tee·*me*·dyas
pantyhose · stockings
pantiprotectores ⑩ pl
pan·tee·pro·tek·*to*·res panty liners
pañal ⑩ pa·*nyal* nappy · diaper
papa ① *pa*·pa potato
Papa ⑩ *pa*·pa Pope
papá ⑩ pa·*pa* dad
papanicolaou ⑩ pa·pa·nee·ko·*low*
pap smear
papel ⑩ pa·*pel* paper
— **higiénico** ee·*khye*·nee·ko
toilet paper
— **para cigarros** *pa*·ra see·*ga*·ros
cigarette papers
paquete ⑩ pa·*ke*·te package · packet
para *pa*·ra for
— **siempre** *syem*·pre forever
parabrisas ⑩ pa·ra·*bree*·sas
windscreen
parada ① pa·*ra*·da stop
— **de camiones** de ka·*myo*·nes
bus stop
paraguas ⑩ pa·*ra*·gwas umbrella
parapléjico/a ⑩/①
pa·ra·*ple*·khee·ko/a paraplegic
parar pa·*rar* stop
pared ① pa·*red* wall (inside)
pareja ① pa·*re*·kha pair (couple)
parlamento ⑩ par·la·*men*·to
parliament
paro ⑩ *pa*·ro dole
parque ⑩ *par*·ke park
— **nacional** na·syo·*nal* national
park
parte ① *par*·te part
partido ⑩ par·*tee*·do match (sport) ·
party (political)
pasado ⑩ pa·*sa*·do past

mexican spanish-english

pasado mañana pa·*sa*·do ma·*nya*·na
day after tomorrow
pasajero ⓜ pa·sa·*khe*·ro *passenger*
pasaporte ⓜ pa·sa·*por*·te *passport*
Pascua ⓕ *pas*·kwa *Easter*
pase ⓜ *pa*·se *pass*
— **de abordar** de a·bor·*dar*
boarding pass
paseo ⓜ pa·*se*·o *ride*
paso ⓜ *pa*·so *step*
pasta ⓕ *pas*·ta *pasta*
— **de dientes** *pas*·ta de *dyen*·tes
toothpaste
pastel ⓜ pas·*tel* *cake*
— **de bodas** de *bo*·das *wedding
cake*
— **de cumpleaños** de
koom·ple·*a*·nyos *birthday cake*
pastelería ⓕ pas·te·le·*ree*·a *cake shop*
pastillas ⓕ pl pas·*tee*·yas *pills*
— **antipalúdicas**
an·tee·pa·*loo*·dee·kas *antimalarial
tablets*
— **de menta** de *men*·ta *mints*
— **para dormir** *pa*·ra dor·*meer*
sleeping pills
pasto ⓜ *pas*·to *grass*
paté ⓜ pa·*te* *pate (food)*
patear pa·te·*ar* *kick*
patinar pa·tee·*nar* *rollerblading*
patineta ⓕ pa·tee·*ne*·ta *skateboard*
pato ⓜ *pa*·to *duck*
pavo ⓜ *pa*·vo *turkey*
pay ⓜ pay *pie*
paz ⓕ pas *peace*
peatón ⓜ pe·a·*ton* *pedestrian*
pecho ⓜ *pe*·cho *chest*
pechuga ⓕ pe·*choo*·ga *breast
(poultry)*
— **de pollo** de *po*·yo *chicken breast*
pedal ⓜ pe·*dal* *pedal*
pedazo ⓜ pe·*da*·so *piece*
pedir pe·*deer* *ask (for something)*
— **aventón** a·ven·*ton* *hitchhike*
— **prestado** pres·*ta*·do *borrow*
pedo ⓜ *pe*·do *fart*
peinar pay·*nar* *comb*
peine ⓜ *pay*·ne *comb*

pelea ⓕ pe·*le*·a *fight • quarrel*
película ⓕ pe·*lee*·koo·la *film • movie*
— **en color** en ko·*lor* *colour film*
peligroso/a ⓜ/ⓕ pe·lee·*gro*·so/a
dangerous
pelo ⓜ *pe*·lo *hair*
pelota ⓕ pe·*lo*·ta *ball*
— **de golf** de golf *golf ball*
peluquero/a ⓜ/ⓕ pe·loo·*ke*·ro/a
hairdresser • barber
pene ⓜ *pe*·ne *penis*
pensar pen·*sar* *think*
pensión ⓕ pen·*syon* *boarding house*
pepino ⓜ pe·*pee*·no *cucumber*
pequeño/a ⓜ/ⓕ pe·*ke*·nyo/a *small •
tiny*
pera ⓕ *pe*·ra *pear*
perder per·*der* *lose*
perdido/a ⓜ/ⓕ per·*dee*·do/a *lost*
perdonar per·do·*nar* *forgive*
perejil ⓜ pe·re·*kheel* *parsley*
perfume ⓜ per·*foo*·me *perfume*
periódico ⓜ pe·*ryo*·dee·ko
newspaper
periodista ⓜ&ⓕ pe·ryo·*dees*·ta
journalist
permiso ⓜ per·*mee*·so
permission • permit
— **de trabajo** de tra·*ba*·kho
work permit
permitir per·mee·*teer* *allow • permit*
pero *pe*·ro *but*
perro/a ⓜ/ⓕ *pe*·ro/a *dog*
perro ⓜ **guía** *pe*·ro *gee*·a *guide dog*
persona ⓕ per·*so*·na *person*
pesado/a ⓜ/ⓕ pe·*sa*·do/a *heavy*
pesar pe·*sar* *weigh*
pesas ⓕ pl *pe*·sas *weights*
pesca ⓕ *pes*·ka *fishing*
pescadería ⓕ pes·ka·de·*ree*·a *fish
shop*
pescado ⓜ pes·*ka*·do *fish (as food)*
peso ⓜ *pe*·so *weight*
petate ⓜ pe·*ta*·te *mat*
petición ⓕ pe·tee·*syon* *petition*
pez ⓜ pes *fish*
picadura ⓕ pee·ka·*doo*·ra *bite
(insect)*
pico ⓜ *pee*·ko *pickaxe*
pie ⓜ pye *foot*

piedra ① *pye*·dra *stone*
piel ① *pyel skin*
pierna ① *pyer*·na *leg*
pila ① *pee*·la *battery (small)*
píldora ① *peel*·do·ra *the Pill*
pimienta ① pee·*myen*·ta *pepper (spice)*
pimiento ⓜ pee·*myen*·to *pepper (bell)*
piña ① *pee*·nya *pineapple*
ping pong ⓜ peen pon *table tennis*
pintar peen·*tar paint*
pintor(a) ⓜ/① peen·*tor*/peen·*to*·ra *painter*
pintura ① peen·*too*·ra *painting*
pinzas ① pl *peen*·sas *tweezers*
piojos ⓜ pl *pyo*·khos *lice*
piolet ⓜ *pyo*·le *ice axe*
piso ⓜ *pee*·so *floor*
pista ① *pees*·ta *racetrack (runners)*
pistache ⓜ pees·*ta*·che *pistachio*
plancha ① *plan*·cha *iron (for clothing)*
planeta ⓜ pla·*ne*·ta *planet*
plano/a ⓜ/① *pla*·no/a *flat*
planta ① *plan*·ta *plant*
plástico ⓜ *plas*·tee·ko *plastic*
plata ① *pla*·ta *silver*
plataforma ① pla·ta·*for*·ma *platform*
plátano ⓜ *pla*·ta·no *banana*
plateado/a ⓜ/① pla·te·*a*·do/a *silver*
plato ⓜ *pla*·to *plate*
playa ① *pla*·ya *beach*
playera ① pla·*ye*·ra *T-shirt*
plaza ① *pla*·sa *market*
 — de toros de *to*·ros *bullring*
 — mayor ma·*yor main square*
pluma ① *ploo*·ma *pen*
pobre *po*·bre *poor*
pobreza ① po·*bre*·sa *poverty*
pocos/as ⓜ/① pl *po*·kos/as *few*
poder po·*der power*
poder po·*der (to be) able* · *can*
poesía ① po·e·*see*·a *poetry*
polen ⓜ *po*·len *pollen*
policía ① po·lee·*see*·a *police*
política ① po·*lee*·tee·ka *politics* · *policy*

político/a ⓜ/① po·*lee*·tee·ko/a *politician*
póliza ① po·*lee*·sa *policy (insurance)*
pollo ⓜ *po*·yo *chicken*
ponchar pon·*char puncture*
poner po·*ner put*
popular po·poo·*lar popular*
póquer ⓜ *po*·ker *poker*
por (día) por (*dee*·a) *per (day)*
por ciento por *syen*·to *percent*
por qué por ke *why*
por vía ① **aérea** por *vee*·a a·*e*·re·a *by airmail*
poro ⓜ *po*·ro *leek*
porque *por*·ke *because*
portafolios ⓜ por·ta·*fo*·lyos *briefcase*
portero/a ⓜ/① por·*te*·ro/a *goalkeeper* · *concierge*
posible po·*see*·ble *possible*
postal ① *pos*·tal *postcard*
póster ⓜ *pos*·ter *poster*
pozo ⓜ *po*·so *well*
precio ⓜ *pre*·syo *price*
 — de entrada de en·*tra*·da *admission price*
preferir pre·fe·*reer prefer*
pregunta ① pre·*goon*·ta *question*
preguntar pre·goon·*tar ask (a question)*
preocupado/a ⓜ/① pre·o·koo·*pa*·do/a *worried*
preocuparse por pre·o·koo·*par*·se por *care about something*
preparar pre·pa·*rar prepare*
presidente/a ⓜ/① pre·see·*den*·te/a *president*
presión ① pre·*syon pressure*
 — arterial ar·te·*ryal blood pressure*
prevenir pre·ve·*neer prevent*
primavera ① pree·ma·*ve*·ra *spring (season)*
primer ministro ⓜ pree·*mer* mee·*nees*·tro *prime minister*
primera ministra ① pree·*me*·ra mee·*nees*·tra *prime minister*
primera clase pree·*me*·ra *kla*·se *first class*
primero/a ⓜ/① pree·*me*·ro/a *first*
principal preen·see·*pal main*
prisa *pree*·sa *in a hurry*

prisionero/a ⓜ/ⓕ pree·syo·*ne*·ro/a
prisoner
privado/a ⓜ/ⓕ pree·*va*·do/a *private*
probadores ⓜ pl pro·ba·*do*·res
changing room
probar pro·*bar* try
producir pro·doo·*seer* produce
productos ⓜ pl **congelados**
pro·*dook*·tos kon·khe·*la*·dos
frozen foods
profundo/a ⓜ/ⓕ pro·*foon*·do/a *deep*
programa ⓜ pro·*gra*·ma *programme*
promesa ⓕ pro·*me*·sa *promise*
prometida ⓕ pro·me·*tee*·da *fiancee*
prometido ⓜ pro·me·*tee*·do *fiance*
pronto *pron*·to *soon*
propietaria ⓕ pro·pye·*ta*·rya
landlady
propietario ⓜ pro·pye·*ta*·ryo
landlord
propina ⓕ pro·*pee*·na *tip (gratuity)*
prórroga ⓕ *pro*·ro·ga *extension (visa)*
proteger pro·te·*kher* protect
protegido/a ⓜ/ⓕ pro·te·*khee*·do/a
protected
protesta ⓕ pro·*tes*·ta *protest*
protestar pro·tes·*tar* protest
provisiones ⓕ pl pro·vee·syo·nes
provisions
proyector ⓜ pro·yek·*tor* projector
prueba ⓕ *prwe*·ba *test*
— **de embarazo** de em·ba·*ra*·so
pregnancy test kit
pruebas ⓕ pl **nucleares**
prwe·bas noo·kle·*a*·res *nuclear
testing*
pueblo ⓜ *pwe*·blo *village*
puente ⓜ *pwen*·te *bridge*
puerta ⓕ *pwer*·ta *door*
puerto ⓜ *pwer*·to *harbour • port*
puesta ⓕ **de sol** *pwes*·ta de sol
sunset
puesto ⓜ **de periódicos** *pwes*·to de
pe·*ryo*·dee·kos *news stand*
pulga ⓕ *pool*·ga *flea*
pulmones ⓜ pl pool·*mo*·nes *lungs*
punto ⓜ *poon*·to *point*
puro ⓜ *poo*·ro *cigar*
puro/a ⓜ/ⓕ *poo*·ro/a *pure*

Q

qué ke *what*
quedarse ke·*dar*·se *stay (remain)*
— **sin** seen *run out of*
quejarse ke·*khar*·se *complain*
quemadura ⓕ ke·ma·*doo*·ra *burn*
— **de sol** de sol *sunburn*
quemar ke·*mar* burn
querer ke·*rer* want
queso ⓜ *ke*·so *cheese*
— **cottage** ko·*tash* cottage cheese
— **crema** *kre*·ma cream cheese
— **de cabra** de ka·bra *goat's cheese*
quién kyen *who*
quincena ⓕ keen·*se*·na *fortnight*
quiste ⓜ **ovárico** *kees*·te o·*va*·ree·ko
ovarian cyst
quizás kee·*sas* perhaps

R

radiador ⓜ ra·dya·*dor* radiator
rally ⓜ *ra*·lee rally
rápido/a ⓜ/ⓕ *ra*·pee·do/a *fast •
quick*
raqueta ⓕ ra·*ke*·ta *racquet*
raro/a ⓜ/ⓕ *ra*·ro/a *rare • strange •
unusual*
rastrillo ⓜ ras·*tree*·yo *razor*
rastro ⓜ *ras*·tro *track (footprints)*
rasurarse ra·soo·*rar*·se *shave*
rata ⓕ *ra*·ta *rat*
ratón ⓜ ra·*ton* *mouse*
raza ⓕ *ra*·sa *race (people)*
razón ⓕ ra·*son* *reason*
realista re·a·*lees*·ta *realistic*
recámara ⓕ re·*ka*·ma·ra *bedroom*
recibir re·see·*beer* receive
recibo ⓜ re·*see*·bo *receipt*
reciclable re·see·*kla*·ble *recyclable*
reciclar re·see·*klar* recycle
recientemente re·syen·te·*men*·te
recently

recolección ⓕ **de fruta**
re·ko·lek·*syon* de *froo*·ta
fruit picking

recomendar re·ko·men·*dar*
recommend

reconocer re·ko·no·*ser recognise*

recordar re·kor·*dar remember*

recorrido ⓜ **guiado** re·ko·*ree*·do
gee·*a*·do *guided tour*

recostarse re·kos·*tar*·se *lie (not stand)*

red ⓕ red *net*

redondo/a ⓜ/ⓕ re·*don*·do/a *round*

reembolsar re·em·bol·*sar refund*

reembolso ⓜ re·em·*bol*·so *refund*

referencia ⓕ re·fe·*ren*·sya *reference*

refractario/a re·frak·*ta*·ryo *bowl*

refresco ⓜ re·*fres*·ko *soft drink*

refrigerador ⓜ re·free·khe·ra·*dor*
refrigerator

refugiado/a ⓜ/ⓕ re·foo·*khya*·do/a
refugee

regadera ⓕ re·ga·*de*·ra *shower*

regalar re·ga·*lar give a gift*

regalo ⓜ re·*ga*·lo *gift*
— **de bodas** de *bo*·das
wedding present

reglas ⓕ pl *re*·glas *rules*

reina ⓕ *ray*·na *queen*

reír re·*eer laugh*

relación ⓕ re·la·*syon relationship*

relajarse re·la·*khar*·se *relax*

religión ⓕ re·lee·*khyon religion*

religioso/a ⓜ/ⓕ re·lee·*khyo*·so/a
religious

reliquia ⓕ re·*lee*·kya *relic*

reloj ⓜ re·*lokh clock*
— **de pulsera** de pool·*se*·ra *watch*

remo ⓜ *re*·mo *rowing*

remoto/a ⓜ/ⓕ re·*mo*·to/a *remote*

renta ⓕ *ren*·ta *rent*
— **de coches** de *ko*·ches *car hire*

rentar ren·*tar hire • rent*

reparar re·pa·*rar repair*

repartir re·par·*teer deal (cards)*

repelente ⓜ **contra mosquitos**
re·pe·*len*·te *kon*·tra mos·*kee*·tos
mosquito repellent

repetir re·pe·*teer repeat*

repisa ⓕ re·*pee*·sa *shelf*

república ⓕ re·*poo*·blee·ka *republic*

reservación ⓕ re·ser·va·*syon*
reservation

reservar re·ser·*var book • reserve*

resfriado ⓜ res·free·*a*·do *cold (illness)*

residuos ⓜ pl **tóxicos** res·*see*·dwos
tok·see·kos *toxic waste*

resorte ⓜ re·*sor*·te *spring (wire)*

respaldo ⓜ res·*pal*·do *back (of chair)*

respirar res·pee·*rar breathe*

respuesta ⓕ res·*pwes*·ta *answer*

restaurante ⓜ res·tow·*ran*·te
restaurant

revisar re·vee·*sar check*

revista ⓕ re·*vees*·ta *magazine*

rey ⓜ ray *king*

rezar re·*sar worship*

rico/a ⓜ/ⓕ *ree*·ko/a *rich • wealthy*

riesgo ⓜ *ryes*·go *risk*

río ⓜ *ree*·o *river*

ritmo ⓜ *reet*·mo *rhythm*

robar ro·*bar rob • steal*

roca ⓕ *ro*·ka *rock*

rock ⓜ rok *rock (music)*

rodilla ⓕ ro·*dee*·ya *knee*

rojo/a ⓜ/ⓕ *ro*·kho/a *red*

romántico/a ⓜ/ⓕ ro·*man*·tee·ko/a
romantic

romper rom·*per break*

ron ⓜ ron *rum*

ropa ⓕ *ro*·pa *clothing*
— **de cama** de *ka*·ma *bedding*
— **interior** een·te·*ryor underwear*

rosa *ro*·sa *pink*

rosadura ⓕ ro·sa·*doo*·ra *nappy rash*

roto/a ⓜ/ⓕ *ro*·to/a *broken*

rueda ⓕ *rwe*·da *wheel*

ruidoso/a ⓜ/ⓕ rwee·*do*·so/a *loud •
noisy*

ruinas ⓕ pl *rwee*·nas *ruins*

ruta ⓕ *roo*·ta *route*

S

S

sábana ① *sa*·ba·na sheet (bed)
Sabbath sa·bat Sabbath
saber sa·ber know (something)
sabroso/a ⓜ/① sa·bro·so/a tasty
sacerdote ⓜ sa·ser·do·te priest
sal ① sal salt
sala ① **de espera** *sa*·la de es·pe·ra
waiting room
sala ① **de tránsito** *sa*·la de
tran·see·to transit lounge
salami ⓜ sa·*la*·mee salami
salario ⓜ sa·*la*·ryo rate of pay • salary
salchicha ① sal·*chee*·cha sausage
saldo ⓜ sal·do balance (account)
salida ① sa·*lee*·da exit • departure
saliente ⓜ sa·*lyen*·te ledge
salir con sa·leer kon date (a person) •
go out with
salir de sa·leer de depart
salmón ⓜ sal·mon salmon
salón ⓜ **de belleza** sa·lon de be·ye·a
beauty salon
salsa ① *sal*·sa sauce
— **de soya** de *so*·ya soy sauce
— **picante** pee·*kan*·te chilli sauce
saltar sal·*tar* jump
salud ① sa·*lood* health
salvar sal·var save
sandalias ① pl san·*da*·lyas sandals
sandía ① san·*dee*·a watermelon
sangrar san·grar bleed
sangre ① *san*·gre blood
santo/a ⓜ/① *san*·to/a saint
sarampión ⓜ sa·ram·*pyon* measles
sartén ⓜ sar·ten frying pan • pan
sastre ⓜ *sas*·tre tailor
sauna ⓜ *sow*·na sauna
secar se·*kar* dry
secretario/a ⓜ/① se·kre·*ta*·ryo/a
secretary
sed ① sed thirst
seda ① *se*·da silk
seguido se·*gee*·do often
seguir se·geer follow
segundo ⓜ se·*goon*·do second (time)

segundo/a ⓜ/① se·*goon*·do/a
second (place)
seguridad ① **social** se·goo·ree·*dad*
so·*syal* social welfare
seguro ⓜ se·goo·ro insurance
seguro/a ⓜ/① se·goo·ro/a safe
sello ⓜ se·yo stamp
semáforos ⓜ pl se·*ma*·fo·ros
traffic lights
Semana ① **Santa** se·*ma*·na *san*·ta
Holy Week
sembrar sem·*brar* plant
semidirecto/a ⓜ/
① se·mee·dee·*rek*·to/a
non-direct
señal ① se·*nyal* sign
sencillo/a ⓜ/① sen·*see*·yo/a simple
sendero ⓜ sen·de·ro path
senos ⓜ pl se·nos breasts
sensibilidad ① sen·see·bee·lee·*dad*
film speed
sensible sen·*see*·ble sensible
sensual sen·*swal* sensual
sentarse sen·*tar*·se sit
sentimientos ⓜ pl sen·tee·*myen*·tos
feelings
sentir sen·teer feel
separado/a ⓜ/① se·pa·*ra*·do/a
separate
separar se·pa·rar separate
ser ser be
serie ① se·rye series • TV series
serio/a ⓜ/① se·ryo/a serious
seropositivo/a ⓜ/①
se·ro·po·see·tee·vo/a HIV positive
serpiente ① ser·*pyen*·te snake
servicio militar mee·lee·*tar* military
service
servilleta ① ser·vee·*ye*·ta napkin
sexismo ⓜ sek·*sees*·mo sexism
sexo ⓜ sek·so sex
— **seguro** se·goo·ro safe sex
sexy sek·see sexy
si see if
sí see yes
SIDA ⓜ see·da AIDS
sidra ① see·dra cider
siempre *syem*·pre always

DICTIONARY

242

silla ⓕ *see·*ya chair
— de montar de mon·*tar* saddle
— de ruedas de rwe·*das* wheelchair
similar see·mee·*lar* similar
simpático/a ⓜ/ⓕ seem·*pa·*tee·ko/a nice
sin seen without
— hogar o·*gar* homeless
— plomo plo·mo unleaded
sinagoga ⓕ see·na·*go·*ga synagogue
síndrome ⓜ premenstrual
*seen·*dro·me pre·men·*strwal*
premenstrual tension
Singapur ⓜ seen·ga·*poor* Singapore
sintético/a ⓜ/ⓕ seen·*te·*tee·ko/a synthetic
sitio ⓜ de taxis *see·*tyo de tak·*sees* taxi stand
sobornar so·bor·*nar* bribe
soborno ⓜ so·*bor·*no bribe
sobre ⓜ so·bre envelope
sobre so·bre about
sobredosis ⓕ so·bre·*do·*sees overdose
sobrevivir so·bre·vee·*veer* survive
socialista ⓜ&ⓕ so·sya·*lees·*ta socialist
sol ⓜ sol sun
soldado ⓜ&ⓕ sol·*da·*do soldier
soleado so·le·*a·*do sunny
sólo so·lo only
solo/a ⓜ/ⓕ so·lo/a alone
soltero/a ⓜ/ⓕ sol·*te·*ro/a single
sombra ⓕ som·bra shadow
sombrero ⓜ som·*bre·*ro hat
soñar so·*nyar* dream
sonreír son·re·*eer* smile
sopa ⓕ so·pa soup
sordo/a ⓜ/ⓕ sor·do/a deaf
sorpresa ⓕ sor·*pre·*sa surprise
su soo his • her • their • your (polite)
submarinismo ⓜ
soob·ma·ree·*nees·*mo diving
subtítulos ⓜ pl soob·*tee·*too·los subtitles
sucio/a ⓜ/ⓕ soo·syo/a dirty
sucursal ⓕ soo·koor·*sal* branch office
sudar soo·*dar* perspire

suegra ⓕ swe·gra mother-in-law
suegro ⓜ swe·gro father-in-law
sueldo ⓜ swel·do wage
suelto/a ⓜ/ⓕ swel·to/a loose
suerte ⓕ swer·te luck
suertudo/a ⓜ/ⓕ swer·*too·*do/a lucky
sueter ⓜ swe·ter jumper • sweater
suficiente soo·fee·*syen·*te enough
sufrir soo·*freer* suffer
supermercado ⓜ soo·per·mer·*ka·*do supermarket
superstición ⓕ soo·per·stee·*syon* superstition
sur ⓜ soor south
surfear sor·fe·*ar* surf
suvenir ⓜ soo·ve·*neer* souvenir

T

tabaco ⓜ ta·*ba·*ko tobacco
tabaquería ⓕ ta·ba·ke·*ree·*a tobacconist
tabla ⓕ de surf *ta·*bla de sorf surfboard
tablero ⓜ de ajedrez ta·*ble·*ro de a·khe·*dres* chess board
tacaño/a ⓜ/ⓕ ta·*ka·*nyo/a stingy
tal vez tal ves maybe
talco ⓜ de bébe *tal·*ko de be·be baby powder
talla ⓕ ta·ya size (clothes)
taller ⓜ ta·*yer* workshop
tamaño ⓜ ta·*ma·*nyo size
también tam·*byen* also
tampoco tam·po·ko neither
tampones ⓜ pl tam·po·nes tampons
tapón ⓜ ta·*pon* bath plug
tanga ⓕ *tan·*ga g-string
tapones ⓜ pl para los oídos ta·po·nes pa·ra los o·ee·dos earplugs
taquilla ⓕ ta·*kee·*ya ticket office
tarde ⓕ tar·de afternoon
tarde tar·de late
tarjeta ⓕ de crédito tar·*khe·*ta de kre·dee·to credit card

tarjeta ⓕ **de teléfono** tar·*khe*·ta de te·*le*·fo·no *phone card*

tarjeta ⓕ **SIM** tar·*khe*·ta seem *SIM card*

tasa ⓕ **de aeropuerto** *ta*·sa de a·e·ro·*pwer*·to *airport tax*

taxi ⓜ *tak*·see *taxi*

taza ⓕ *ta*·sa *cup*

té ⓜ te *tea*

teatro ⓜ te·*a*·tro *theatre*

teclado ⓜ te·*kla*·do *keyboard*

técnica ⓕ *tek*·nee·ka *technique*

tela ⓕ *te*·la *fabric*

tele ⓕ *te*·le *TV*

teleférico ⓜ te·le·*fe*·ree·ko *cable car*

teléfono ⓜ te·*le*·fo·no *telephone*
— **celular** se·loo·*lar mobile phone*
— **público** *poo*·blee·ko *phone box* • *public telephone*

telegrama ⓜ te·le·*gra*·ma *telegram*

telenovela ⓕ te·le·no·*ve*·la *soap opera*

teleobjetivo ⓜ te·le·ob·khe·*tee*·vo *telephoto lens*

telescopio ⓜ te·les·*ko*·pyo *telescope*

televisión ⓕ te·le·vee·*syon television*

temperatura ⓕ tem·pe·ra·*too*·ra *temperature (weather)*

templado/a ⓜ/ⓕ tem·*pla*·do/a *warm*

templo ⓜ *tem*·plo *temple*

temporada ⓕ tem·po·*ra*·da *season (in sport)*

temprano tem·*pra*·no *early*

tendedero ⓜ ten·de·*de*·ro *clothes line*

tenedor ⓜ te·ne·*dor fork*

tener te·*ner have*
— **gripa** *gree*·pa *have a cold*
— **hambre** *am*·bre *(be) hungry*
— **sed** sed *(be) thirsty*
— **sueño** *swe*·nyo *(be) sleepy*

tenis ⓜ *te*·nees *tennis*

tercio ⓜ *ter*·syo *third*

terco/a ⓜ/ⓕ *ter*·ko/a *stubborn*

terminar ter·mee·*nar finish* • *end*

ternera ⓕ ter·*ne*·ra *veal*

terremoto ⓜ te·re·*mo*·to *earthquake*

terrible te·*ree*·ble *terrible*

tía ⓕ *tee*·a *aunt*

tiempo ⓜ *tyem*·po *time* • *weather*
— **completo** kom·*ple*·to *full-time*

tienda ⓕ *tyen*·da *shop* • *convenience store*
— **de abarrotes** de a·ba·*ro*·tes *grocery*
— **de campaña** de kam·*pa*·nya *tent*
— **de campismo** de cam·*pees*·mo *camping store*
— **de deportes** de de·*por*·tes *sports store*
— **de fotografía** de fo·to·gra·*fee*·a *camera shop*
— **de ropa** de *ro*·pa *clothing store*
— **de suvenirs** de soo·ve·*neers souvenir shop*
— **departamental** de·par·ta·men·*tal department store*

Tierra ⓕ *tye*·ra *Earth*

tierra ⓕ *tye*·ra *land*

tijeras ⓕ pl tee·*khe*·ras *scissors*

tímido/a ⓜ/ⓕ *tee*·mee·do/a *shy*

tina ⓕ *tee*·na *bathtub*

típico/a ⓜ/ⓕ *tee*·pee·ko/a *typical*

tipo ⓜ *tee*·po *type*
— **de cambio** de *kam*·byo *exchange rate*

título ⓜ *tee*·too·lo *degree*

tlapalería ⓕ tla·pa·le·*ree*·a *hardware store*

toalla ⓕ to·*a*·ya *towel*

toallas ⓕ pl **femeninas** to·*a*·yas fe·me·*nee*·nas *sanitary napkins*

toallita ⓕ **facial** to·a·*yee*·ta fa·*syal face cloth*

tobillo ⓜ to·*bee*·yo *ankle*

tocar to·*kar touch* • *play (instrument)*

tocino ⓜ to·*see*·no *bacon*

todavía (no) to·da·*vee*·a (no) *(not) yet*

todo/a ⓜ/ⓕ *to*·do/a *all* • *everything*

todos/as ⓜ/ⓕ *to*·dos/as *all (of them)*

tofu ⓜ *to*·foo *tofu*

tomar to·*mar drink* • *take (the train)* • *take (photos)*
— **fotos** *fo*·tos *take photographs*

tomates ⓜ pl **deshidratados** to·*ma*·tes des·ee·dra·*ta*·dos *sun-dried tomatoes*

torcedura ① tor·se·*doo*·ra *sprain*
tormenta ① tor·*men*·ta *storm*
toro ⓜ *to*·ro *bull*
toronja ① to·*ron*·kha *grapefruit*
torre ① *to*·re *tower*
tos ① tos *cough*
tostador ⓜ tos·ta·*dor toaster*
trabajar tra·ba·*khar work*
trabajo ⓜ tra·*ba*·kho *job* • *work*
 — **de casa** de *ka*·sa *housework*
 — **de limpieza** de leem·*pye*·sa
  cleaning
 — **eventual** e·ven·*twal casual work*
traducir tra·doo·*seer translate*
traer tra·*er bring*
traficante ⓜ&① **de drogas**
 tra·fee·*kan*·te de *dro*·gas *drug
 dealer*
tráfico ⓜ *tra*·fee·ko *traffic*
traje ⓜ **de baño** *tra*·khe de *ba*·nyo
 bathing suit • *swimsuit*
trámites ⓜ *tra*·mee·tes *paperwork*
tramposo/a ⓜ/① tram·*po*·so/a *cheat*
tranquilidad ① tran·kee·lee·*dad
 quiet*
tranquilo/a ⓜ/① tran·*kee*·lo/a *quiet*
transparencia ① trans·pa·*ren*·sya
 slide
transporte ⓜ trans·*por*·te *transport*
tranvía ⓜ tran·*vee*·a *tram*
tren ⓜ tren *train*
triste *trees*·te *sad*
truzas ① pl *troo*·sas *underpants
 (men)*
tu sg inf too *your*
tú sg inf too *you*
tumba ① *toom*·ba *grave*
turista ⓜ&① too·*rees*·ta *tourist*

U

ultrasonido ⓜ ool·tra·so·*nee*·do
 ultrasound
una vez *oo*·na ves *once*
uniforme ⓜ oo·nee·*for*·me *uniform*
universidad ① oo·nee·ver·see·*dad
 university* • *college*

universo ⓜ oo·nee·*ver*·so *universe*
urgente oor·*khen*·te *urgent*
usted sg pol oos·*ted you*
ustedes pl pol oos·*te*·des *you*
útil *oo*·teel *useful*
uva ① **pasa** *oo*·va *pa*·sa *raisin*
uvas ① pl *oo*·vas *grapes*

V

vaca ① *va*·ka *cow* • *beef*
vacaciones ① pl va·ka·*syo*·nes
 holidays • *vacation*
vacante va·*kan*·te *vacant*
vacío/a ⓜ/① va·*see*·o/a *empty*
vacuna ① va·*koo*·na *vaccination*
vagina ① va·*khee*·na *vagina*
vagón ⓜ **restaurante** va·*gon*
 res·tow·*ran*·te *dining car*
validar va·lee·*dar validate*
valiente va·*lyen*·te *brave*
valioso/a ⓜ/① va·*lyo*·so/a *valuable*
valle ⓜ *va*·ye *valley*
valor ⓜ va·*lor value*
varios/as ⓜ/① *va*·ryos/as *several*
vaso ⓜ *va*·so *glass*
vegetariano/a ⓜ/①
 ve·khe·ta·*rya*·no/a *vegetarian*
vela ① *ve*·la *candle*
velocidad ① ve·lo·see·*dad speed*
velocímetro ⓜ ve·lo·*see*·me·tro
 speedometer
velódromo ⓜ ve·*lo*·dro·mo *racetrack
 (bicycles)*
vena ① *ve*·na *vein*
vendaje ⓜ ven·*da*·khe *bandage*
vendedor(a) ⓜ/① **de flores**
 ven·de·*dor*/ven·de·*do*·ra de *flo*·res
 flower seller
vender ven·*der sell*
venenoso/a ⓜ/① ve·ne·*no*·so/a
 poisonous
venir ve·*neer come*
venta ① **automática de boletos**
 ven·ta ow·to·*ma*·tee·ka de bo·*le*·tos
 ticket machine
ventana ① ven·*ta*·na *window*

ventilador ⓜ ven·tee·la·*dor fan (machine)*

ver ver *see*

verano ⓜ ve·*ra*·no *summer*

verde ver·de *green*

verdulería ⓕ ver·doo·le·*ree*·a *greengrocery*

verduras ⓕ ver·*doo*·ras *vegetables*

vestíbulo ⓜ ves·*tee*·boo·lo *foyer*

vestido ⓜ ves·*tee*·do *dress*

viajar vya·*khar travel*

viaje ⓜ *vya*·khe *trip*

vid ⓕ veed *vine*

vida ⓕ *vee*·da *life*

videocassette ⓕ vee·de·o·ka·*set video tape*

viejo/a ⓜ/ⓕ *vye*·kho/a *old*

viento ⓜ *vyen*·to *wind*

vinagre ⓜ vee·*na*·gre *vinegar*

vinatería ⓕ vee·na·te·*ree*·a *liquor store*

viñedo ⓜ vee·*nye*·do *vineyard*

vino ⓜ *vee*·no *wine*

violar vyo·*lar rape*

virus ⓜ *vee*·roos *virus*

visa ⓕ vee·*sa visa*

visitar vee·see·*tar visit*

vista ⓕ *vees*·ta *view*

vitaminas ⓕ pl vee·ta·*mee*·nas *vitamins*

víveres ⓜ pl *vee*·ve·res *food supplies*

vivir vee·*veer live*

vodka ⓕ *vod*·ka *vodka*

volar vo·*lar fly*

volumen ⓜ vo·*loo*·men *volume*

volver vol·*ver return*

votar vo·*tar vote*

voz ⓕ vos *voice*

vuelo ⓜ **doméstico** *vwe*·lo do·*mes*·tee·ko *domestic flight*

W

whiskey *gwees*·kee *whiskey*

Y

y ee *and*

ya ya *already*

yerbero/a ⓜ/ⓕ yer·*be*·ro/a *herbalist*

yo yo

yoga ⓜ *yo*·ga *yoga*

yogurt ⓜ yo·*goort yogurt*

Z

zanahoria ⓕ sa·na·o·rya *carrot*

zapatería ⓕ sa·pa·te·*ree*·a *shoe shop*

zapatos ⓜ pl sa·*pa*·tos *shoes*

zócalo ⓜ *so*·ka·lo *main square*

zodíaco ⓜ so·*dee*·a·ko *zodiac*

zoológico ⓜ so·o·*lo*·khee·ko *zoo*

INDEX

don't just stand there, say something!

see the full range of our language products, go to:

lonelyplanet.com

What kind of traveller are you?

A. You're eating chicken for dinner *again* because it's the only word you know.

B. When no one understands what you say, you step closer and shout louder.

C. When the barman doesn't understand your order, you point frantically at the beer.

D. You're surrounded by locals, swapping jokes, email addresses and experiences
   – other travellers want to borrow your phrasebook or audio guide.

If you answered A, B, or C, you NEED Lonely Planet's language products ...

- **Lonely Planet Phrasebooks** – for every phrase you need in every language
  you want

- **Lonely Planet Language & Culture** – get behind the scenes of English as it's
  spoken around the world – learn and laugh

- **Lonely Planet Fast Talk & Fast Talk Audio** – essential phrases for short trips and
  weekends away – read, listen and talk like a local

- **Lonely Planet Small Talk** – 10 essential languages for city breaks

- **Lonely Planet Real Talk** – downloadable language audio guides from
  lonelyplanet.com to your MP3 player

... and this is why

- **Talk to everyone everywhere**
  Over 120 languages, more than any other publisher

- **The right words at the right time**
  Quick-reference colour sections, two-way dictionary, easy pronunciation,
  every possible subject – and audio to support it

Lonely Planet Offices

Australia
90 Maribyrnong St, Footscray,
Victoria 3011
☎ 03 8379 8000
fax 03 8379 8111
✉ talk2us@lonelyplanet.com.au

USA
150 Linden St, Oakland,
CA 94607
☎ 510 893 8555
fax 510 893 8572
✉ info@lonelyplanet.com

UK
72-82 Rosebery Ave,
London EC1R 4RW
☎ 020 7841 9000
fax 020 7841 9001
✉ go@lonelyplanet.co.uk

lonelyplanet.com